Wakefield Press

Now in Remission

Ken Clezy is a general surgeon with a special interest in leprosy. He spent most of his working life in the Third World, in government and mission hospitals, and now lives in Adelaide.
Photo: Ken and Gwen Clezy

Now in Remission
A Surgical Life

Ken Clezy

Wakefield Press

Wakefield Press
16 Rose Street
Mile End
South Australia 5031
www.wakefieldpress.com.au

First published 2011
Reprinted 2012, 2017

Copyright © Ken Clezy, 2011

All rights reserved. This book is copyright. Apart from any fair dealing for the purposes of private study, research, criticism or review, as permitted under the Copyright Act, no part may be reproduced without written permission. Enquiries should be addressed to the publisher.

Edited by Julia Beaven
Cover photograph of Jibla, Yemen, by the author
Maps by Ian Ross
Designed and typeset by Wakefield Press

National Library of Australia Cataloguing-in-Publication entry

Author:	Clezy, Ken.
Title:	Now in remission: a surgical live / Ken Clezy.
ISBN:	978 1 74305 014 9 (paperback).
Subjects:	Clezy, Ken.
	Missionaries, Medical – Biography.
	Surgeons – Australia – Biography.
	Missions to leprosy patients – Biography.
	Leprosy – Treatment.
	Christian life.
Dewey Number:	266.0092

Contents

Chapter 1	Muslim rage up close and personal	1
Chapter 2	Selkirk, Nairne and Naracoorte	10
Chapter 3	Growing up	18
Chapter 4	To Adelaide	32
Chapter 5	A taste of New Guinea	41
Chapter 6	Graduation, marriage, children	50
Chapter 7	Ship's doctor to England	62
Chapter 8	Rabaul	79
Chapter 9	To India	106
Chapter 10	To Madang	121
Chapter 11	Port Moresby	133
Chapter 12	Dean and professor of surgery	143
Chapter 13	Goroka	155
Chapter 14	Home invasion and worse	171
Chapter 15	Travels and travellers	180
Chapter 16	Around the world on two rolls of film	195
Chapter 17	Burnie, Tasmania	227
Chapter 18	Jibla Baptist Hospital, Yemen	241
Chapter 19	Over and out	261

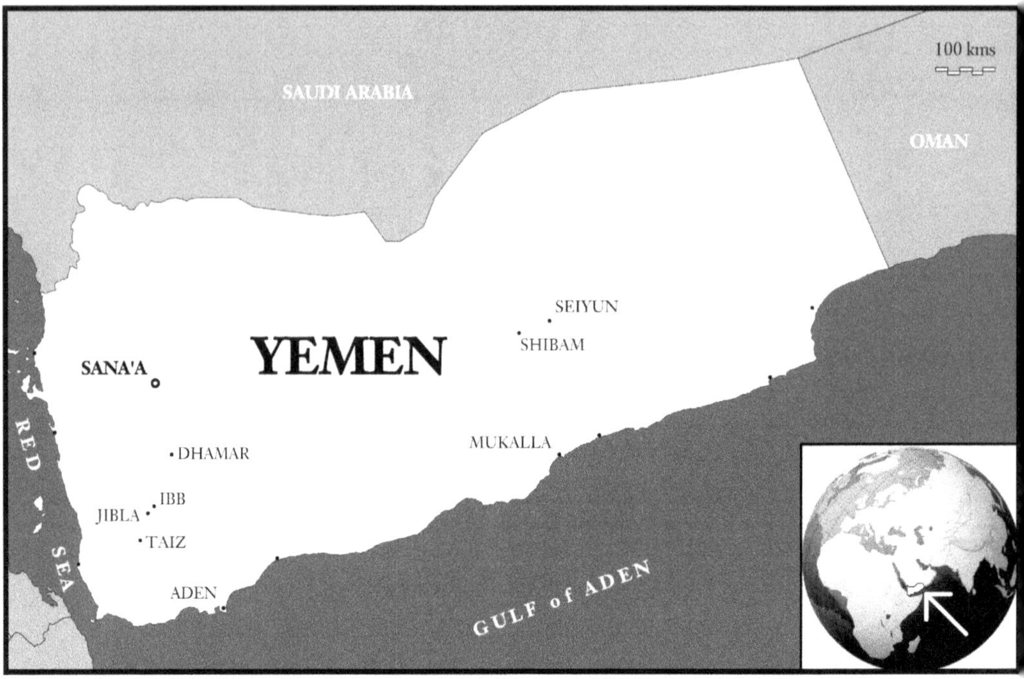
100 kms
SAUDI ARABIA
OMAN
YEMEN
SANA'A
SEIYUN
SHIBAM
MUKALLA
DHAMAR
IBB
JIBLA
TAIZ
ADEN
RED SEA
GULF of ADEN

200 kms
MANUS
KAVIENG
NEW IRELAND
RABAUL
NISSAN IS.
NEW BRITAIN
BUKA
SOHANO
BOUGAINVILLE
AITAPE
IRIAN JAYA
WABAG
MADANG
MT HAGEN
GOROKA
MENDI
LAE
BALIMO
DARU
PORT MORESBY
NORMANBY IS.
SAMARAI
PAPUA NEW GUINEA

Foreword

Ken Clezy's career, and indeed his whole life, has been marked most of all by an overarching sense of duty; a duty to his family, his profession, his country, and indeed to many other countries less fortunate than this one, but perhaps, most of all, to his God. He has been an unpaid and unsung ambassador for this country in New Guinea, India, Africa and other parts of the developing world. Not for Ken the relatively comfortable affluent existence of an Adelaide surgeon. He forsook all of that to work in relatively primitive, at least by our standards, surroundings and for little income, but undoubtedly for immense personal satisfaction and a sense of great achievement.

Perhaps the person who knows Ken best professionally is Sankar Sinha, who first met him in Port Moresby in 1979. Sankar described Ken to me as a surgical hero; a man who in the same day would remove a pituitary tumour, a meningioma, a liver tumour and perform a tendon transfer and then in the evening go on to fix a fractured neck of femur. This is a man who was a founder of leprosy surgical services in Papua New Guinea and saved many limbs. He is a man who, as Sankar stated, craved nothing for himself and is always available to help others.

Always an inventive surgeon, Ken has been to some extent a man before his time. He was amongst the first to manage splenic trauma in adults non-operatively. They were managed this way, of course, by necessity, as splenectomy in a malarial country such as New Guinea will often mean death from overwhelming sepsis. His work was published in the *Australian and New Zealand Journal of Surgery* and, as is typical of the man, he gave himself no credit for this. He did not put his name as an author on the paper, giving the credit instead to the other surgeons involved throughout the country in the management of splenic trauma.

Ken's leprosy work is famous and internationally acknowledged. More recently, since returning to Australia and working in Burnie, he has been one of the leading national and international advocates of mini-cholecystectomy. He and others who have followed have shown the importance and the safety of this technique. Perhaps most of all he has shown the relevance of this technique, particularly in the developing world where laparoscopic surgery is never likely to be available for the majority of the population.

By his every action, word and deed, Ken has demonstrated that all human beings – regardless of race, creed, nationality, gender and age – deserve care and compassion. We all believe this but how many of us have had the faith, determination and courage to put our beliefs into practice? He has shown by his work in New Guinea and elsewhere that one human being can make a very big difference to people's lives. His life is a testimony to Robert Burn's belief that what unites humanity is far greater than what divides it. Ken has truly looked upon every human as his brother or sister.

He is a role model, not just a good surgeon, but an exemplary human being capable of compassion and humanity; someone who cares for and can communicate with staff, patients and their relatives. Ken has, in addition, a laconic sense of humour, perhaps typically bush Australian, and which from time to time transcends crises and defuses various situations. And he has an immense skill in teaching, as well as an ability and will to try and resolve conflict.

Ken Clezy is a man who has translated his Christian beliefs into practical action; a man worthy of any honour we can bestow upon him. Ken Clezy, a remarkable surgeon, a truly remarkable Australian.

Dr Alan Scott
*Edited from a speech given on the occasion of
Ken's RACS retirement dinner, 28 November 1998*

Chapter 1

Muslim rage up close and personal

Most news is bad, and some say it can't be news if CNN isn't there, so when the cameras descended on our little hospital at Jibla, high in a remote Yemen valley, the news about to hit the airwaves and front pages around the world was very bad indeed.

Jibla is a picturesque tourist town crammed with superb examples of the stonemason's art, the multi-storey houses that terrace the valley's steep sides. Proud to the point of narcissism at having been the seat of Queen Arwa, the overdriven ruler of all Yemen a thousand years ago, it boasts the QA mosque, the QA museum, the crumbling remains of her palace, and much else. But for me it's the place where my good friends Jibla Baptist Hospital administrator Bill Koehn, GP/obstetrician Martha Myers and medical store boss Kathy Gariety were shot dead on 30 December 2002 while I breakfasted with my wife, a stone's throw away. Firecrackers, gunshots – whatever – were prosaic pedal points to the music of life around Jibla, and I heard nothing.

Told-you-so types wondered why we didn't see it coming, because communal anti-American feeling soared during and after the First Gulf War, when Yemen was the lone and quixotic UN Security Council member touting an exclusively Arab response to Iraq's invasion of Kuwait.

One of the World Bank's basket cases, Yemen is the only dirt-poor Arabian state, with rampant population growth, a critical water shortage, and little oil. Notionally a parliamentary democracy but riven by tribalism with Sunni-Shiite overtones, and choking on world-class institutionalised corruption, cronyism and nepotism at many levels, it is a top-heavy conservative republic, where journalists learn, the hard way, to tread very carefully. Ruling for three decades and counting, Yemen's hard-nosed autarch Ali Abdullah Saleh ruthlessly suppressed the popular ferment of mid-2011, confidently ignoring how often transfer of power in this corner of the Arabian Peninsula has been by assassination.

Al-Qa'ida's audacious 2002 bombing of the USS *Cole* in Aden harbour brought the country to world attention, adding to the bad press stemming from the 1998 shooting deaths of four kidnapped tourists, including a Sydney man. Exasperated tribesmen had been kidnapping foreigners for years, as their one and only road-tested method of squeezing the government for improved infrastructure or other reasonable services. Hostages were usually treated well, even cosseted, and after parleying between their captors and the authorities they were released unharmed. Some dined out on their adventures for years.

Instead of fractious villagers the 1998 kidnappers were ruthless Aden-Abyan Islamic Army zealots determined to spring a bunch of gaoled fellow travellers. When they threatened to kill the tourists the government wouldn't budge, and made a widely criticised military response when negotiations stalled.

Many countries followed the US State Department in underscoring the Yemen entry in their black books. The struggling tourist industry collapsed but, like most expats, we felt safe enough. An already fragile security situation deteriorated after 9/11, and our hospital's protection was beefed up, with a gun-truck parked outside the compound for weeks. Soldiers accompanied us on trips out of town, but Gwen felt faintly ridiculous entering a city supermarket with her escort toting an AK-47, so did it infrequently.

Matters might have settled down but for America's campaign in Afghanistan. Despite the Pentagon's protestations, the Islamic world understandably saw this conflict as Christians waging war on Muslims, given that Islam doesn't recognise, and most Muslims cannot begin to comprehend, the God/Caesar dichotomy that pertains elsewhere. Muslim lands are theocracies, theoretically at least, and wars against them are ipso facto wars against Islam. Add a dash of racism and any such fracas is a highly flammable situation.

Our Yemeni co-workers, even those who longed in vain to be called to a Palestinian jihad, kept telling us that everybody knew we weren't part of the problem, but we sensed mounting communal anti-Western feeling. More boys were being named Osama, a social indicator more resonant than official expressions of solidarity with the USA.

In late 2002 the British embassy asked UK citizens to leave, and every week or two the US embassy sent our warden another strident email. We had enough problems already, because our hospital was slated to close, the result of a drawn-out and hotly disputed decision by its proprietor, the International Mission Board of the Southern Baptist Church, headquartered in Richmond, Virginia. This represented the ascendancy of those IMB heavies who held that evangelism was one thing and medical work quite another.

Such opinions reflect differing conceptions of the Christian gospel. The Bible says that after calling His disciples, Jesus both taught and healed, but church history shows that all too often one of these activities is pursued at the other's expense. The IMB seemed to believe that if effective verbal evangelism was impossible, social action was pointless and worthless.

There is another view. If Jesus is the light of the world, His followers should cast sharp shadows even if their mouths are shut, as is necessarily so in most Muslim countries. At Jibla these shadows were exemplified by three decades of good medical work and social action. Just as a shadow is inseparable from its cause, appropriate social involvement should be intrinsic to the Christian gospel, but the IMB was resistant, if not blind, to this concept.

JBH was its last hospital anywhere, and the IMB was prepared to walk away at close of business on 31 December 2002, which grieved and disgusted most of us working there. Maybe quality services were available elsewhere in north Yemen, but patients still flocked in from all over. Our fees were far lower than those in regular private clinics, and we provided the only good, affordable inpatient care available to millions. To the end we hoped for continuity, but a projected handover to a Yemeni charity seemed certain to fail.

Monday 30 December was to be the darkest day in 150 years of IMB history, but began ordinarily enough with our 6.30 am chapel service. I was rostered to lead it, and aimed to encourage my downcast colleagues. After our hymn I spoke from Hebrews 11:4. We know little about Abel, I said. He seems to have died unmarried (and, strangely, I thought of Martha and Kathy as I spoke) so we don't honour him as a patriarch. We read that in faith he offered his best to God, which pleased Him. Abel is dead, but the Bible says 'he still speaks today'.

'So,' I said, 'if you're downhearted because JBH is closing when there's so much yet to be done, try looking at it this way: if, like Abel, we've been giving our best to God this has pleased Him, and He will continue using it long after we've all gone.' An hour or so later three of us were dead.

I wondered if Bill had picked up clues overnight that could hint at a positive outcome to the last-ditch mission–government negotiations that were due onsite at 10 am, so after prayers I gave him the floor. He had no news, but simply and sombrely thanked us all for working at Jibla.

Admissions had ceased a fortnight earlier, but a few old cases needed review. Bill had two of mine waiting, so I followed him to the clinic before going home for breakfast. I left the house again at 8.30 to meet incoherent Yemeni staff shrieking, 'Mr Bill, Mr Bill.' I wondered if he'd had a heart attack.

I reached the theatre suite as the stretchers were wheeled in. Martha looked serene, dead from a bullet that left no more than a smudge like a caste mark in the middle of her forehead. A bullet through Bill's right eye-socket exploded his brain. His wife Marty arrived in time to clasp his hand as he died. Kathy had a chest wound and no pulse, but her neck veins were bulging. Judy Williams, our American surgeon, correctly diagnosed cardiac tamponade and opened her chest in a flash, but she had a hopeless heart injury.

I phoned Gwen with a précis of the situation before we operated on the survivor, pharmacist Don Caswell, who had taken two bullets in the belly. We found no serious damage, and after dealing with him I rushed home to talk to Gwen and phone our family. Bad news travels fast, and both our daughter Meredith in Tasmania and our son John in Germany called first.

The train of events was this: months previously a man from a distant village known to be an extremists' nursery brought his wife to Martha who, as always, took the necessary time with her. The lady felt she'd been given a proper hearing for the first time, and on the way home told her husband, perhaps taunting him, that no Muslim doctor had ever treated her so kindly. (She was unfortunate – we know many good, kind and considerate Muslim doctors.) The implicit unfavourable comparison of Islam with Christianity so needled him that he decided to kill Martha. Later he thought he could do better – might as well be hung for a sheep as a lamb. In December they rented a house in Jibla and saw Martha again. She issued a return ticket for 26 December, which the husband changed to 30 December on the assumption that this was our last day, because he'd learnt that Yemeni workers were to be paid off that day. And he knew he'd find a worthwhile cluster of foreign staff in the office area shortly after 8 am.

The soldier on the gate frisked him routinely but missed the pistol strapped to the inner side of his arm. In the front office he asked for a phone card, but instead of producing the money for it he drew his weapon and felled Martha at the telephone two metres away. Within seconds he was in Bill's office and killed Kathy. Bill, rising from his desk, was next. It was all over in less time than it takes to tell.

In the pharmacy next door he put two bullets into Caswell, but nothing happened when he pulled the trigger at radiographers Prince Rajan, an Indian, and Daniel Cajiuat, a Filipino–American. Our security squad appeared so he dropped his gun and invited arrest, proudly identifying himself as Abid Abdul Razzaz al Hamidi, and announcing that, having done some cleansing, he felt closer to God. (In court he said he'd killed Christians for evangelising, and for sterilising Yemeni women. The Qur'an says nothing that most Muslims construe as specifically interdicting sterilisation, but many conservatives oppose it.)

Yemenis were aghast nationwide. Bill had 28 years' service, and was well known as a straight, fair and even-tempered manager with a big heart for prisoners, orphans and the destitute. We all respected him as an outstandingly gracious, generous and godly man who used his authority with discrimination, and who was the ideal leader for JBH in good times and bad. As a faithful Southern Baptist he was bound to obey his superiors, despite his conviction that the hospital's closure was a serious mistake. Being the boss, he couldn't share this personal conflict with us in any detail.

Martha had spent 25 years at Jibla, was known all over the country, and took her elderly Land Cruiser on mountain tracks where even Yemeni drivers feared to go. Clerics excoriated her as the mother of all prostitutes, but when the chips were down they usually brought their wives to her. If it be proper to call anyone generous to a fault, this was Martha, who gave to the needy with rare liberality. She worked late, and often called at our house around 10 pm to unwind and regale us with the day's highlights or stories from the past, before driving home a few kilometres to Ibb, the capital of our governorate. With an ear close to the ground and many Yemeni friends, she was the first of us to detect community undercurrents.

Kathy, 53, was a mover and shaker with an acute business sense, a detailed mental inventory of the store, and a vivacity that made her valuable far beyond her official position. With a rare ability to entertain and amuse all ages, she was the tireless organiser of compound dinners and celebrations that were invaluable social cement.

All three revelled in their faithful service to their God and to the Yemeni people, and were saddened beyond words by the IMB's determination to unload JBH for what most of us saw as unworthy reasons.

The authorities took charge immediately, and carloads of Ibb police, US embassy and FBI personnel poured onto the compound. The IMB ordered evacuation to Sana'a, the capital. All but a skeleton staff were to pack for two weeks and leave at 1 pm next day.

Numbed male Yemeni staff hung around the boundary all day, and it seemed essential that someone senior meet them. Judy was busy with the FBI crowd, so I went out and assured them that they retained our confidence. Many were deeply affected, and I told them, 'They weren't killed because they loved Yemen or because they loved Yemenis, which you know they did; they were killed because they loved Jesus. Think about that.'

After a simple, tearful service next morning, Bill and Martha were buried in the lonely little missionary graveyard among the eucalypts at the top of the compound. (Kathy's body was sent to the USA.) The site wasn't ready on time because the ground was rocky and the gravediggers were slow, so we went back to drink tea, commiserate and continue packing. Even the smallest child was unnaturally quiet. The interment took place after lunch, and our police convoy crawled out at 2.30, watched by hundreds of sad and silent Jibla residents lining the road well out into open country. Five hours later we pulled in at the Sana'a Sheraton, to spend two days being debriefed by a team including, ironically, IMB personnel who had long advocated JBH's closure.

Others could have died. Yemen Baptist Mission chief Al Lindholm and our Sana'a office manager Abraham Chacko were due for a 'premeeting' session in Bill's office at 8 am. They left Sana'a before daylight and clipped a roundabout, which broke a front wheel. They'd have been more sitting ducks, so the time they lost finding another vehicle probably saved their lives.

Bill usually breakfasted from 8 to 8.30, but with Lindholm due and Yemeni staff to pay off, he worked on. Otherwise Lee Hixon, an American with young children, would have occupied that fatal chair.

Soon we saw Jibla on TV, and Dr Jerry Rankin, the IMB president, proclaiming to the world that JBH would go on; the poor man didn't seem to know the Ministry of Health had taken it over. IMB talking heads spouted frothy assurances for days, which suggested that people in high places were drowning in guilt. Some had wanted to be shot of JBH for years, but closure by pistol-shot was too much.

Hyper-Calvinists interpret such tragedies effortlessly, but others will at least wonder why a sovereign God allowed it. We won't know everything this side of glory, and it is presumptuous to second-guess God, but some will do it anyway, so what can be said? JBH's impending closure greatly distressed all three martyrs. I think Bill saw it as the IMB gutting Baptist work in Yemen, and on his watch, so close to his retirement, that hurt.

Martha intended staying on regardless, continuing her village health work, but without a hospital base she'd have been unable to offer inpatient treatment to women in need. She knew Third World villagers have scant interest in health education and immunisations if their perceived acute needs are ignored. Our recently expanded Community Health Service, offering preventive measures but not treatment, had suffered disheartening responses, and Martha saw endless frustration ahead.

Kathy saw the situation as Martha did. She handled her job superbly, and loved Yemenis and the service we provided. Her home church had caught her enthusiasm, and sent us container loads of useful donations every year. The most vocal protester against the hospital's expected transfer to a non-Christian organisation, Kathy was prepared to stay on, but would have been unable to tolerate the accounting sleight of hand that was to creep in under new management.

Writing on 5 January 2003: I see a gracious God sparing these three servants the distress of seeing what is yet to happen to Jibla hospital. They died as they lived, working faithfully for almost 70 years between them. Dying in happy harness has much to be said for it, by comparison with a tedious, often problematic, descent into old age.

Perhaps these deaths will reinvigorate Southern Baptist missionary vision. Long ago Tertullian said, 'The blood of the martyrs is the seed of the church.' Maybe changes are ahead here, and across the region, that will enable local Christians to identify themselves to each other in safety, and form the churches that are essential if believers are to mature and Christian communities to grow. Perhaps JBH will be necessary no longer, with another entity assuming its functions.

This interpretation doesn't belittle the grief of families and friends. Marty Koehn, Bill's widow, has great spiritual strength, and her grace was a challenge to Yemenis, to supporters in the US, and to us. Days after the shootings she led the remaining foreign staff through Jibla in a well-received demonstration that nobody held Yemenis, as a people, responsible, and many townsfolk asked them in to sit on the floor and drink tea. Marty knew that many Muslims (and Christians, let it be said) are long on vengeance, but short on sacrificial love. After home leave she returned in April 2003 and worked in the medical store until her 2007 retirement.

The apostle Paul told the Philippian church he wanted to 'depart to be with Christ, which is far better, but it is expedient that I remain with you for a time.' When he died many must have wondered why, because world evangelisation was far from over, but they accepted that in God's economy Paul's work was done. Likewise, it is no longer expedient that these our friends and co-workers remain with us, so God has taken them to be with Himself. We grieve that they have left us, but must rejoice that they have gone to their reward.

'Unfinished business' may be a threadbare cliché, but it's no figment. Days after the funerals the three-year-old son of Dutch friends in Ibb dug a hole in their garden. When his mother questioned him about it he said it was for Auntie Kathy. 'We buried Uncle Bill and Dr Martha,' he said, 'but not her,' as he carefully laid a few stones in the grave and covered them with gravel. Business completed.

Many have asked how we coped. My standard reply has been that having a child die in adult life must be preparation for almost anything. (Our second daughter Robyn died at 41, after a long, extremely distressing illness.) I know of nothing to suggest that the faith of any of our fellow missionaries was shaken, but the emotional trauma ended some careers.

At a political rally two days before the Jibla murders a Yemen Socialist Party leader was assassinated for calling for more democracy, anathema to Muslims on the far right. So extremism was biting as never before.

On 6 January 2003 a *Yemen Times* columnist wrote: 'As for the Americans who worked at the Jibla Baptist Hospital, the fact of the matter is that the overwhelming majority of Yemenis find no religious doctrine in Islam that supports their murder. Surely, it is dishonorable for a Moslem to kill anyone who is a guest and who is providing assistance, *as long as that guest does not seek to disrupt the religious convictions of the people of Yemen*. Thus, most Yemenis clearly condemned the killing. Even those opposed to any religious missionaries echoed their displeasure at the killing of unarmed innocent people, who were motivated by philanthropic ideals, albeit under a different religious persuasion. Humanitarianism is a common trait of all God-fearing people everywhere.' (Italics mine.)

He was having it both ways, as he was obliged to do. In Islamic law apostasy is a capital offence, as it is for anyone seen as responsible for the conversion. Every Christian in the Muslim world knows this.

Gwen and I left Jibla convinced that the hospital was finished. We were wrong. But how did an Australian couple in their seventies come to be so far from home in the first place? That, as they say, is a very long story.

Chapter 2

Selkirk, Nairne and Naracoorte

Many families have traditions, affectations even, when naming their children. Some use a maddening alliteration of initials, or stock names, as in the Alice Duer Miller poem, *The White Cliffs*, in which the first son was always called Percy. We call him John.

Should he ape American usage, my son's eldest boy could style himself John Clezy VII, or even better if he trumps us with incontrovertible details of earlier ancestors than our family tree's taproot, my great-great-grandfather John Clezy, rector of Selkirk Grammar School in Scotland from 1825 to 1837. Old John was an austere and pernickety dominie, judging from the diary that describes the petty irritations that peppered the Clezys' voyage from Liverpool to Adelaide in 1849. But he was a good headmaster, and when he left Selkirk his was amongst the best academies outside Edinburgh, judged by the quality of student it sent up to university.

We know little about him. One tradition has him born around 1790 at Berwick-upon-Tweed, a walled and moated seaport long past its glory now, but notable for having the first purpose-built infantry barracks in the UK. Clezys lived in nearby villages, and records suggest that Old John's father, another John, was born to George and Agnes Claise/Claizy in 1755, at Coldstream. He became an officer in the Royal Artillery, and perhaps was at Woolwich Barracks when Old John was born. We have no birth certificate, but other documents describe him as born in Kent, which then included Woolwich. He said he learnt English there, but Greek and Latin in Berwick. His English accent was described as refined, which suggests that he was at least a teenager before the family returned to Berwick. Perhaps transfers between it and Woolwich meant that his father spent time in both barracks.

A distant Canadian relative has another angle, with Old John born at Longformacus, a tiny village at the sharp end of a gloomy glen north-west of Berwick. Calling it a village is an exaggeration; Longformacus is a mansion hidden by tall trees, with the laird's kirk in a corner of the front garden and a few cottages over the road. These are yuppie-smart now, but were workmen's accommodation originally. We'd know if John came from the manor or the church, and if a labourer's cottage was home, where did the money for university come from? So Longformacus sounds unlikely.

A teacher's testimonial describes him as English, so whatever his birthplace he must have been brought up south of the border. He was at Edinburgh University intermittently between 1810 and 1820, and in 1817 took a prize given by the city burghers for an English essay. He also won awards for rhetoric and Latin poetry, distinctions that no descendant has achieved. For four years he tutored the children of Colonel Robertson Macdonald of Kinlochmoidart, on Scotland's west coast, and while there tried unsuccessfully for a junior post at Selkirk. He then taught at a subscription school at Eccles, Berwickshire, for three years before applying for the rectorship of Perth Grammar School. Such preferment was more than a young man could reasonably expect, but his 1824 application to Selkirk, bolstered by a raft of hyperbolic testimonials from his Edinburgh professors, secured him its rectorship. Selkirk was a prosperous mill town, and the school's fees enabled Old John to support a wife. On 27 December 1825 he married Mary Steele and moved into Byethorn, the schoolhouse. He was to build his own Byethorn in the Adelaide Hills, at Nairne, where it still stands.

More distant family details are a mystery, but some believe we were Huguenots. The nearest French name is le Clezio, with some in Paris and more in Mauritius. The French connection is consistent with the Clezys' friendship with Sir Walter Scott, whose French wife's family had fled the Revolution. The Scotts lived near Selkirk, at Abbotsford, an extravagant Victorian Gothic baronial pile that squats above terraced lawns on the bank of the Tweed.

In 1993 Gwen and I visited Selkirk to pursue details of my ancestry. The town archivist went to her microfiche cabinet looking bored, but she brightened when she found dozens of us. In the late 1700s the spelling hadn't crystallised, and there were Clezie, Clezia, Clazy, Clezy and other versions. The name has disappeared locally, but internet searches have identified it elsewhere in the UK and in North

America. We enjoyed Selkirk, which is still prosperous, and is set amongst smooth hills resembling those around Nairne. We admired the tidy streetscape, in particular the proud memorial to the town's most illustrious son, the African explorer Mungo Park. We saw the school but not Byethorn, which had been demolished long ago to make way for more classrooms.

Months later a miner was referred to my Burnie rooms. After hearing the details of his current complaint I asked, as we do, about previous illnesses. These included tuberculosis in childhood, in Scotland.

'Where?' I asked.

'In the lowlands,' he replied.

'But where?' I persisted.

'Selkirk.'

So I described our visit, and mentioned that Old John's house had gone. 'You mean Byethorn?' he sparkled. 'I was brought up in that house.'

When I asked if he had a photo of it he promised to track one down, and a few weeks later his wife brought us a much better picture than the spotty Brownie job taken by a relative long ago.

Old John didn't come to Australia direct from Selkirk. In 1837 he resigned the rectorship to be master of the boarding house, which he dubbed Byethorn Academy. He offered extra tuition, which apparently paid well, but nevertheless he moved to another private school, in Rothesay on the Isle of Bute, in 1841 or 1842.

He was a strong Presbyterian, and his next move, to the Isle of Man, may have been partly prompted by the disruption that brewed for years before the 1843 split. A tangible focus of this complex dispute was the ministerial appointment process, which was in the gift of the local laird. In view of his innate conservatism – he was the type for whom rolling over in bed amounts to a paradigm shift – it is remarkable that Old John supported the idea of congregations calling their ministers rather than having them foisted on them. This preternaturally democratic stance may have alienated him from those best able to send their boys to his academy. Whatever caused his move, it followed an invitation from Mary's brother, Alexander Steele, to teach at his Crescent Academy in Douglas. This position promised further profit.

He had prospered already. In 1840, when John Fife Angas's South

Australian Company offered free settlers prime land at a pound an acre, Old John was able to buy two 80-acre blocks on the Nairne town boundary. This risky action by a middle-aged schoolmaster perhaps reflected his friendship with Sir Walter Scott. Two enthusiastic Scott nephews had bought Charles Sturt's station near Nairne, on what is now called Scott's Creek, and did well. Mary Clezy's brother-in-law, John Disher, had farmed in the colony since 1839. He agreed to run the Clezy land, which was near his own, and did well out of it, but he seriously overgrazed, so another settler wrote to Old John urging him to come out and take over before his property was ruined.

Despite his restless nature it is surprising that he took this advice, a tall order for a man steeped in the classics but lacking real farming experience. And he was no unencumbered adventurer – he had Mary and seven children in tow, plus Mary's sister, Isabella, and son-in-law David Moffatt, newly married to his eldest girl. They sailed on the *Anna*, 1099 tons, departing Liverpool on 12 June 1849, and after an uncomfortable voyage docked in Melbourne on 20 September. Most passengers disembarked there, but the Clezys stayed aboard for five weary weeks, and reached Port Adelaide on 6 November.

Old John was pleased with his property, which proved to be 30-bushel-an-acre wheat land. This would have satisfied most people, but with optimism born of ignorance he aimed higher, and imported seed from Scotland – of Italian origin. He shared it with a neighbour, John Frame, who developed an early-maturing strain, known as Purple Straw or Tuscan. Its introduction has been described as the key to the establishment of the South Australian wheat belt, for long the granary for the Australian colonies. Apart from this serendipitous venture Old John was essentially a smalltime gentleman farmer, living by renting out his land.

In 2000 local historical societies gained National Trust support for a memorial to John Clezy, commemorating his contribution to the South Australian wheat industry. It was erected near Byethorn, where numerous descendants saw the plaque unveiled and enjoyed a weekend of concentrated, almost saccharine, nostalgia, many of us meeting distant cousins for the first time.

Old John bought more land, and also ran a general store in Nairne until his death in 1864. John II carried it on until 1880, with his wife Jane (nee Stockham) being the brains of the business. A skilled milliner, she had a large clientele. Naturally, her daughters were hatted properly, and the line of Clezy girls sailing into church on Sunday mornings was said to be one of the sights of Nairne. Old John educated his children according to his lights, which was anything but appropriate preparation for farming life. John II followed his father, but James's eyes were opened to a wider world and he went off to the University of Melbourne, where he became a highly regarded classical coach.

The Presbyterians didn't build in Nairne, and our family put their energies into the Primitive Methodist Church. In 1884 John II laid the foundation stone for their new building. His religion was no mere cultural gloss, but permeated his life. He was much in demand in the pulpit, and briefly was Nairne Council chairman, serving as honest broker during a turbulent period in 1886. He died in 1913, leaving Jane and thirteen children who lived into their 80s, except for George who was hit by a train in his prime.

Byethorn remained in the family until 1939, except for acreage sold in 1881 after the survey for the Adelaide–Melbourne railway line cut it into two unequal and dysfunctional pieces. It might have been ours to this day if my grandfather's bachelor brother Willie hadn't so objected to a rate rise that he chose to sell up rather than pay up. After a literal cooling-off period he offered the buyer a good premium for Byethorn's return, but this was in vain, so he retired to Adelaide to live with his spinster sisters. He rarely darkened the door of a church, so the tidy sum he left to the Presbyterians occasioned some surprise.

John III (my grandfather) was born at Nairne in 1864. After an elementary education he worked Byethorn, which was never so successful as in his time. He also did seasonal work on wool boats on the Darling–Murrumbidgee system, for long the lifeline of western New South Wales. At 40 he married Margaret Munro from Beechworth, Victoria, and settled on land fifteen miles north of Naracoorte, in the south-east of South Australia, near the Victorian border. He built a house named Alves on the wooded slope that marks the eastern edge of the Mosquito Plains. Dad was born there in 1906.

When Cooee, three miles north of Naracoorte, came onto the market, the family moved there in the interests of the children's education. Cooee was prime land originally taken up by the Barr-Malcolms, and was graced by a fine sandstone farmhouse, built on a rise near the road. The homestead therefore lacks the long tree-lined drive so favoured by broad-acre proprietors all over Australia.

My earliest Cooee memories are of the elegant acetylene lamps in the foyer and principal rooms, the window seats, and the wide circumferential verandah bordered by mauve wisteria espaliered on wire. I marvelled at the stone lavatory 20 yards from the house, with a standard adult seat plus a mini-job for us children, perched high above a pit. Other outbuildings were as substantial as the house and the lav. A stable doorjamb bears a pencilled record of Barr-Malcolm children's heights, still as fresh as yesterday.

Grandpa was a good farmer and owned up to 8000 acres, 640 around the house and the rest in several parcels on the almost treeless Mosquito Plains. This ancient seabed slopes almost imperceptibly from a western border stuttering into the scrub that reaches a hundred kilometres to the coast, down to a sharp eastern edge where the Adelaide road skirts a line of low sandhills. Originally the black-soil plains were covered with onion grass and tussocks, but Grandpa planted rye and other nutritious fodder. His main effort went into raising merino wethers, for which Cooee was ideal, as the South East rarely suffered a drought. Even in 1914, when most of Australia was parched and thousands of farmers were ruined, Cooee prospered.

Grandpa was short, broad and strong, easily able to lift two bags of wheat at the same time. He was quiet, not given to rash decisions or unjustifiable anger. Like his father and grandfather he could be called, tautologically, a born-again Christian, with his faith much more than a convenient philosophy. Bishop Ambrose of Milan put it perfectly: 'I will not glory because I am righteous; I will glory because I am redeemed. I will not glory because I am free from sin; I will glory because I am forgiven.'

Grandpa was a Presbyterian elder, and with his brother-in-law Trevor Williams ran a young people's Bible class before the morning service. Around 1930 the minister scrubbed their notes off the blackboard – he wouldn't have this rubbish taught in his church. The family had long chafed at this man's liberalism, so worshipped temporarily with the Anglicans, whose minister, their friend Walter Corden, was an evangelical. Our families have now been friends for four generations.

Grandpa and Uncle Trevor preached during ministerial absences but neither was a natural, so they read their sermons. One of them (not Grandpa, according to his youngest daughter) once turned over two pages without noticing, although the puzzled congregation did. At least he must have had their attention. Grandpa was briefly a Justice of the Peace and sat on the bench with another JP, as the custom was. His fair and gentle nature made judging between two plausible but contradictory stories too difficult, so he soon resigned.

When domestic duties included such tasks as soap-making, and good housekeeping was time-consuming, he held that the girls had quite enough work in the house so forbade them learning to milk, for example, in case this tempted the boys to do another round of ploughing or whatever and leave the cows to them.

Five children arrived in fifteen years. My father was John Beresford, his second name indicating Grandma's admiration for Lord Beresford, sent too late to save 'Chinese' Gordon at Khartoum in 1885. The third child was Wilfred Grenfell, named for the pioneer medical missionary to Labrador. The daughters were Margaret, Jean and Alethe.

Uncle Wilf farmed successfully, initially on land he bought from Grandpa. He married Peggy Oxley of Melbourne after meeting her at Upwey, an annual conference modelled on the Keswick (England) holiness meetings. Their children are Judith and Pamela.

Margaret and Alethe never married, but Jean did at 32, to the Rev. John Coombe, a 64-year-old family friend widowed in India. They produced Margaret and Geoffrey, to the immoderate disgust of those who held that such an old man couldn't possibly sire healthy offspring. Geoffrey broke the mould by becoming a Roman Catholic priest, and worked in PNG before relocating to a slum parish in Manila.

Margaret Clezy was mother's help to a degree that vanished long ago. Her smocking was a byword and she fitted out nieces and others with their favourite clothes. When the family moved to Adelaide they entertained more visiting Christians than they ever saw in Naracoorte. I thought guests were always in the house. Margaret enjoyed it; like her mother, she was 'given to hospitality', to quote the King James Version.

Alethe spent a lifetime with Christian organisations, and helped establish the Scripture Union movement in the Philippines in the 1960s. Later she worked in Christian publishing in India and when over 80 ran pottery master classes for Fusion Australia at Poatina, Tasmania.

All five children followed their parents in faith and practice. Uncle Wilf ceased church gardening and maintenance in 2001 after a coronary bypass at 89. Despite decades of driving Caterpillar tractors long before the days of earmuffs or exhaust mufflers, at 99 he had excellent hearing. We have familial deafness, but somehow the bent gene missed him.

After retiring to Adelaide in 1941 Grandpa was at a loose end, but brightened his Fridays, whatever the weather, by tramming it to the Gepps Cross saleyards to see how stock were doing. He visited his Adelaide sisters often but still had time on his hands, so delighted in returning to Cooee at shearing time to keep sheep up to the holding yards. Performing this lowly task on what had been his own domain was no problem until the horse pulling his jinker jerked away from a gate and tipped him out. The ground was soft and his injuries were trivial but this accident convinced him that a man of 80 should truly retire.

There are no Clezys around Naracoorte now. Grandpa's brother James farmed near Cooee, and with Aunt Illeret produced a pigeon pair. Their Cyril never married, was slightly odd, and ended his days in a mental hospital. He refused to feed uncooked offal to his dogs, and I remember shearers ridiculing him for this eccentricity. He was right, of course, when hydatid disease was rife. If Grandpa had followed his crazy nephew's example he may have saved Grandma several major operations for hydatids.

Another Naracoorte brother, Bob, a stock agent of high repute, had one daughter. Even in Mount Gambier, 100 kilometres south, where brother Herbert's brood included five sons, the name will disappear, except for the Clezy Crescent sign. One son never married, two had daughters, and the male line of another is extinguished. Only Herbert's eldest, John Alexander, has male direct descendants, far from Mount Gambier. Even in Grandpa's line some saw the name disappearing, as my parents had twelve grand-daughters before our John appeared. He has six sons, so the name seems secure.

Chapter 3

Growing up

My father, known as 'Jack' or 'JBC', was no student, but he took a prize for efficiency – whatever that meant in the 1920s. He'd always aimed to go on the land and grudged the year and a bit he spent at high school before leaving to work Cooee with Grandpa. An attraction (which was mutual) at school, and at church, was Juanita, Albert Schinckel's youngest daughter. Albert's parents were Schleswig-Holsteiners who came to South Australia in 1848 in the second wave of Lutherans fleeing persecution. In the 1880s he settled near Goroke in Western Victoria.

My mother's primary schooling was at Moreah, a speck on the map, more of a concept than a place. She and her sister Mollie rode to school along a furrow their father ploughed through miles of scrub lest they get lost. They had three days' school one week and two the next because their teacher also served Booroopki, another tiny settlement. Such limited teacher–pupil interaction would be unacceptable now, but they survived.

Bush life was no deprivation. They had books galore, and learnt piano from old Uncle Boehm, who lived with them. A stepsister and three stepbrothers were at home until the Great War. Albert's father had farmed near Naracoorte for many years, and for the sake of the younger children's secondary schooling they all moved there after the war.

With an excellent apprenticeship behind him and marriage ahead, in 1927 Jack bought 2000 acres in Victoria, fifteen miles east of Naracoorte, from Bob Laidlaw of Newlands, a pioneer Western District sheep run in the same league as Bringalbert, Benayeo and Mortat. Newlands stretched seven or eight miles from Apsley to the South Australian border, and how far in other directions I never knew. Like many similar spreads, much of it remained undeveloped until after World War II, when thousands of acres were cut up for soldier settlement.

Dad's property was well drained and treed with bull oak and red gum. He named it Wahronga, and built a small weatherboard house close to the Naracoorte–Apsley road. Another block on higher ground a few miles away was called King Billy after a long-dead Aboriginal leader. He was well on with his clearing, burning the red gum but saving the bull oak for firewood, when he married Nita on 27 December 1928.

I was born in Naracoorte on 16 November 1929 and, of course, was named John, Kenneth to identify me, and Albert for Grandpa Schinckel. Ailsa arrived in 1931, Trevor in 1935 and Norman in 1937.

Mother was never robust and did no outside work. She suffered with post-partum depression, so employed a housemaid for many years. In our simplicity we children perceived her as eventually recovering, but Alethe says she never regained the glow and sparkle of her youth.

Her rose garden was her delight but it asked too much of our rainwater tanks, so Dad laid pipes from a windmill over a deep bore 400 yards away. When a workman laughed at him, being fooled by an optical illusion that put the bore-head below the house, Dad rested a spirit level on a fence-post and invited the doubter to sight along it. So Mother was never short of water for her roses.

The Presbyterians worshipped in a little stone building on the edge of Apsley town, and our week revolved around the Sunday service there. Our minister lived miles away at Edenhope and had several preaching places, as in many rural charges, so our services could be morning or evening. Soon Dad was on the Board of Management and later became an elder.

I was taken to that church when I was three weeks old, and I've rarely missed a Sunday since. Even as children, when concentration can be difficult, we didn't find church irksome. We even took it home. I was about six, preaching to a line of Ailsa's dolls propped up on the sitting-room couch, when Mother called us to lunch, so I adjourned for half an hour. I'd heard on the wireless that Parliament sometimes adjourned and I reckoned that this would be OK for church services too. Without fail Mother read Bible stories and prayed with us at bedtime, which helps explain why we all grew up as believers, with adult understanding of our faith developing in due course.

Except on Sunday, his day of rest, Dad worked long hours, often feeding his horses in the dark. He transformed virgin bush into a prizewinning sheep farm, and a silver cup described his pasture as the best around Apsley in 1936. I found such achievements of no interest. I was bookish, and by the time I was knee-high anyone with half an eye could see I'd never be a farmer. Instead of revelling in it all I was frightened of the turkey gobblers, thought dogs and horses stank, and was revolted by milk straight from the cow. Still am.

What my parents made of my aversion to all things bucolic I'll never know. Perhaps they linked it to my left-handedness, then regarded literally as sinister, so much so that Mother wrote at least one anguished letter to Grandma about it. Her concern was compounded when Ailsa too was left-handed.

If our grandchildren know no more than this about Mother her image will be distorted, unless they remember that they too are products of their times. In some respects she had it better – she was sheltered to a degree that is rare nowadays, in a close household headed by godly parents. Grandma Schinckel was a particularly gracious lady who bore years of disabling rheumatoid arthritis without complaint. Perhaps this explained Mother's heightened concern about aches and pains.

In her childhood mirrors were turned to the wall when lightning was about, a practice she continued until Dad talked her out of it. She believed in homeopathy; after all, didn't the King have a homeopathic doctor? Her standby was aconite. She was timid rather than bold, but didn't panic if we were ill. The doctor was 20 miles away, and I remember no urgent visits. If we were off-colour Dad's standard remedy was castor oil, so we cracked hardy in his presence.

Dad was too busy to pay much attention to his children. Mother read to us, taught us reading and writing, and saw to it that we learnt piano, which Ailsa and I began with a Naracoorte lady on Saturday afternoons. When Norman arrived with infantile hemiplegia, and needed extra care, we saw a new side to our father. We'd never known him open a book apart from his Bible, but he read to Norman and, amazingly, concocted stories for him.

A tree-lined creek ran through Wahronga, and Ailsa and I sometimes paddled in it, hunting for yabbies that always got away. Returning from one such expedition we came upon a glistening newborn calf struggling uncertainly to its feet, while its mother stood by, as cows do, munching mournfully on the afterbirth. I was bewildered: where on earth had this calf come from? Ailsa (aged four) knew instinctively, and gently explained it all in monosyllables to her dumbfounded brother. This incident, amounting to a rite of passage, led to some doctors and nurses business that flummoxed Mother. ('We're only playing, Mummy!')

Wahronga was four miles from Apsley, and with transport problematic there was no rush to send me to school. I thought reading and writing was enough, and had no higher ambition until I saw a woodwork class in action on Open Day. I eagerly enrolled at Apsley Primary School, number 1208 in the Victorian system, in mid-1936, the year that left-handers, at least in Apsley, were no longer forced to write right-handed. But I never did learn woodwork.

And I lack other skills that most farm-bred boys absorb unconsciously. Like Grandpa, Dad was no handyman, and his tools were few. He could erect a good line of fencing and pull up a windmill if rubbish got under the clack, but otherwise he was unusually dependent on tradesmen. He knew nothing about internal combustion engines, not that he needed to at first, when he drove a buggy and pair.

Apsley was the archetypical Sleepy Hollow. Like many settlements, it began as a utilitarian but indispensable appendage to a squatter's spread, in this case Newlands. It was a crossroads in the bush, with the pub, the post office and a general store bunched on the cross. Other small businesses and simple weatherboard houses spread out thinly in all directions. The postmistress operated the telephone exchange, so knew everything of importance going on in the district, and much more. Beyond the post office was the police station, whose finely attired constable seemed inseparable from his even finer horse.

Not every farmer's credit was good but Dad's was, and I sometimes tagged along when he paid our grocery bill at Geo. Chapman & Son's store. While Dad wrote his cheque Mr Chapman solemnly handed me a boiled sweet as a sort of discount. Otherwise we saw few luxuries, but didn't lack good food. Home-killed mutton was always on, along with our home-grown vegetables. Occasionally we tasted beef, when a neighbour killed an old cow to share around. No money changed hands, and next time beef was due another struggling cocky killed the best beast he could spare. Chook was a Christmas luxury. We knew nothing of pork because Dad detested pigs forever after a sow almost killed him in his childhood.

In hard times, with high unemployment, swaggies were a common sight. The law of the jungle as it evolved in rural Australia meant that they usually tramped alone. Often a hungry unwashed man would wander up the 200 yards from the road to our house. Mother always produced something, usually a thick mutton sandwich (we regarded rabbit as dog-food) but one gaunt chap was more interested in methylated spirits to rub on his rheumaticky knee, and carried a bottle for it. He was excessively grateful when she found him a few ounces. ('Oops, lady, that's enough. Ta.') These men were harmless, but Mother was nervous and always peered through the sitting room's lace curtains to watch them off the property. This time the man with the knee trouble was at the garden tap, diluting the meths. She was mystified, much to Dad's amusement when she told him about it that night.

The day I began school Dad drove me there in his second-hand 1927 Chevrolet. Miss Cawthra took the first four grades and sat me in a heavy double desk with another farmer's son, Lindsay Cross. He and his sister were the first, and for long the only, children I knew who were allowed and expected to use their parents' Christian names. This aberration had no apparent philosophical basis, and otherwise the Crosses were a typical farming family.

That first morning I was turned out in new clothes and shiny black boots, and near Jackie White's waterhole, Apsley's favourite swimming spot on the edge of the common, we picked up two skinny barefoot lads. That night I wondered aloud why they went unshod; it was mid-winter, with horse-troughs and puddles iced over in the mornings. Dad explained that their father drank his wages at the Border Inn, Apsley's pub. There was no liquor at Wahronga, so why a man spent money on it rather than on his children was a mystery. I was ignorant of alcohol and its effects for many years, apart from an indelible memory of the sour smell wafting through the squeaky swing doors of the Border Inn's front bar. In the 1930s there was little building activity around Apsley, but I remember the Border Inn being done over in about 1938. Seventy years later the exterior is unchanged, apart from more layers of paint, but the building looks smaller.

My new school lore included a string of four-letter words, and when I trotted these out Mother knew some were unacceptable but was uncertain of others, so I had to recite them to Dad, who soaped my mouth out for each item below the line. I'm unaware of scars from this crude but effective behaviour therapy.

By mid-1936 getting to school was easy because Reg Ansett's Naracoorte–Hamilton bus passed Wahronga at the right time each morning. Three days a week I rode home with a baker returning to Naracoorte, but for months I hoofed it on Tuesdays and Thursdays. I detested this lonely walk, fearing attack, which never came, by an Old English sheepdog belonging to Bob Laidlaw's sister, and which often waited at the roadside for me. Sometimes the coast seemed clear, and then the fearsome beast would rush in my direction from behind the trees that hid the vast Newlands homestead.

My anxiety ceased when Dad bought me a fat little pony. This frisky animal, named Black Magic after a horse in a favourite storybook, served me well but knew she had my measure. I paddocked her behind Louie Simpson's house in the main street, and whenever she felt mischievous Louie had to catch her for me after school. We knew the Simpsons because they were Presbyterians, and also because Dad was one of many who shore at The Depot, the communal shearing shed at the bottom of the Simpsons' garden.

Most of us began school believing that our teachers were paragons but in time all lost their bloom. Miss Cawthra was the first to fall. An insipid city girl in her first post, she boarded at a rundown cottage with a lady whose husband worked away for most of the year. Whenever he came home poor Miss C slept on the verandah, whatever the weather. We pitied her because even her barefoot students did better than that, or said they did.

When I joined the Gould Bird League, and my precious membership certificate finally filtered through the system to Apsley, she was dim enough to sign her name in my space. When she realised her error she said it didn't matter, but she'd wrecked it. Disgusted, I took the irreparably defaced document home and burnt it. We feared she would last forever, but her transfer out came when I was in third grade. Her replacement was a complete contrast. Miss C was pale and willowy, with enough hair to have safely sold half to a wigmaker. The newcomer was red-faced and shaped like a teapot. He sported an apology for a moustache, an idiosyncrasy rarely seen in Apsley, and the parting in his thinning hair was broad and crooked, reminding one wag of a sheep pad up a hill. We thought little of his curious accent until the day a story in the Victorian Grade 3 reader exposed his inability to articulate medial Ts. We could say 'a little bottle of milk' but he couldn't. The class had a mimic, and, despite ignorance of what a plosive might be, he repeated the magic phrase in a creditable Cockney accent at increasing volume until we almost wet ourselves. Our teacher pretended not to notice but we knew we'd got to him. For months we thought 'a li'le bo'le of milk' sounded funnier than anything else we'd ever heard.

There was little to laugh about during the Great Depression. With produce prices falling Dad struggled to find mortgage repayments for Bob Laidlaw, who invariably appeared for his cheque on the due date, once when Mother was baking. When he rang the doorbell she thought it was another of Dad's jokes, for no good reason, so she stomped to the door covered in flour, jerked it open, and stuck her tongue right out. Mr Laidlaw, after a moment's goggle-eyed astonishment, hooted good-naturedly while Mother went purple.

We survived the Depression and by about 1940 Dad was doing well enough to build a woolshed, but my shearing memories are of The Depot. After school I watched the rouseabouts scramble to whisk the fleeces, white and fluffy as cumulus clouds, from the four-stand shearing board and throw them expertly onto the wool table for Louie Simpson to skirt and class them. He sometimes let the juniors try their hands at this arcane skill, but he was never satisfied, and if they graded a fleece as AA or whatever he always found reason to disagree.

Each afternoon Louie ground the shearers' combs and cutters, and I was fascinated by the sparks flying upwards from the emery wheel in the gloom of the engine shed. And I still see sweat pouring off men bent double in greasy singlets and trousers, barely pausing between sheep, like gun shearers aiming for a record tally. A bell, precise as a starter's pistol, timed four two-hour periods during which the handpieces flashed through the fleece-skin interface with surgical precision. The smell of new wool was pleasant enough, but this strenuous life wasn't for me.

No children lived near Wahronga so school was my first real experience of other boys. I was shy and soft and attracted the attentions of a bully, the first genuine fatty I'd ever seen, a juvenile bruiser as pretty as a pit bull with pimples. He kept going for my tender spots until I complained to Dad who promised me threepence if I punched his nose next time around. I mustered the necessary courage, with a beneficial result.

This was a one-off and didn't save me from becoming the butt of the class, saddled with the galling nickname of Professor Nimbus, a hydrocephalic comic strip character in the Melbourne *Sun*. He was a thick little twit, the personification of bumbledom, and some smart aleck saw a resemblance. I don't know when or why I earned it, unless it was the morning I breathlessly informed a boy, late for school the day the duck season opened, that a shooter, Cliff somebody, had drowned at dawn in the Newlands swamp. How was I to know it was his uncle?

Schoolwork was a breeze. I mastered the lead pencil and slate in no time, so Miss C wanted to put me in Grade 2, but I'd taken a liking to another Grade 1 pupil, Elaine Munn, and promotion would seat me two rows away so I refused to move. I did Grade 2 the next year and then grades 3 and 4 in one year, thus catching up with my age group.

Life was different in the senior classroom, for grades 5 to 8. For one thing we had much more homework and for another there was a high drawer where the headmaster kept his strap. We feared it all the more because he used it so rarely. I felt it after several of us threw gravel onto the tin roof of the dunny behind the Oddfellows' Hall next door. Tom was one of a sour pair of bachelor brothers living across the lane behind the school, in a dark tumbledown house surrounded by dead farm implements. He needed a pit stop on his way home from his regular liquid lunch at the Border Inn, and we gave him a minute to get going before throwing our stones. By the time he emerged we had vanished, which annoyed him wonderfully, so we kept it up until he complained to the head. We soon felt the swish of leather, the traditional six of the best.

Occasionally a huge rusty red van brought the Western District Touring Talkies to the Oddfellows' Hall, but few children saw them. In their courting days Dad sometimes took Mother to the silent movies in Naracoorte, but life was serious now, and if they could spare the money they no longer had time for such frivolity.

The school lacked sportsgrounds so we played Australian Rules football in the back lane. There were no goal posts and I forget how we scored. In summer we played cricket of a sort. For much of the year it was marbles, for which the gravel-covered playground was far from ideal.

Dad was a good manager in lean times and in January 1938 bought a new car, a Ford V8, with headlamps set into the mudguards, which I thought looked extremely smart. He turned up in it at Robe, west of Naracoorte, where Mother and Auntie Margaret had taken us for our first seaside holiday. Robe was a shabby fishing village, a far cry from today's selfconsciously elite resort. It didn't grab me. Cold water in my ears and grit in my gills were bad enough without the pervasive stench of rotting seaweed. And who wanted to make silly sandcastles anyway? To me the simile 'happy as a sandboy' was sick, sick, sick, but I was the exception, so we went back for more next year.

All except Dad, that is. Until his prostatectomy took him to Adelaide for a month in his mid-70s he never had a holiday, his rationale being that in winter he was too busy and in summer the risk of bushfires was too great. True as far as it went perhaps, but I was to learn that other farmers managed to take holidays. Dad loved his farm, and his greatest pleasure was work.

His bushfire concerns were well founded, and during the terrible fires of 1939 I remember Mother frantically packing suitcases lest we need to abandon Wahronga. We smelt smoke long before we saw the jagged, jerking flames through the lattice of gum trees a mile away, on the far side of Newlands swamp. It fizzled out before it reached us, but I'll never forget next day's trip around the district. From Apsley to Naracoorte thousands of sheep lay roasted, anywhere from rare to well done, belly-up like giant black beetles with their legs pointing skywards. Trees and fences smouldered and great piles of ash under twists of blackened roofing iron indicated where precious buildings had been.

I finished in Apsley at Grade 5. Melbourne friends, George and Elsie Coombe, whose son Sidwell, about my age, was to enrol at Ivanhoe Grammar School in 1941, suggested that I live with them and become an Ivanhoe boy too. My secondary schooling would pose a problem sooner or later, so we all saw this as an excellent solution, and I spent a happy 1941 in Form 4 with Sid. Chapel introduced me to the prayer book, different from the Presbyterian rubric, but that didn't faze me. I knew Christians came in many brands.

Our most memorable master was an excitable Lebanese who taught French. He was fluent in Arabic too, but barely spoke English. His party piece was scribbling our names on the board in a wiry Arabic script, and when I came to that language 60 years later I could still remember the wild swirl he made with mine. He taught me little

French but masters of other subjects did better, so that Sid and I took two of the first three prizes, and won house colours.

In 1941 Grandpa Clezy, then 76, had a hernia operation. Grandma chose to believe that he'd never work again and persuaded him to retire to Adelaide. Dad gladly bought Cooee, selling Wahronga well to an Adelaide investor whose wife had no time for roses, so their first act was to bulldoze Mother's precious garden. Our move put us within easy distance of a high school. The timing was right because Ivanhoe's buildings were commandeered for the RAAF in 1942, with boarders moving to Yea, north-east of Melbourne, while dayboys crowded into an Ivanhoe church hall complex. Much as I enjoyed the Coombes, even I saw that it was better to switch to the high school in Naracoorte.

Cooee's acetylene lamps and their carbide batteries were gone, replaced by a 32-volt plant. This was because Naracoorte's electricity supply was privately owned and we were beyond its service area. Later the government bought out the private concern, so we graduated to 240 volts, with new appliances except for the Silent Knight kerosene fridge that worked well for years.

Naracoorte retained its strong Scots ambience, with the St Andrew's Presbyterian Church spire visible for miles. Most local farmers were into sheep and the town's prosperity paralleled theirs. A bank was on every corner, always a good sign. The Adelaide–Mt Gambier railway passed through, with a branch line to the port of Kingston. The railway workshop was the major employer of non-farm labour until long after World War II.

The high school syllabus was slim, with no French or German. The foreign language on offer was Latin, still regarded as the *sine qua non* for a real education. There was a basic general curriculum and a commercial stream. Biology was available only in Adelaide. Our school's library was built during my time and was the first local illustration that, in practice as well as in theory, education was progressing beyond talk and chalk.

The library had other uses. At irregular intervals teachers took us there for singing sessions. (They could hardly be called lessons.) When my class teacher Phil Howlett learnt that I played piano he bought me Duke Ellington's 'Solitude'. Its discords seem benign now but they were a severe jolt then, and sounded even worse on the out-of-tune school piano than they did at home. All except PH were happier with common chords than with elementary Ellington, and he can't have rated this timid musical adventure a success.

Schoolwork was neither troublesome nor engaging but I enjoyed sport. In summer we played cricket, and although I was a hopeless batsman I was a good slow bowler. Left-handers who spin it both ways are useful, and I made the town A side for a few games. When coaches from Adelaide introduced baseball I proved to be an above-average pitcher, with an awkward curve ball. Once again, being left-handed gave me an edge.

Two state examinations were the first steps towards any career beyond labouring or housework. The Intermediate Certificate took two or three years, depending on the student's ability. Shortly before my Intermediate I developed catarrhal jaundice and was judged unfit to sit the exam. Presumably this decision was made with help from our friend Lloyd Tiver, a pharmacist who provided much medical advice for Naracoorte people. It was wartime, and the town's one doctor was too busy to be bothered with trivia. So I repeated the year, and being doubly prepared I passed with credit in four of the seven subjects, which was regarded as an excellent performance for a country student. Next year the much smaller Leaving class cut me down to size and I managed straight passes only.

I made few school friends. Milton Smith became an economist and went abroad with the Colombo Plan when he was about 20, at a time when overseas employment was almost beyond imagining. Lester Russell, the son of a Bordertown minister, became a high school teacher. These friendships were of no great depth, and we lost touch almost completely. I can boast of no lifelong friend except Sidwell Coombe, and this relationship has suffered gaps of many years.

Like married primary producers generally, Dad wasn't called up for war service. We were almost self-sufficient food-wise, and apart from the innovation of cuffless trousers, which we thought low-class and ugly, the austerity talk meant little. Austerity was the posh British catchword for the exigencies of rationing. I heard a circus clown ask his mate if he'd seen the austerity chamber-pot.

'Nah. Wot's it like?'

'It's on'y a rim'n'a handle. Ya gotta put ya own bottom in it.'

We knew men who had joined up, the wireless constantly fed us grisly news about the evil deeds of the Axis, and twice a day I rode past

Naracoorte's Air Raid Precautions post, manned by volunteer spotters, binoculars at the ready, waiting for the Japs who never came. Despite these insistent reminders the war seemed unreal until one Friday a RAAF Avro Anson chugged across the Cooee sky and flopped onto 'the sixty-six', a flat paddock two back from the road. No aeroplane had landed on Cooee before, so we rushed down to see the silvery wonder. The crew spoke of obscure engine trouble and the pilot came up to the house to phone the base 60 miles away, asking engineers to come up next morning. Suddenly a bubbly Comforts Fund girl arrived from Naracoorte to collect the crew, just as one of Dad's far-from-gullible workmen noticed a cowling open and a split pin missing from the starter motor. The poker-faced airmen growled that regulations forbade them touching it, and went off to Naracoorte where there just happened to be a gala ball in the Town Hall that night. This was the social event of the year and much hair was expected to be let down. It was. Late next morning an engineering corps vehicle rumbled into our driveway, followed by the Comforts Fund girl and the revellers. I forget how many men it took to replace the split pin, but it was done in a flash and the bleary-eyed, hung-over flyers took off.

The war came no closer to us than this, and I never stopped to wonder what I'd do if it was still on when I left school. A vague desire to become an architect arose from my interest in the construction of the house the Coombes built while I was with them. Whatever ideas my parents may have had about careers for their scion they didn't influence me directly, and I remember no discussion about it. If Dad was upset that the land didn't enthuse me he hid it well. He was mildly contemptuous of neighbours who were lazy or muddlers or both, and must have known I'd be no better. Perhaps his undisguised pride in his children's modest academic achievements helped him handle any disappointment.

Again, we worshipped at the Presbyterian Church. As in Apsley, we children happily attended church and Sunday school, free of the miseries that many people admit to, or bemoan, when describing their childhood. This was because our parents led by quiet unfeigned example. They were deeply committed Christians who saw separation from the world as more important than community engagement. For my parents and theirs, the core of their religion was their life-transforming assurance that they served the living God as revealed in Jesus

Christ. As children of God, they aimed to love and serve Him, living out their conviction that the abundant Christian life totally discounts much that unbelievers find supremely important.

Friends in other denominations had the same outlook. I cannot criticise them or my parents for their withdrawal from whatever they perceived as worldly and ephemeral, because the greatest names in Christian history share one characteristic with the humblest believer: they see the eternal as infinitely more important than the temporal. My parents served God wholeheartedly as they believed best, and their practical Christian lives had a positive influence on many others. If ever a man did good by stealth it was my father, but I was unaware of its extent for many years, and learnt of his munificence quite accidentally.

Members of Christian mission societies on deputation always found a welcome in our home, and we met many interesting people this way. Letters from one such couple, George Coombe's brother John and his first wife, working on the India–Nepal border, provided the spark that fired my lifelong interest in postage stamps. Not much charm, perhaps, in a scrap of paper bearing a deep olive portrait of the King and Emperor George V, but this unpromising item sparked my greatest hobby. Nowadays myriad forms of active and passive entertainment compete for our time, so stamp collecting has gone the way of many hobbies and is commonly held to be on a par with collecting teddy bears or salt and pepper shakers, but a hard core of enthusiasts remains undeterred by the attempts some countries make to kill the goose. There is abiding interest in many areas of philately, and although fashions come and go, the classic period will keep its devotees forever. At medical school two of our teachers regularly pored over each other's treasures, with their juniors supposing that the only logical explanation for such strange activity was that it gave them opportunities to toast each stamp.

My parents had no serious hobbies but Mother enjoyed her German piano that had the richest bass I've ever heard in an upright. She had a small collection of gramophone records and soothed me in infancy by playing Beethoven symphonies on her spring-powered His Master's Voice machine. We had a Fisk Radiola in a stylish cabinet, powered by A and B batteries, which I remember best for the long-running comedy, *Dad and Dave*. These hayseeds lived in Snake Gully, nine miles from Gundagai, according to the signature tune. Despite the program's name most of the action seemed to involve Dave and Mabel.

When Australia played cricket in England Dad would lie on the carpet with his head near the wireless, untroubled by the crackling and whistling that went with short-wave broadcasts. Later in life he allowed himself to listen by day if the temperature after lunch was over 104°F, when he applied his rule that in such heat cricket took priority over anything else. He had Grandpa's relentless work ethic, and no weather prevented him getting on with whatever was waiting to be done – but cricket could.

He often spent Friday afternoons at the saleyards, an important meeting place for graziers whether or not they were actually in the market. When I dropped in after school I hoped he hadn't bought sheep, which would mean me tailing them home. Even worse, sheep he put in mightn't reach his reserve, and would have to be driven back to Cooee. Most boys enjoyed bossing sheep about with dogs, but I saw nothing in it but sore feet and wasted time.

Although the Leaving Certificate allowed matriculation, almost everyone aiming to go to university did a Leaving Honours year. This wasn't offered in country high schools, so a move to the Adelaide High School was ahead. At first the plan was for me to live with my grandparents in Linden Park, but Grandpa Clezy's tedious dotage was making enough demands on the household, so it seemed better that I board elsewhere. The family worshipped about a mile up the road at the Burnside Christian Church, one of Adelaide's few surviving union churches. Although styled non-denominational it was, in essence, an independent Baptist congregation. Pastor Burrow and his wife had a son about my age, due to enter dental school. Thinking that they would welcome a little extra money, Grandma asked them about taking me in. Her bright idea did more than solve our immediate problem; it determined the course of my life. So I thank God for Grandma.

Chapter 4

To Adelaide

Living with the Burrows solved my problem. Reg and Hettie were warm and extroverted, so putting a country lad at ease was second nature, and John was glad to have a boy his own age in the house. We meshed well, and I remember no major disagreement in my years with them.

Reg was a fine preacher and an exceptional pastor. From 1912 to 1926 he and Hettie worked as pioneer missionaries in Bolivia, combining evangelistic and medical work – not that he was a doctor, although he certainly had the makings. While he was at Bible college the Royal Adelaide Hospital senior staff had taken him into the wards with their regular students – and with Florey and Cairns in the class the standard was high. This preparation made Reg a particularly useful missionary in remote Andean villages, and the Burrows were greatly loved throughout the Bolivian Indian Mission field. They raised three boys and lost another before returning to Adelaide, where John was born. Reg maintained a lifelong interest in medical matters, which often dominated table conversation.

Adelaide High School competition was stiff. I enrolled for the maximum five subjects but soon was advised to drop English. I remained unpleasantly close to the bottom of the class all year, with miserable percentages I'd never turned in before that presumably indicated some unperceived difficulty in adjusting to city life. I was happy with the Burrows and enjoyed the church, and even with hindsight I can see no convincing reason for my slump. It didn't last; I passed Leaving Honours.

Our cricket coach was Clarrie Grimmett, Australia's greatest slow bowler until Shane Warne. At my first session in the nets the wizened little man hobbled over excitedly because my action resembled his. He maintained his interest and pushed me to practise until I could land the ball on a threepence, as he did, but unfortunately I didn't realise how great was my opportunity, and failed to put in the necessary effort. In winter we had baseball, and as in Naracoorte I was in demand as a pitcher. This continued at university, and although I never made it to a senior level I pitched at the 1949 intervarsity carnival in Brisbane. The highlight was a match between the Queensland side and a combined universities' team, the first ballgame played under lights in Australia. Brisbane's lord mayor pitched a wildly erratic first ball, and I was little better when I took over for two innings. Our other pitchers were more accurate but no more effective, and we were trounced.

Sport came a poor second to church, where there was a good range of youth activities, and our social lives were centred there. I had no solo voice but enjoyed singing in the choir's bass line alongside John Burrow. An additional attraction was the pastor's niece, Gwen Burrow, a year older than me. She was a contralto, played piano beautifully, and worked for the British and Foreign Bible Society. She was of surpassing beauty and a scintillating new colour in the rainbow, but it was ages before my admiration was acknowledged, let alone encouraged. She was the youngest of Hettie's widowed sister's six children, and lived two doors away. Her father, Reg's brother, a carpenter–joiner, had died young.

Before the morning service the Christian Endeavour class met for an hour. Now in decline worldwide, CE was a valuable interdenominational link for young people, and provided excellent leadership training. We learnt to plan and conduct meetings, lead Bible studies, pray in public extemporaneously without crippling self-consciousness, to preach, and much else.

The main speaker at the 1946 state CE convention was the Rev. Ben Butcher, a London Missionary Society pioneer in Papua. A Congregational minister, he was the first to venture onto Goaribari Island after Papuans killed and ate James Chalmers and eleven others there in 1901. He challenged us to offer our lives to God for His purposes. I was a convinced Christian, but hadn't properly understood that God has a plan for each of His children, who should follow wherever He leads. This meant praying for guidance about such matters as career choices. Mr Butcher seemed to speak directly to me, so when he appealed for commitment I responded, along with many others. Helpers prayed with us in small groups, after which I went home and wrote Mother a letter that she treasured all her life. (After her death

I learnt that she'd prayed for years that I become a missionary, 'but, Lord, not to the lepers'. When I began leprosy work she had overcome her fears, because she had read about Paul Brand, the pioneer of reconstructive surgery in leprosy.)

Pondering Ben Butcher's challenge, I felt God calling me for overseas service, so architecture (or stamp dealing!) seemed inappropriate. Lacking an evangelist's temperament, and with medical influences surrounding me in the Burrow home, my obvious next move was to study medicine, but my limited experience of doctors had been so disagreeable that this seemed impossible. After consultation with Uncle Reg I embarked on a science degree with a view to doing laboratory work in a mission hospital. Some lectures were with the med students, and late that year I decided that if these boys and girls (who were ten per cent of the class) could do it, so could I. This change of attitude was almost miraculous, and illustrates an important truth: if we are willing to obey God He won't let us wander off the road, but will steer us in the right direction, shutting some doors and opening others.

Switching courses wasn't simple, and to my dismay I couldn't enter second year medicine directly because my Biology 101 course was deemed to include insufficient zoology. The botany component was adequate but I had to take the half-unit medical zoology. In addition, matriculation for medicine required another language at Intermediate level. Based on my Ivanhoe memories I plumped for German. Gwen's friend Joan Hallewell excelled at languages and promised to get me up to speed, so I spent a year studying zoology and Intermediate German. Such a waste of time would be unthinkable now.

I first saw a pipe organ when I was fourteen and longed to play it. Now came my opportunity. A light study load allowed time for lessons from Fred Finlay, a well-known organist, and I still recall the tingle I felt at managing to coordinate hands and feet and read three staves simultaneously. Our church's instrument was a harmonium so I practised on the Dodd organ at St Matthew's, Marryatville. I was to spend many years far from pipe organs but in my 60s I became organist at Burnie Baptist Church, Tasmania, and in retirement began relearning works I'd struggled with intermittently for 50 years.

There was nothing medical about first year medicine; second year was the real introduction. Anatomy was massively detailed, requiring long hours at the dissecting table. Today's students take shortcuts so may not remember their first session as we did, when we entered the dissecting room in some trepidation. The orderly had laid out a dozen bodies made decent with sheets. Ex-servicemen were still entering the course and took this in their stride, but some of us had never even been to a funeral. Few had seen a corpse, but now we would spend half our time with one. Happily the almost overwhelming stench of formalin countered any other disagreeable sensations.

We began on the arm, four to a side, while third years dissected the head and neck. My group included Rod Westerman, Tony Parham and John Thompson. Our body was thin, which made it easier. Three afternoons a week we took turns perching on a stool, reading instructions from 'little *Cunningham*' while the others patiently did the dissection. Departmental staff circulated to make sure we didn't make a hash of it. We absorbed a mountain of poorly digested facts, aided by lectures from Ross Adey and Dudley Packer, and became experts on the geography of dead bodies. But few of us understood the more important living, functional anatomy.

Lectures and lab work in biochemistry and physiology were much easier than anatomy, largely because the mass of detail was far less. Sir Cedric Stanton Hicks, a dapper little chap and a stand-up comic, taught physiology, but without textbooks we'd have been lost. Hilarious accounts of his wartime responsibility for army nutrition were of little relevance. We also endured lectures and pracs in pharmacy's mortar-and-pestle mysteries that were Dickensian even then.

From fourth year we became real medical students, with lengthy attachments to one of the six pairs of general medical and surgical units. These corresponded strictly, referring cases to each other only. While I was a junior registrar free consultation was introduced. This brought its own problems, one being that some specialists were more popular than others, for the usual reasons. Most honoraries were good doctors by any standards, and some were fully aware of it. We didn't have the rigid pyramidal system seen in Germany, where unit heads exerted total control over staff who would function independently here, but some of our great men swept, even strutted, into the wards like lords of creation, basking in their minions' subservience.

Most students feared a certain gruff senior surgeon who took himself exceptionally seriously. Even after graduating I was uncomfortable riding in the lift with him, as were others. After Sir Philip

Messent retired this man was the top surgeon by seniority and by right, but few of us chose to work for him. Later he was involved in a zoo scandal to do with the illegal and highly profitable sale of rare birds. His precise role in this felonious enterprise never became clear, but we now no longer feared him. We already knew he was mortal; I watched him perform his first hindquarter amputation, no superhuman feat, and to my astonishment his anatomy book lay open.

In 1973, when I was on study leave with the RAH neurosurgical unit, I was in radiology collecting films and noticed this great man on a trolley, waiting patiently for service. A crumpled caricature of his former self, he had the big C written all over him and was in pain, with his wife wringing her hands at his side. When I approached them he said, 'You're Clezy, aren't you?' I was amazed, as we'd last met eleven years before, when he examined at the FRACS finals. After some small talk I said I'd push things along, and asked the chief radiographer, 'D'you know who that is?' He'd worked at the RAH for years, so surprised me when he didn't.

'It's not long since that man was all but king around here,' I said, and suggested that he give him priority over healthier-looking people awaiting X-ray. This incident was an exquisite reminder that the transition from 'Who's Who' to 'Who's He?' can be painfully short.

Adelaide boasted no clinical professors when I began, although Melbourne and Sydney had had them for generations. Our professor of medicine arrived during my sixth year, and was a breath of fresh air. He was a Scot, H.N. Robson, later Sir Hugh Robson, the revered Principal of Edinburgh University. An outstanding diagnostician and teacher, he struggled for beds because the senior physicians, who had resisted his appointment, were unwilling to share theirs. (The surgeons were made of sterner stuff, and a surgical professorship was delayed for some years.) Prof Robson spoke with us instead of at us, so not knowing the answers to questions no longer felt embarrassing and shameful. Our mornings were spent in the wards where we were allotted new patients as they were admitted, and had to know all about them for twice-weekly ward rounds with our senior honorary. Most patients enjoyed having students and accepted us as part of the deal in a free hospital.

Adult medicine and surgery were the backbone of the course but we also spent short periods at the maternity and children's hospitals. I was briefly attracted to obstetrics because of the evident perfection of most newborns, in pleasant contrast to the average RAH inpatient, but I have few memories of this period, except for seeing chloroform given by a midwife under the nominal direction of the attending obstetrician. Considering the importance of paediatrics in general practice (where most students were heading), the time allocated to it was pitifully inadequate. I found sick children of no interest and have never been truly comfortable with them, but somewhere I learnt a useful adage: a vomiting child always does it more than once, so don't be in a hurry to change everything.

Gynaecology was taught by a group of specialists different from the rest. The two seniors, both knighted, were highly skilled and superbly attired, but comically pompous. We had doubts about their suede-shoed juniors, all quite ordinary except for a good-looking lady whose exceptional ability aroused the jealousy of her male colleagues. Her husband was an eminent scientist, which probably didn't help. As in all branches of surgery, gynae students spent hours standing in operating theatres, with the worth of all this time dependent on the procedure being performed and on how informative the operator was. The head of gynaecology was a chatterer and enjoyed teaching while he worked. Treating the condition known as cervical erosion, he asked, 'What's the treatment for erosion?' One student opined, *sotto voce*, 'Contour ploughing.' The stony-dull theatre sister exploded in laughter with the rest of us, but our teacher was most unimpressed and barked over his shoulder, 'Any more of that, boy, and I'll plough you in November.'

Much gynae teaching was done in the outpatients department, and could be disgustingly insensitive. Fresh out of our teens, most of us found history taking and examination slightly awkward, as did our patients. After answering our questions each lady was displayed supine, her feet up in stirrups. A minuscule sheet was token recognition that there was a decent way to do these things. With the class of six or eight in a semicircle around him, the student stood between the patient's legs and performed a pelvic examination, with commentary so that the teacher could assess technique. After the student was through the teacher confirmed (or failed to confirm) the findings. If an operation was indicated the patient went on the waiting list and was hurried away to make room for the next victim.

A quivering eighteen-year-old with a mundane complaint – three months, no period — endured her ordeal at the hands of a burly full-back. While he struggled our worldly-wise teacher broke the silence by whining superciliously, 'Well now, she's had connection, hasn't she?' which the student had difficulty confirming. He did battle with the hymen while we discussed the causes of missed periods until a nurse rushed in and reported 4-plus sugar on urine testing. A few well-directed questions now uncovered glaring symptoms of diabetes, the sole reason for the problem. Her nightmarish humiliation and clumsy public digital deflowering had been entirely unnecessary.

It was well known that a substantial proportion of every GP's patients had psychological problems, but our time in psychological medicine and psychiatry was brief. Teachers in these specialties were aware of their subjects' importance, but lacked clout at faculty level, in keeping with the lowly status of psychiatry in society in general and within the medical hierarchy in particular. Other 'minor' specialties (eyes, ENT, dermatology, anaesthesia, forensic medicine, radiology) fared little better, being regarded as lightweight additions to the main game.

Many students learn the hard way that a little knowledge is a dangerous thing. Tuberculosis was still surrounded by myth and mystery, with rigid protocols at every turn. The TB ward was off limits to all but those with business there, and we had to be demonstrably clean and safe before being allowed in. Cleanliness was established by a miniature film chest X-ray and a Mantoux skin test; if these were negative we were inoculated with BCG. I was recalled one Friday to hear about a spot on my lung, which meant a large film the following Tuesday. If anyone mentioned that most spots were artifacts I didn't hear it. I had no suggestive symptoms and was most unlikely to have TB, but spent a tense weekend pondering the prospect of eighteen months of treatment, a two-year gap in my training, and therefore that much extra delay before I could marry Gwen. After Tuesday's X-ray I was pronounced clean, and rejoined the human race.

Like many other Christian students I joined the Evangelical Union, a conservative group with interdenominational backing that was the offspring of the British Inter-Varsity Fellowship. We held Bible study, prayer and other meetings, and although our local impact was slight in my time, EUs were powerful influences in tertiary institutions. Many Christian leaders here, as in Britain, traced the beginning or the strengthening of their faith to the EU.

Early on I was talked into a staff position with the university paper, *On Dit*. For my first item, about an upcoming music festival, I interviewed the professor of music, who strolled around his office dictating program details. Some young lady would play a Brahms intermezzo. 'That's B - r - a - h - m - s,' he declaimed from a great height. This is my only memory of my *On Dit* time. I didn't stay long. As many others have discovered, the perpetual frenzy of a medical student's life all but prohibited activities that allegedly enriched the university experience. And like many others, I was developing a mindset that carried over into later life, with work appearing to be the be-all and end-all. I always denied that this was the case. They all do.

Trevor better handled the competing claims of medicine and everything else. He'd have made a good farmer but I saw a good doctor in him too, and persuaded him to follow me. On my say-so he matriculated on his Leaving Certificate, so graduated younger than most, and married Nancy Royal that much earlier. We were good friends but saw little of each other for 30 years until Gwen and I went to Burnie. Trevor was in general practice in Launceston, 150 kilometres away.

Trevor's leaving the land must have been a blow to our dad, but he didn't show it. Norman enjoyed farming and eventually took over Cooee. A moderately severe infantile hemiplegic, he was born during the 1936–37 infantile paralysis epidemic that closed Victorian schools for months. Polio hit Apsley when a vaguely ill nurse at the Austin Hospital, Melbourne (where Victoria's cases were treated), was sent home early for Christmas. She partied with siblings and cousins, several of whom went down with it three weeks later. This disease cluster illustrated several features of polio's natural history that were poorly understood.

Although Norman found most sports difficult he played the best tennis in the family. He married Rosalie Murrell of Penola, but died young in a fire. Rosalie then married John Gething, and later they sold Cooee and moved to Victoria, but we have kept in touch. Subsequently Cooee fell into the wrong hands, and when I last saw it the house I remembered as a wonderful home looked irrecoverably derelict.

Next door to Cooee the Malone sisters ran a farm successfully, demonstrating that girls could do it. Ailsa wasn't their outdoor type, but married a farmer, Laurie Davie, who owned land at Kybybolite, a few miles away. This was our family's last connection with the land as their daughters married away from it. Ailsa and Laurie were our last link with the Naracoorte Presbyterians, whose minister once told them he believed them to be the only couple in the congregation whose children were practising Christians. This says something about the compelling depth and sincerity of the faith we saw expressed in the lives of our own parents.

Chapter 5

A taste of New Guinea

Nowadays every medical student completes an elective in progressively more exotic locations, but such adventures were almost unheard of in the 50s. An ex-naval officer in our cohort went the whole hog and dropped a year to help crew the *Passat*, a four-masted clipper, on what was touted as her last voyage to Europe with South Australian wheat. His action was generally regarded as eccentric and/or a wicked waste of time.

During my fifth year the Public Health Department (PHD) of the Territories of Papua and New Guinea (TPNG) offered summer employment to students from each Australian medical school. Ever since hearing Ben Butcher speak at that CE meeting in 1946 I'd felt drawn to the mysterious bird-shaped island north of us. A trip there promised to be far better than digging post-holes or mending fences in the blazing sun at Cooee, as we did every summer. Good fencing means a good farm, and Dad surely had a good farm. If it wasn't fencing we bagged wheat, a hand-blistering task that demanded tougher palms than mine.

The med-students-to-New-Guinea thing happened because two Melbourne undergraduates, Len Champness and Neville York, couldn't face spending Christmas 1950 counter-jumping at Myers or Birks, and asked the Department for External Territories (DET) for employment in New Guinea. A rare imaginative official kicked this idea along until they had work and were issued entry permits. This was some achievement, in view of Canberra's paranoid policy on admitting visitors to New Guinea for fear they introduce uppity nationalistic aspirations and other unseemly ideas that were loosely labelled communism.

After the war the PHD had trouble in recruiting doctors, especially when the new director, Dr Gunther, was an outsider. Clearly, 'Buggins' turn next' no longer applied, so some prewar medicos declined re-employment. Gunther had so few Australians that he was reduced to employing European migrants, who jumped at the opportunity to exchange menial work in Australia for medicine in New Guinea. Apart from Brits and near-Brits, foreign doctors were deemed to have abilities and qualifications dangerously inferior to the standards white Australians were entitled to. Most migrants wishing to practise here had to do the full medical course, but many were too old, poor, proud, discouraged or otherwise unprepared to face it. Some saw working in New Guinea as far better than cracking stones or minding a potato peeler, and most proved to be far better doctors than the DET's xenophobes could have believed possible. Unsurprisingly, the characteristics that made them exchange the uncertainties of postwar Europe for the hazards of life down under fitted them well for Territory doctoring.

Other countries had colonies but our dependency was deemed to have a special relationship with us, never clearly defined, but somehow it wasn't exactly a colony. By rights Australian doctors should be working there. York and Champness, exuberant about their experiences, suggested to Gunther that he invite more students to sample life and work in New Guinea in the expectation that some would be hooked. They were right. Champness was the first to return.

So in 1952 the Department offered paid summer jobs to a few senior students, with three places for Adelaide. I was accepted along with Andrew Cockburn and John Thompson. None of my immediate family had been abroad but my parents were happy for me to blaze the trail. With almost juvenile excitement, one evening Andrew and I boarded the Qantas Empire Airways DC-3 at Sydney's Kingsford Smith Airport and lugged our carry-on baggage up the narrow aisle. A white-haired Dr Giblin, one of the few prewar doctors in the service, was one of three other passengers. More boarded at Brisbane, Rockhampton and Townsville, where we had a leisurely cooked breakfast on the ground. At Mackay and Cooktown we collected a few more. When we left the Australian coast at Lizard Island I felt, at long last, that I really was on an overseas journey.

In mid-afternoon we made Jackson's Strip, Port Moresby, where the brutal blast from the shimmering, steaming, sunstruck tarmac almost flattened us. Dr Giblin got us aboard a rickety Qantas bus for the nine-mile trip to Konedobu, the Administration suburb. We arrived long after closing time (4.06 pm) but found the senior PHD clerk at the Kone Club bar. After sounding off about Canberra's failure to give him our time and date he found us space in the Kone single quarters, bleak roughcast wartime buildings.

That evening we had our first and forever memorable sight of sunset over Fairfax Harbour. Towering masses of fluffy cloud slowly rolled through many shades at the red end of the spectrum, their fiery glow starkly silhouetting the thin line of coconut palms along the beach. We were in wonderland. After wolfing dinner at the Kone mess we crawled under musty mosquito nets for the first time.

Next day we were driven to the native hospital, discreetly hidden in an out-of-the-way section of Ela Beach and consisting of half-a-dozen wooden wards on stilts over the water. The slat floors were virtually self-cleaning, and more substantial rubbish, including oddments from the operating theatre, went through empty window frames into the sea. Two New Australian GPs had sessional help from Janos Loschdorfer, an eye specialist, and Charles Haszler, a large and hearty Hungarian surgeon.

As is common in primitive hospitals, the admissions clerk was the pivotal staff member. Here he was an elderly Papuan whose diagnoses were correct surprisingly often. The native staff duty roster, chalked on a board above his head, listed absentees in four categories: off duty, sick, on leave, and in gaol, the last usually on account of a liquor offence. Natives were prohibited alcohol until the early 1960s when the law changed after extensive token public consultation. I say 'token' because change was inevitable, regardless of paternalism, teetotalism or any other ism.

The wards were crammed with a fascinating variety of patients, many with fractures. Many pulmonary TB cases awaited launch transport to the isolation hospital on Gemo Island in the harbour. Staffed by London Missionary Society nurses, Gemo catered for leprosy as well as tuberculosis. Judging from my diary, when Andrew and I visited it I showed particular interest in the various manifestations of leprosy. Patients seemed remarkably happy, and sang in pitch-perfect unaccompanied four-part harmony. I couldn't have dreamed that I would become one of the specialists who visited Gemo regularly until it closed.

A lady at Ela Beach was said to have actinomycosis (a fungus infection) of the jaw. With hindsight this seems unlikely, but in the early

1950s it was still widely believed, even by Dr Gunther, that cancer was rare in New Guinea. This case must have been a slow-growing mouth cancer, an almost avoidable malignancy, common in betel chewers anywhere.

The provision for mental patients was a toilet-sized galvanised-iron building well away from the other wards. It was an oven, and held a man who was released for exercise of a kind each afternoon with a ball and chain on one ankle.

Being the first arrivals, Andrew and I had our pick of the available postings and chose Rabaul, New Britain and Sohano, Bougainville respectively. Soon we were off in one of the most exhilarating aircraft ever built, a four-engined Sandringham flying boat. It was cramped and painfully noisy during take-off, but there can be few more thrilling ways to travel than on this craft. It charged across the harbour, bow waves thrown high and drumming on the fuselage, totally obscuring any view until it shot clear of the water like a cork from a bottle and headed eastwards, with the smoky green, cloud-crowned Owen Stanley Ranges amazingly close on our left, rising to 10,000 feet. We enjoyed the excitement of the take-off twice more because the weekly Rabaul flight also served Samarai, the Milne Bay District's frangipani-scented island capital, and Esa'ala in the d'Entrecasteauxs. We had time to stroll right around tiny Samarai but at Esa'ala the aircraft waited in the channel while a native canoe ferried the mailbags back and forth. Before dusk the volcanoes and steep hills that almost surround Rabaul's Simpson Harbour came into sight, and Matupit volcano's sulphurous stench caught our breath just before we splashed down. Much of New Britain is volcanic, and its high rainfall makes the soil exceptionally productive. I'd never seen a greener place.

The onwards service to Bougainville was fortnightly, and as this was the off week I had time to see Rabaul, where I was to be posted eight years later. We put up at the rebuilt beachfront Cosmopolitan Hotel, and that first night saw an hilarious Rabaul Dramatic Society performance of *The Man Who Came to Dinner*, with the principal character played by J.K. McCarthy, the District Commissioner, then in the middle of a notable career.

By day we scarcely noticed the muddy streets, being more impressed by the profuse, multicoloured tropical foliage lining them, the film-set backdrop made by the conical Mother and Daughter volcanoes and the almost vertical jungle-clad hills that surrounded the town in every shade of green. As much a bougainvillea and hibiscus garden as a town, Rabaul hugged the harbour, with Chinatown at the north-eastern end. The 150 Chinese shops, run by descendants of Cantonese labourers brought in by the Germans 50 years previously, and most other structures in town, including the banks, were timber framed and panelled with material looking like sun-bleached plywood, except its components were layers of coarse paper and tar rather than wood and glue. Rabaul businesses served plantations and outstations over a wide area. The deep harbour with its narrow eastern entrance was cluttered with sunken wartime ships but otherwise was ideal for large vessels, so Rabaul remained the Islands Region's major port.

European, Chinese and native hospitals served three distinct communities. We spent several days at the flimsy native hospital where again the general duties doctors, Con Salemann and Jan Saave, were New Australians. The English surgeon, R.K. Wilson, a world-renowned firearms expert, didn't see students as part of his brief, but Dr Saave found time to teach us about tropical diseases.

Local male orderlies, trained on the job, did the nursing. I admired their skill, far superior to mine, at giving intravenous injections. NAB, an organic arsenical compound, was the standard treatment for yaws, a common non-venereal spirochaetal infection whose early stage produced weeping yellowish cutaneous lumps. By 1952 penicillin was better treatment and made the lesions shrink within hours, but it was in short supply. Many adults with joint pains ascribed them, rightly or wrongly, to past yaws infection, for which great quantities of intravenous NAB were given. I seized the opportunity to improve my skills with the needle. We visited the strikingly clean Catholic Mission hospital at Vunapope, near Kokopo, 20 miles or so from Rabaul. The German doctor, Hubert Langer, welcomed us and apologised for his wife's inability to entertain us – he had just operated on her ectopic pregnancy. He showed us the hospital and the cathedral, where I enjoyed a few minutes at their fine Hammond organ.

After my Rabaul week I re-boarded the Sandringham for two hours until we splashed down in Buka Passage, the strait barely separating Buka and Bougainville. A launch put me ashore on Sohano, the rocky islet in mid-passage that was the district administrative centre. Once again no medical student was expected, but Ken Pike, the only government doctor between Rabaul and the British Solomon Islands, greeted me warmly.

A softly spoken, bearded bachelor with a non-threatening manner, Pike was popular with all communities. He ran a busy native hospital on the flat near the beach, assisted by a European Medical Assistant (EMA) and local orderlies. EMAs were the backbone of the service and performed a wide range of medical and administrative work. Most were ex-army medical orderlies with pioneering personalities and remarkable competence. Many would have bettered themselves by taking ex-servicemen's scholarships to do medicine. Sohano's EMA was Rob Lorimer, whose wife was ill in Sydney. He was quieter than the characteristically extrovert EMAs I met years later, but willingly took a boarder. His *hausboi* cooked and washed for us. Rob worked at entertaining me, even taking me out on Buka Passage in an outrigger canoe, my only boating experience apart from the Gemo trip. It was great fun until a squall caught our sail and lifted the outrigger clear of the water. Rob put about before we could capsize – just as well, because I couldn't swim and there were no life jackets.

Two Australian nurses staffed the tiny European hospital on the island's upper level. Inpatients were rare, which would have meant a dreary existence for them but for extra duties such as supervising vaccinations and helping in the native hospital theatre.

Pike feared operating, and it was my Sohano time that decided me on a surgical career. New Guinea entranced me from day one, but I soon saw that general duties doctors in places like Sohano, where medical evacuations were possible at fortnightly intervals only, faced surgical emergencies that I'd be unable to handle. The range of other skills an isolated doctor needed was frightening, and as the necessary omnicompetence would be forever beyond me I felt compelled to narrow my sights. Surgical skill was the obvious deficiency here and presumably in other places too. So Bougainville pointed me in a previously unthinkable direction.

Keeping a somewhat passive student occupied can be a full-time job but if that was a problem Pike soon had a solution. There were reports of recent hurricane damage on Nissan, in the Green Islands, a pair of atolls about 120 miles north of us. There had been no proper postwar patrol there, so the Administration decided to inspect the storm damage, take a census and make long-overdue war damage payments to villagers who had lost coconut palms, houses and other property during Japanese occupation or when the US air force constructed landing strips. The PHD was to supply someone to inspect village aid posts and provide otherwise unavailable treatment. Pike saw me as a suitable candidate so I was kitted out and put on board the MV *Poseidon*, the government workboat, with two ADOs (Assistant District Officers) who were to assess claims and make payouts from their cache of £5000 in marks. (The Germans had departed almost 40 years before, but shillings were still called marks.)

We slipped into the elliptical Nissan lagoon late that day and dropped anchor opposite the Catholic mission, where two American nuns ran a primary school and supervised several aid posts, with backup from a Canadian priest. The sisters rarely saw visitors so invited us to dinner. We ate well, lounging in the lukewarm air and retailing the news to a background accompaniment of interminable booming on the atoll's seaward side, a contrast to the silence of the mirror-flat lagoon, yards below us. We talked late before rowing back to the *Poseidon* through water teeming with brilliantly luminescent creatures; our oars stirred liquid silver.

Storm damage wasn't severe, but a few villages needed food so we bought rice from the island's Chinese trade store. While the ADOs recorded war damage details in quadruplicate as required by the much-excoriated Canberra bureaucracy, and reduced 'think-of-a-number' claims to acceptable levels, I patrolled the villages with a medical orderly. His limp, due to Japanese bayonet wounds, didn't prevent him setting such a pace that I suspected he was testing me, and within minutes I was drowning in sweat. Every hour or two I was resuscitated with a long draught of fresh coconut milk. We began with a general inspection of each village, usually finding houses clean and pig-proof fences in good order. We then lined the populace for quick medicals, concentrating on those with suggestions of disease. Some had problems beyond my diagnostic skills or which needed treatment at Sohano, and others, desperate for injections, lined up for the famous NAB. Long queues of people marched up with arms thrust out for me to find veins at the elbow. One day the second man dropped halfway through his injection, which must have been a rare occurrence, because it caused quite a stir. I thought I'd killed him and, as is usual when someone faints, I had difficulty finding his pulse. He quickly recovered, but the shock of being a lone student far out in the Pacific, surrounded by a thunderstruck gallery for what could have been the ultimate medical disaster, threw me off balance. The canny old orderly saw I needed moral support and took charge for the rest of the day. Things improved from then on, and we saw every village and most of the population of 1200, including the few on Pinipel, north of Nissan.

After a fortnight we returned to Sohano to finish our paperwork. While I tried to compose a readable patrol report Pike received news of his transfer to Rabaul as Regional Medical Officer (RMO), a promotion that displeased him because Bougainville catered perfectly for his interest in birds. Ten days later we were patrolling on Buka when DO Colin McLean and Fred Archer, an influential plantation owner, rode out and asked him to refuse the transfer, without success.

The Buka patrol was to give me experience, and to investigate the incidence of infestation with hookworm, a parasite believed to be a major cause of anaemia in the tropics. We carried a microscope, and after lining villagers for inspection we gave out cardboard containers for stool specimens. I prepared slides and passed them to Pike who identified any parasites and called each 'positive' to look down the microscope, which produced a gamut of reactions. Hookworm incidence was high, so we asked everybody to fast next morning for mass medication, and urged stricter use of latrines.

One teenager had pointy gravity-defying breasts that interested and amused the boys. She was acutely aware of it, so jury-rigged a skimpy shawl that only drew more male sniggers and condescending smirks from the other girls, all half-naked and unashamed.

That night we slept in a Chinese bakery that had lost its licence over a regulation breach. It seemed a good resthouse until tick-ridden pigs began scratching themselves on the stilts. Their grunting and the vibration of the rickety building made sleep impossible until Pike had our cook-boy fetch a bucket of boiling water, which he poured through the slats with great effect. Squealing pigs scattered in all directions while we laughed until we cried. I was half-asleep when a land crab dropped from the rafters onto my bare chest, flailing wildly. I jumped as if I'd been shot and lay awake for hours, waiting for the next one.

After the bad night I wasn't too disappointed when a runner arrived before breakfast, calling Pike back to Sohano. After he tried to mollify an old man whose scalded pig was still missing we lined the village and dispensed hookworm treatment while our carriers packed up. A few villagers had eaten coconut meat, and as the medicine was fat-soluble they were mildly poisoned, but none seemed severe so we tracked through the jungle back to base.

Nocturnal emergencies were rare because villagers feared travelling in the dark, but one wet night a young man was canoed in from afar with a week-old strangulated hernia. My task was to pour on the ether, which needed more experienced hands than mine. With rain thudding on the roof I couldn't hear his breathing, which didn't help. Poor Pike was commendably patient, with every extra minute postponing the operation he dreaded. Eventually he said, 'Help him, Arampip,' and an old man who was an orderly when I was still in three-cornered pants stepped forward to take over. Pike excised loops of dead bowel but felt incapable of joining the good ends together, so stitched them to the skin. This was lifesaving, but meant an awkward groin stoma and a tedious secondary procedure in Rabaul. I escorted the patient on my way home and watched Dr Wilson put him together again, while fuming about his soon-to-be RMO and outstation doctors in general. 'Easiest operation in the book,' he growled. Not so, but he reinforced my desire to master the surgery of such emergencies.

I returned home thoroughly sold on New Guinea. My final year flashed by, packed with ward work and revision in all clinical subjects. I was preparing for the last hurdle, but for my aim to specialise in surgery.

Chapter 6

Graduation, marriage, children

At last! Although failing MBBS finals was uncommon, most students were like over-wound clocks and approached the exams very seriously because a bad long case in the orals meant disaster. But enough was enough. Gwen and I had planned our wedding for 11 December 1953, a week after the exam results were due. The entire class milled around the noticeboard late on 4 December. I was staggered – my name was missing. Then somebody pointed out the honours and credits lists. There I was, twelfth amongst 120.

The Rev. Allan Burrow, Gwen's cousin, married us at Burnside Christian Church. Trevor played the organ with his usual panache, but was on edge on this momentous occasion and forgot to bring a copy of the second hymn's rousing tune. He wrote out the melody line early in the service and carried it off faultlessly. My best man was Sidwell Coombe, now well established in the wool business, and Gwen's bridesmaid was Joan Hallewell, her friend who had taught me German.

After our Melbourne honeymoon I did a locum in Burra, a two-doctor town in the Mid North of South Australia. As others have found, many people choose to wait for their regular doctor rather than risk an unknown, and one fresh out of school at that. But some problems won't wait; a curious case of pneumonia in a parrot fancier was psittacosis, which I've never met again. Another puzzle was the most insulin-resistant diabetic I've ever seen. With the other doctor available for consultation, my job amounted to a honeymoon on full pay.

Ah, those ecstatic weeks. Our beliefs had made premarital sex unthinkable, or if not literally that, unquestionably and absolutely a no-no. I had no car, so we'd enjoyed little secure solitude, thus escaping some of the ineluctable pressures that predictably and stridently attend prolonged propinquity, so we had plenty left for the honeymoon. After being outside the fence for so long we found the grass in these Elysian Fields even greener than expected, and as we blithely and breathlessly unveiled the ambrosial delights of the Song of Solomon they took on indescribably delicious new dimensions, all in technicolour!

Unsurprisingly, soon Gwen was pregnant with Meredith, who was born on my 25th birthday, 16 November 1954, when any expectant father, especially a young doctor, hanging around a maternity ward was an intolerable nuisance. Anyway, I was on duty, and was called from the billiards table to hear the news.

In 1954 internship wasn't yet compulsory in South Australia so a few graduates entered general practice directly, but most went to the RAH for a year. I landed a good roster except for its rude beginning in the Casualty department. Students spent many hours in Cas sewing up cuts in drunkards' heads with horsehair, and doing other minor procedures under direction, but being the one giving the directions was quite another matter. The Cas rotation was frightening, and wouldn't be legal now. Three new chums worked for a month on a three-day cycle of 24, three and ten hour shifts. We treated simple acute problems, steered outpatients to the appropriate specialist clinic, and assessed accident and other cases for admission. With the bed-state chronically at bursting point the relevant duty registrar had to approve admissions, which usually meant seeing them. Registrars were busy, and some were displeased, in varying degrees, when called to a patient that they decided didn't need admission. We relied on two senior Cas sisters for much advice, and without them I'd have sunk without trace.

Patients seen in Casualty had to be dealt with promptly and definitively; leaving them lying around under observation was strictly forbidden. I saw a drunk at midnight with a dislocated shoulder, a problem I'd treated several times, but this one wouldn't go back so I phoned the duty surgical registrar, a surly chap with a notoriously short fuse. He strode down in undisguised disgust, his white coat-tails flying, reduced the dislocation in a flash, and stormed out muttering inaudibly. I felt very small.

At 6 am another man came in with a dislocated shoulder. Better luck this time, I thought. Not likely. I tried every trick I knew (not many) before calling the same registrar. He was in bed, and seemed to think I was joking. He appeared minutes later with steam coming out of his ears and again put the shoulder back with humiliating ease. This time his parting remarks were quite audible. I went off at 8 am feeling thoroughly squashed.

Rules insisted on a provisional diagnosis on the admission slip. This could be a trap, because our diagnoses sometimes sneaked right through the system with the apparent status of expert sworn statements. Many patients had problems obviously warranting admission, but with the diagnosis unclear. With little time to think, and rules to be satisfied, we sometimes used our imaginations. This became habitual, and when a mental hospital patient dismantled his wire mattress and swallowed a huge spring I wrote 'inner spring' without hesitation. This was enough to prise a laugh out of the sober-sided honorary who dealt with him.

An intern in Melbourne, working under similar pressure, certified a woman brought in dead drunk as dead on arrival (DOA). A cold hard ride to the city morgue aroused her, allegedly just in time. Her family went to the newspapers, which scathed the wretched intern for his casual, perhaps criminally careless, examination in the gloom of the ambulance.

Next morning our med super made a rare appearance to check on our DOA routine. We too examined them in the ambulance, so he issued an edict that all bodies were to be brought into a cubicle for half an hour's observation. Those at the coalface felt that observing the dead was nonsensical when it was forbidden in the living. 'Overkill' seemed the right description for the practice, which soon died.

We all made terrible mistakes. One night a pregnant girl near term was brought in, pale as a ghost and with a classical fear-of-death face, complaining of severe abdominal pain that had hit her like a bullet. I'd never seen a case of ruptured uterus and wasn't smart enough to realise that this couldn't be the diagnosis, as she wasn't in labour. Obstetric patients were managed miles away at the Queen Victoria Hospital, but I hesitated to transfer someone so desperately ill, and called the gynae registrar as the most appropriate in-house opinion. He examined her, phoned around for advice, and sent her to the maternity hospital.

By the time blood was cross-matched and she arrived in the operating theatre she was near death, and reached it without her obstetrician discovering the cause of her bleeding. Autopsy disclosed a ruptured splenic artery aneurysm, an almost unheard-of oddity then, but now a recognised but admittedly rare condition, rather less so in pregnancy. Whether she would have survived if we'd bucked the system and admitted her to the RAH is uncertain. The next case of ruptured splenic artery aneurysm I saw (in an elderly woman) also died after an experienced surgeon failed to identify it at operation. Happily the inflexibility that mandated this girl's transfer to the Queen Vic in 1954 could scarcely exist now.

After handling or mishandling such crises I was glad when that frantic month ended. Life in the wards was busy, but after Casualty it was a dream. My two months of general surgery was with Alan Hobbs. Above me was a prickly junior registrar, and above him the much more laid-back Mervyn Smith. With responsibility for two units they were always busy elsewhere, so for practical purposes I was ruled by Sister Thomas. She was a tense but good-hearted spinster who in spasms of agitation grabbed her glasses like a Formula One steering wheel and snapped the bridge repeatedly. She'd managed the Hobbs ward for years, and as the Casualty sisters had done, saved me from many pitfalls.

Usually we were in-house before midnight to look after our own patients until we were next off duty, so many young wives were left alone for long periods. Not Gwen; we had the advantage of living with her mother until Robyn was born in 1956.

Each surgical unit was 'on take' for 24 hours every sixth day. Most emergency operations were performed at night because the theatres were fully booked with routine work by day. Registrars did most procedures – but before midnight, or if we were deemed to deserve it, minor cases were interns' work, assisted or supervised by a registrar. Control was extreme in some units, with appendicectomies impermissible without notification to the senior honorary, complete with lab work. In other units the senior registrar, who by definition had one or more surgical fellowships, used his/her discretion. (Only one 'her', Lena McEwan, in my time.) All this meant a very good deal indeed for public hospital patients.

Next I spent a month with TAR (Jim) Dinning, a boyish-looking dynamo recently returned from Guy's Hospital, London as Adelaide's first trained neurosurgeon, with a pedigree going back to Harvey Cushing, the father of neurosurgery at Harvard, via Murray Falconer and Sir Hugh Cairns. He took over from Leonard Lindon, a talented generalist with a special interest who had performed Adelaide's neurosurgery since 1932.

TARD was widely regarded as a man-eater, not unjustifiably, but the high standards he demanded of others he certainly maintained himself. In true neurological tradition he was systematic in the extreme, as we soon found out if we risked a shortcut. He allowed no room for error, and before an elective craniotomy a typed case summary had to be prepared and discussed. Woe betide us if all X-rays and lab reports weren't immediately available. On-call 24 hours a day, he barely noticed if we'd been up all night. His only RAH assistant was an intern who changed monthly, which meant that just as one approached familiarity with his methods he had to train the next. He maintained a private office across the road and operated in several private hospitals.

TARD was into audit long before it was common, and on Saturday mornings we went through the week's discharges, classifying symptoms and signs, diagnoses, procedures, complications and outcomes. To some this seemed an obsessive and pernickety undertaking, but audit is now a mandatory feature of surgical practice.

My month on anaesthetics was terrifying. By day we caddied for honorary anaesthetists, most of them GPs. We were 'it' at night, unless the sole anaesthetic registrar was also on duty. Emergency anaesthesia can be taxing at any time, and leaving it to interns seems preposterous now. We had help from surgical registrars who had been down this road themselves a year or two previously, and while this scratch back-up was far from ideal, to my knowledge no deaths that year were attributable to our being too junior. A few close calls, certainly, but someone else always managed to take charge when necessary.

Duodenal perforation was common in Friday night boozers. Urgent operation was usual, for which we poured on ethyl chloride and open ether. This could be a challenge, and once I struggled to get underway, taking in more ether than my poor patient did, until the junior honorary 'Big Bob' Magarey, who happened to be in theatre, rescued me. After patiently watching me getting nowhere he asked gently, 'May I have a go? I reckon I've done a few more of these than you have.' He was right, and all was well.

One anaesthetist refused to work after 5 pm so if his list wasn't finished the intern was summoned to take over. Often the operation had been in progress for hours and needed an experienced person in charge, but we managed somehow, helped by an anaesthetist from a nearby theatre if need be.

Andrew Cockburn, son of a paediatrician who was no oil painting, received one such 5 pm call to Sid Krantz's theatre. Sid, a fine surgeon but a rough diamond, was still unmarried in his 50s, with a reputedly overbearing mama in the background. Years later marriage made him meek as a lamb, but we feared him then, even though his staff said his bark was much worse than his bite. Sid had eyes in the back of his head, and when Andrew sneaked in he spotted him and whined, 'And who are you?'

'Cockburn, sir,' he replied politely. Sid was thunderstruck.

'Cockburn?' he shrieked, as only he could, his question mark bouncing off the ceiling. 'Not as ugly as ya father, are ya?'

The rest of the year was less taxing and has left few memories. I was on medical wards for two eight-week terms, first with Eugene McLaughlin, a mildly cantankerous and idiosyncratic man who ran a pathology lab as well as his physician's practice. Lastly I went to the professorial unit, with fewer patients and stifling supervision by the string of Robson underlings. Otherwise, working there was one of the most enjoyable terms on the roster.

I had one success on that unit. A woman was admitted with chest pain without apparent cause until I realised that the problem was in her shoulder muscles, which were in constant spasm. This had to be tetanus, I decided correctly. Instantly she was whisked off to a special darkened, silenced room, to be managed by the specialist responsible for all tetanus cases. Such subspecialisation is common now, but at the RAH tetanus was the only disease believed to warrant this distinction then.

Most house staff disliked dealing with death. We were taught almost nothing about its social aspects but often were expected to seek post-mortems from grieving relatives. This could be awkward for all concerned, so at a 1956 staff meeting the med super proposed eliminating the problem by adding a compulsory 'permission for autopsy' form to the papers people signed on admission. Mine was the only vote against. It seemed ghoulish, and whether the hospital board ever approved it I do not know.

Many patients were ill-informed medically, and some doctors believed that in general they should be kept ignorant of a bad prognosis. I remember a discussion – it couldn't be called a debate – about telling the truth. A senior surgeon boasted that he never told patients they had cancer. Another described a dying man he had left in ignorance, who then borrowed heavily to expand his business, which left his family in financial chaos. Maybe we go too far the other way now, sometimes overloading patients or relatives with unbalanced fine print, but all agree that questions must be answered clearly, truthfully and comprehensively.

The year's experiences didn't tempt me to reconsider my New Guinea plans, so systematic surgical training was ahead. There were two tough fellowship examinations, Part 1 (the primary) and Part 2 (finals.) Most would-be specialists did a year or two at home before going abroad, usually to Britain, and in the case of surgical trainees, preferably with the primary under their belts. Royal colleges recognised each other's primaries, but we all aimed to sit the London Part 2 and become Fellows of the Royal College of Surgeons of England. Every surgical tyro in the English-speaking world outside the USA dreamed of one cachet – a post-nominal FRCS.

I applied for a 1955 junior surgical registrarship but the single post available went to Mick Hone. TARD heard of this, and as we'd had a good month together he suggested I spend a year with him, which should give me front running for the next available general surgical registrarship. Management had said he could have a neurosurgical resident – a hollow offer because they expected nobody would touch it. I jumped at it, which was to be of lifelong benefit.

TARD was without a specialist colleague until 1956, when Donald Simpson, one of the best-read surgeons I know, returned from Oxford. He began as a general neurosurgeon but went on to carve out a distinguished career in paediatric neurosurgery at the Adelaide Children's Hospital. So in 1955 TARD's staff consisted of the hapless intern-by-the-month and me.

General surgeons still insisted on managing most head injuries (except at weekends!) so much of our operative work was tumour surgery. Modern imaging techniques hadn't yet revolutionised the diagnostic process, and tumour localisation was by serially X-raying the skull after ventriculography (injecting air into the brain cavities) or direct-puncture carotid, or occasionally vertebral, angiography (injecting dye into arteries).

Early in the century Cushing relied on clinical findings and plain X-rays, long after Dandy introduced ventriculography, but even the father of neurosurgery occasionally opened the skull at the wrong site, and at least once on the wrong side. Eventually he relented and used ventriculography, admitting that he should have done so earlier. Everyone else used invasive radiological methods when indicated, but sometimes these had the downside of major unpleasantness for the patient. In Adelaide Lance Perrett, later one of Australia's top neuro-radiologists, did angiography well, but often he was busy with other things. No one else had Lance's dab hand, so most patients up for a craniotomy for tumour had a ventriculogram in the morning and the big operation in the afternoon.

I learnt to bore two holes in the back of the head under local anaesthesia and pass a fine tube into the ventricle on each side. I injected small amounts of air before taking the patient to the X-ray department for a picture series. Before we left the X-ray room I ran across North Terrace, wet films in my hand, for TARD's approval. Sometimes I had to inject more air, or vary the technique. In one way or another we obtained precise tumour localisation. Most patients had headache before we began, and often this became much worse between the ventriculogram and the craniotomy. In addition, the overall clinical state sometimes deteriorated, so ventriculography was no minor procedure. Years later an English EMI executive endured these investigations and asked why such extreme discomfort was necessary in the twentieth century. They said it wouldn't be if only neurosurgeons had a miraculous X-ray machine that showed neat slices of the skull contents. 'Money should fix that,' he groaned, and in due course the CAT (computer-assisted tomography – *tomo* is Greek for 'cut') scan was born. The first machines were called EMI-scanners, for good reason.

Like most neurosurgeons, TARD followed Cushing's methods to the letter, except he didn't always perform the entire operation himself. (An iron man of outstanding genius, Cushing was a barely tolerable martinet, and anecdotes about him still circulate almost a century later. One long-serving first assistant left him to take up a neurosurgical professorship elsewhere, having never performed a solo craniotomy while working for Cushing, who held that people coming to Harvard from all over wanted *him*, not some sidekick.)

But operative procedures were strictly Cushing, and included obsessive attention to the control of bleeding. More than the faintest bruising around the wound was unusual, and serious post-operative bleeding inside the skull was rare. Years later TARD visited Sir

Leonard Lindon the day after his hip replacement and was astonished by the size of his bruise. This was the origin of what Donald Simpson whimsically describes as Dinning's law: there is no operation that wouldn't be better performed by a neurosurgeon.

Post-craniotomy care included daily lumbar punctures to remove cerebrospinal fluid (CSF) until the pressure fell to normal. I became slick at this and often did several before breakfast. As the in-house expert, I had regular calls when young doctors were in difficulties.

Opening the head is a major procedure, and even when all seems straightforward the patient is observed closely for a day or two, particularly for the first few hours, lest a post-operative bloodclot develop inside the skull and require evacuation as a lifesaving emergency. After a craniotomy I stayed in and phoned TARD at 10 pm on the dot to report on the patient's progress. He was a fine operator, and trouble was rare.

Memorable cases included Mr Ecks, a young farmer with months of disabling headache, relieved only by progressively larger tots of whiskey, which added a drinking problem to the headache. When he became incapable of managing his affairs he sold his farm and entered a private institution to be weaned off the booze. His psychiatrist suspected an organic cause for the headache and called an eminent physician who saw him late one afternoon. He agreed with the psychiatrist, and unfortunately decided on a lumbar puncture to allow CSF analysis. Dutifully he examined the optic nerve heads to rule out their engorgement, and judged them to be normal (which they may have been), so he performed the lumbar puncture. To his surprise and horror a jet of CSF like water from a fire-hose hit him in the chest. Instantly he withdrew the needle, but the damage was done. Release of a little CSF from below in the presence of grossly raised intracranial pressure allowed the brain to shift downwards, and the patient became spastic and barely conscious. They called TARD, who put his money on a right frontal lobe tumour. Treating the near-fatal situation was truly urgent, and he phoned me saying the man was on his way by ambulance, to proceed straight to theatre. I was to handle Mrs Ecks with kid gloves as she was aghast that her husband was going to the RAH rather than to a private hospital. This was impossible in such an after-hours emergency, which she seemed unable to comprehend.

No angiographer was available and a standard ventriculogram

would have taken too long so TARD bored a hole in the upper right forehead under local. He hit a mass with a blunt brain needle and knew it was no ordinary tumour. Carefully he exposed something like a boiled egg. 'Hydatid!' he cried, which made sense in a sheep farmer. After emptying the cyst he peeled it from the brain, which became slack, suggesting that all was well, but as we closed the wound Mr Ecks became deeply unconscious and threw a high fever.

TARD came in next morning saying, 'Mr Lindon tells me he had two of these, and they both died of hyperthermia.' Our man was heading the same way so we tried to reverse the situation using current methods. We injected drugs that minimised shivering, stripped him, and for hours I rubbed him down with ice-cold water mixed with alcohol, in front of a fan whirring at full bore. It was midwinter, and soon the patient and I were blue, as was the nurse helping me. We beat his fever and he survived with mild intellectual deficit, a stiff limp, and muscle weakness around his eye. All considered, this was a good result.

At the Ecks's final visit to TARD's rooms they shamefacedly expressed complete satisfaction with their RAH treatment. They made a generous donation towards equipment for the neurosurgical unit, and Mrs Ecks produced a classy pigskin and gold-plate cigarette case and lighter for TARD to give me. He thanked them but said I didn't smoke, so she gave it to him and bought me a pen and pencil set instead. TARD refrained from mentioning that he too was a non-smoker.

The year was so busy that it flashed by. We got on well, and I enjoyed the work so much that I might have sought to train in neurosurgery but for my plan to go to New Guinea, where this degree of specialisation wouldn't be required for many years. As predicted, I secured a 1956 registrarship, and was rostered to the Britten-Jones unit for the first six months. Jonah, as he was known, was a notably gracious man and a fine surgeon with a wide repertoire. He and his junior, 'Big Bob' Magarey, took a real interest in their trainees. Jonah assisted me when I removed my first prostate, which took 45 minutes skin to skin and was almost bloodless.

This beginner's luck didn't hold up for my first gallbladder, a Magarey case. Bob was late and told me to go ahead while he scrubbed up. I made the generous incision he required, but about five centimetres too low. Exposure was unbelievably difficult, but rather than take over Bob pulled hard on the retractors while I struggled for over two hours, a long time for a straightforward procedure.

Otherwise I remember little of my time on the Britten-Jones unit, and I doubt that I demonstrated the native surgical aptitude expected of trainees nowadays. But I'd progressed to supervising interns removing appendices, and because general surgeons still treated most fractures I learnt such things as pinning broken hips in the small hours.

There were a few disasters, such as happened to a Magarey patient who, in the middle of visiting hours, complained of curious chest pain. His was an otherwise straightforward recovery from an elective operation, and while I was putting my mind to his problem he dropped dead in front of his family. That night I discussed this calamity with a registrar who had preceded me on the Britten-Jones/Magarey unit. In an access of candour I said, 'You know, when he carked it my first thought wasn't for him or his rellies. It was, What'll Bob say?' My colleague admitted that in a similar situation his reaction had been identical. We parted in sober agreement that we had much to learn about proper doctoring.

I spent the second six months as one of two Casualty registrars. We provided the support and supervision of new graduates that I'd lacked in my Casualty intern time, and did some ward work to keep in touch with real surgery.

My next goal was the primary. In Australia this hurdle could be attempted twice a year, and the bar was set high enough to eliminate candidates who hadn't studied full-time for months. Anatomy was the killer, with physiology and pathology less troublesome. In early 1957 several of us took part-time jobs as anatomy demonstrators, which gave us entry to the dissecting room where we kept ahead of the medical students. We grilled them weekly as others had dealt with us years earlier, and attended goal-oriented lectures by surgeons and university staff. Nine of us were flat out until we sat the September exams in Melbourne.

All I remember of this event was a disheartening viva conducted by Sir Sidney Sunderland, Melbourne's renowned and gimlet-eyed professor of anatomy, and Pat Kenny, a surgeon with vast anatomical expertise. Amongst other things they produced a single maxillary bone and asked abstruse questions about it. I was all but lost, and accelerated downhill thereafter. I don't know what they inflicted on the others, but despite our months of study only one Adelaide candidate, Joe Savage, passed.

We left Melbourne before the results were out. I arrived home on a Wednesday to find that a shipping company had phoned minutes earlier, looking for a doctor to leave Port Adelaide for England on Friday. After British surgical training, Don Beard had come home as a ship's doctor, and the deck officers threw him a farewell party. A guest from the RAH knew I planned to go to England. The doctor signed up for the homeward journey was ill, and the company was desperate for a replacement, hence the phone-call. Was I interested?

Chapter 7

Ship's doctor to England

A free passage was too good to pass up, but I needed a passport and a tax clearance within 48 hours, and would travel ahead of Gwen and the girls, as this was a cargo ship only. Thursday brought news of my failure in Melbourne, which was sad, if not surprising. I airmailed Bob Britten-Jones (Jonah's son) at Nuffield House, the residential quarters at the Royal College of Surgeons, asking him to book me a room and register me for the next British primary exam.

I was unaware of the rule that repeat primaries couldn't be taken within less than three months after a previous attempt; if a student failed today, it made a mockery of the whole process if he could be ready for another go in a few weeks. The next primary was in London, a fortnight after I arrived, and I was ineligible.

There was a gap then until February, but I was permitted to sit in Glasgow in November. I was in London before I learnt these details. Jonah was a friend of Sir James Paterson Ross, lately PRCS, and I believe I owe my slightly premature Glasgow admission to them.

The SS *Nestor* (Captain W.E. Studley, master) carried a doctor because it had a complement of more than 70. With no passengers and a healthy crew I had ample study time on the five-week voyage. I had a spacious stateroom and ate in style at the captain's table. Apart from an unscheduled stop at Albany to land a stowaway we called at Aden and Genoa only before docking in Liverpool. With no medical work I thought I had landed much more than the famous free lunch – it was full board and free passage. Then one morning, far across the Indian Ocean, we logged a radio from a tanker *en route* from Bahrain to East London. Hours earlier a lascar had fallen through a ladder. The good news (via Morse code) was that he was more or less intact. But, desperate to empty his bladder, he could pass a few drops of blood but no urine. We were the nearest ship. What to do?

This was a ruptured urethra, a serious injury. If both ships changed course we would meet in about eight hours, so Captain Studley issued orders immediately. I sent a radio asking them to give morphine and warn the man not to try urinating. An hour later he was in agony. What now? Most urethral tears are partial, which is bad enough, but catheterisation can inflict more serious damage. I didn't want unskilled people trying it, but with no alternative I suggested that they make a gentle attempt. Hours passed. The purser tried, then the captain, and finally the ship's engineer, who was successful. Having emptied the bladder they asked for more advice, so I told them to strap the catheter in. We felt the agony in their next radio: they'd pulled it out again. There seemed no need to risk more damage so I had them load him with morphine and hope for the best. The ships met late in the afternoon and my patient was hoisted aboard strapped into a Neil Robertson stretcher, his eyes popping. In the ship's hospital I managed to pass a catheter and secured it with great care. Several nights later we reached Aden, where ships using the Suez Canal bunkered anyway. An ambulance took us to the run-down Crater hospital, where the poor man thought I was abandoning him amongst barbarians.

By this time I had another patient, a raving Chinese greaser determined to walk home, so I had to keep him well sedated in the ship's hospital. I expected to land him along with the other man, but Aden had seen too much cabin fever and never accepted psychiatric cases, so we locked him up all the way to Liverpool.

Otherwise the journey was uneventful and we arrived on the due date, a dank and drizzly day. This was long before smoke abatement legislation, so Liverpool's soot and grime made it a disenchanting entrée to England, but in my excitement I took scant notice. I signed off, had a shilling haircut, took the train to London and found my room in Nuffield House, where Bob explained the exam plans. He'd booked me into a legendary anatomy teacher's tutorial series for those taking the forthcoming London primary. I jumped at this extra, but otherwise relied on the well-thumbed books I had with me.

I was preparing for an old-fashioned essay-type examination; the MCQs that torment today's examinees were far in the future. For years I'd been reminded, repeatedly and pointedly, that examiners found poor handwriting a turn-off, so I bought a calligraphy manual and a fountain pen with a spade-pointed nib, and learnt a neat italic script. Another necessity was attire that made me look like a surgeon, so I went to Pope and Bradley in the Savile Row area and was measured for a dark grey suit costing 44 guineas. When I collected it I was ready to pay cash, which bowled them over. They wanted to mail an account but I didn't know where I'd be, so they hunted everywhere for a receipt book, which took some finding. There has to be truth in that adage about gentlemen and their tailors.

A week or so after reaching London I received a finely engraved card from Miss Macdonald of Sleat inviting me to tea in Knightsbridge, so I went along to see if cucumber sandwiches really existed. (They did.) My hostess was an elderly Scots aristocrat who enjoyed entertaining young colonials, Australians on Thursdays. She plomped me on a couch next to a girl gushing about the London music scene; she'd been to concerts almost every night for weeks. When I got a word in edgeways I said we were always sending promising Adelaide musicians to London but rarely heard of them again. Small fish, big pool and all that. Cuts them down to size. The girl bristled and dried up. When I left Miss M said, 'I do hope you enjoyed talking to Miss So-and-so. Lovely girl. She's a promising young violinist from Tasmania.'

This was the extent of my socialising. I kept my nose in my books, with occasional breaks to see a little of the city on foot. Lincoln's Inn Fields is off Kingsway, within easy walking distance of the Strand and the West End. Stanley Gibbons, Britain's leading stamp dealers, had an unprepossessing building in the Strand, with their cramped retail shop on the ground floor. No doubt there was something grander upstairs, but I had no money to spend, and settled for window-shopping. On Sundays I walked to Westminster Chapel where the legendary Welsh physician and preacher Dr Martyn Lloyd-Jones had a 2000-strong morning congregation and perhaps half that at night. For twelve years 1000 or so heard him expound Paul's letter to the Romans on Friday nights. To my mind the published version fails to transmit their greatness.

An Adelaide businessman had written me an introduction to an old friend, the manager of the Mayfair branch of a major American bank, and insisted that I call on him. I did so late one morning in a mixture of fog and drizzle – average November for London – wearing a rather worn but favourite suit, and entered a building more like a palace than a bank. The manager greeted me with stilted warmth and seemed pleased to have direct news of his friend, but small talk soon dried up so I took my leave. It was almost lunchtime so I asked the doorman, a big bruiser dressed like a full colonel in some South American army, for suggestions. He looked down his big red nose, appraised me from head to toe and said plummily, 'I think you'd find the restaurants around here rather expensive, sir, but if you walk two blocks that way' – pointing east – 'you'll find a Lyons on the corner.' I took his advice. A Mt Gambier-born relative, yet another John Clezy, was general manager of the ES&A Bank in Threadneedle Street, but I found him about as communicative as the man in Mayfair. Bankers seemed a strangely taciturn lot, on this sampling at least.

What with concentrated study onboard ship and my time in London I took the train for Glasgow feeling ready for anything. Because that primary was regarded as easier than some others, many under-prepared candidates tried it. I was ahead of most, so passed with ease, nine weeks after crashing in Melbourne. My Scots examiners were gentlemen. The anatomy wasn't troublesome, and two learned professors began my physiology viva by asking why an Australian was in Glasgow. I explained myself slightly obliquely and was then asked why Australians didn't like fish. I said, 'Well, sir, in my country good fish is expensive and good meat is cheap, and in your country it's the other way around.' They grinned approvingly and then asked about goitre in Tasmania and other serious matters. Our results were posted that afternoon. I had passed while my fellow-failures in Melbourne were still licking their wounds.

Overnight I returned to London in a buoyant mood, but was brought down to earth by the taxi driver who rushed to take my bag when I finally made it to the head of the queue outside the railway station. The fare to Lincoln's Inn Fields was a mere half-crown, so the cabbie was mightily disgusted at landing such a dud at six on a chilly morning, after waiting in line for hours. I was barely aboard before he almost slammed the door off. He was annoyed still further when I proffered the exact fare. As others have discovered, failing to tip an English cabbie can be wondrously educational.

At Nuffield House I found a letter from Gwen, posted in Singapore. Meredith's appendix had been removed during a storm in the Timor Sea. Presumably all was well, but I took the boat-train to Southampton a few days later anxious to be sure. Gwen and the girls made the voyage accompanied by Dad's youngest sister Alethe and

Blanche Bourne, an old friend of the family. We took rooms in an Earl's Court boarding house while I continued my search for a job.

After I'd drawn a few blanks Bob B-J recommended St Andrew's Hospital, Billericay, which favoured Australians, and was looking for a locum resident surgical officer (RSO). The local rules were that if the locum was any good he could expect to land the permanent post. St Andrew's had two main attractions: it was only half an hour from London, and the senior surgeon was Peter Martin, a man of great ability and a pioneer in the new specialty of vascular surgery. I got the locum, to begin on 1 January 1958. When I asked the hospital secretary about accommodation he could offer a single room only, and said that vacant housing was almost non-existent, which I confirmed by visiting a couple of estate agents. A few expensive houses were on their books, with more reception rooms than we'd know what to do with. Tenancies changed on quarter days only, with possible vacancies months away.

Some solicitors handled rental properties so I tried the door of a High Street house bearing a lawyer's plate, but the lady answering the bell apologised that they didn't deal with housing. Somehow I picked her as a Christian, so I asked about places of worship. She invited us to the Anglican service at Great Burstead, a nearby village, and offered to take us there in their car. We were to enjoy that ancient church, some of whose dissenting members had been on the *Mayflower*.

I needed a haircut, and when the barber commented on my Australian accent I told him I was looking for family accommodation. So, if he heard of anything … His next customer was a solicitor's clerk with a flat to let above Woolworths, and before I made it back to the hospital for lunch he'd phoned looking for me. I returned to London in high spirits, to tell Gwen I had a job and accommodation. This flat was a good beginning but was rather cramped, with access via a slippery steel external staircase and across an un-railed roof. This was less than ideal for children, so a few months later we moved to a duplex in Hunt's Mead, a new area.

Billericay was best known for being the first town in England to post results on election night. Otherwise it was an undistinguished Essex village, now shrivelling downwind of Basildon New Town, but it was a fine place to begin British surgical training. Bill Hamer, a general surgeon with an interest in urology, was at St Andrew's about half time. Peter Martin came one day a week only, his main appointments being at Chelmsford, the county town nine miles away. He was also the vascular surgeon at the Hammersmith, the London Postgraduate Medical School hospital, and spent Thursdays there. Despite being spread around southern England like this he was always available when on call. When we met he said, 'Clezy, I don't care what you do as long as you don't make a mess of it.' This sounds like reckless *carte blanche* but it worked well. I remember displeasing him twice only at Billericay, first when I operated on a baby's obstructed hernia. On his ward round next day I explained what I'd done. He looked askance over his half-moons and said, 'Never, never operate on obstructed hernias in small children.' I was mystified; I'd followed standard teaching. In future I was to sedate them and put them up in gallows traction. This was treatment for broken thighs in young children, in which they were swung by the ankles from a bar across the cot, just high enough to lift their buttocks off the bed, until the fracture healed. I hadn't heard of its use for obstructed hernias, but I've followed Peter's advice ever since with great success. Sedation relaxes the child and gravity reduces the hernia, which is repaired at leisure, and more easily, next day.

The second incident involved an old lady with a persistently discharging wound months after her gallbladder had been removed. On my registrar's Friday operating list I had to take four sets of tonsils from the ENT waiting list before doing cases of my own choosing. Tonsils were messy and boring, if good technical training. The discharging wound seemed a much more interesting challenge, so I called the lady in and explored it. She was fat and I had to make a deep hole, but I recovered a gallstone and put in a drain. She was doing well when Mr Martin and Mr Hamer made rounds a few days later, but they looked at each other, raised their eyebrows and harrumphed, which told me I'd taken on something that might well have been beyond me.

The standard treatment for peptic ulcer unresponsive to medical treatment was partial gastrectomy, in which a large part of the stomach is removed. PM was a master and I once saw him perform it in 35 minutes, skin to skin, on a man with a bleeding ulcer. At this speed the assistant had to anticipate his every step. I did my first gastrectomy under his tutelage. Ordinarily he didn't use a post-operative nasogastric tube, but he allowed me to pass one as a safety measure. Hours later

I visited the ward and was distressed to find the nurses recovering a few mL of bloodstained fluid each time they aspirated the tube. I was alarmed until the charge nurse, an experienced Irish lady, gave me a motherly pat on the shoulder and bade me leave it to them, go home, and quit worrying.

Perforated peptic ulcers were common, and in Adelaide I'd learnt to operate on them through a short incision to the right of the midline. I opened one suspected case in an elderly lady and found a perforated cancer of the stomach, with metastases in each ovary. Simple closure of the perforation was inappropriate so I performed my first solo partial gastrectomy, which went well.

St Andrew's employed a Casualty registrar, also a surgical trainee, and we shared nights. I did it from home and was often called out. At first we had no car, so this meant a walk of about a mile each way. Callouts were less of a problem after we bought a second-hand Ford Consul with money from my income from J.B. Clezy & Co, the family farming company. (Dad, Mother and their sons were the directors. Ordinarily we boys saw nothing of our notional profits, but could draw on them if there was real need. Our income was ploughed back into the business, or bought part of our parents' acreage, so that after some years each son owned freehold land.)

My time with Jim Dinning soon proved useful. One morning a girl was admitted with a linear skull fracture after crashing her motorbike. She was quite 'with it' but complained of severe headache, far more than the average head injury does. Within minutes she didn't know what day it was, but was otherwise unchanged. I phoned our regional neurosurgeon, half an hour away, and described her. He agreed with my diagnosis of extradural haematoma (a clot just under the skull bone), the classic emergency in head trauma, and asked if we could get her to him inside 30 minutes. We had an ambulance onsite, so while his theatre staff set up we roared down the highway, sirens blaring. He opened her head under local anaesthetic and evacuated blood and clot. Half the cases of extradural haematoma sent to him died in the ambulance before they were anywhere near him, but this girl made a perfect recovery, so I was pleased that I'd recognised her subtle deterioration.

Months later a medical ward took in an old lady with a presumed stroke. Over lunch, where problem cases were on the menu regularly, the medical registrar said she'd been fluctuating in and out of consciousness. 'Ahaa,' I said magisterially, 'chronic subdural haematoma.' (This is another clot on the surface of the brain, with a slow evolution, typically taking three weeks or more to declare itself after an apparently trivial head injury. Headache may be minimal, and a fluctuating level of consciousness is characteristic.) Off I went to find the patient sleeping peacefully, but unrouseably. To me this has always seemed typical of a chronic subdural rather than a stroke, and after examining her I phoned our neurosurgeon. He asked for a skull X-ray, and would see her that evening. The X-ray showed what is commonly but incorrectly called a calcified pineal gland, exactly in the midline. This was disappointing, as I'd expected it to be shifted away from whichever side harboured the haematoma. When our consultant arrived the lady was almost awake and he was unimpressed, but a day or so later she was deeply unconscious again. I felt she had to have a subdural, with the absence of midline shift explained by her having bilateral symmetrical haematomas. Burr-holes proved this diagnosis correct.

Most days were humdrum by comparison with such lifesaving incidents. One hectic Monday morning Dr Zed, a GP on the periphery of our catchment area, phoned apologetically about a Jewish couple whose eight-day-old boy needed circumcision that day.

'Fair go,' I said. 'I'm not a rabbi.'

'I know that,' he said patiently, 'but apparently that doesn't matter. Anyway, the nearest rabbi's in London, and what's more, he wants rather a lot for doing it. Is there any possibility …?'

'I would if I could,' I said, I hoped convincingly, 'but you know what Mondays are like here. I'm absolutely chokka, but I've got an idea. Bill Hamer sees outpatients this afternoon, so I'll book him in there.'

He was greatly relieved, but Mr Hamer's clinic was fully booked. The clerk didn't dare exceed the permitted number of new public patients but suggested I phone Mr Hamer asking if he'd see the baby privately. He said 5.30, and would perform the circumcision straightaway. His fee would be ten guineas. I relayed this information to the GP, who thanked me effusively before hanging up. Two minutes later my pager buzzed for the umpteenth time. The telephonist had Dr Zed on the line again. 'Put him through,' I said.

'I'm terribly sorry,' he groaned. 'That circumcision. The parents think ten guineas is a bit steep. The rabbi would've done it for five.' So it was back to square one, and I did it for free on Friday's list, when the boy was twelve days old.

I knew that by late 1958 I'd have spent enough post-internship time to qualify for an attempt at the FRCS, so after passing the Glasgow primary I tried to enrol for the month-long coaching course at St Thomas's Hospital, London, widely regarded as the best possible preparation for the final fellowship exam. The next was in May. I was dismayed to find it fully booked, but the girl offered to put me on her yards-long waiting list. Adding my name seemed pointless but I accepted her offer and then forgot about it. A senior surgeon at St Thomas's saw my name and worked out that I was a relative of John Clezy, his banker neighbour, hence the offer of a place in the May course.

I'd barely worked myself in at Billericay when I received this news. Mr Martin said the hospital couldn't release me so soon. But I didn't need any course, he said; I was bound to pass if I worked for him and Bill Hamer, and read Ian Aird, plus the orthopaedic text of my choice. (Aird was the Hammersmith's professor of surgery, and renowned for his *A Companion in Surgical Studies*, the last and best of the great single-author British postgraduate texts.)

I decided to sit in November anyway, as a trial run before doing next year's Tommy's course, after which I'd make a serious attempt at Part 2. Unless I was prepared to make a fool of myself, even a trial exam warranted proper preparation, so I took Mr Martin's advice and studied in all my spare evenings, oblivious to our girls' noise.

The written exam suited me, but that was the soft part, and I didn't yet think of regarding this as a serious shot at the finals. The vivas took about a week, with 32 candidates appearing each day. When my turn came on 18 November, Gwen's birthday, I went up to London relaxed and in my Pope and Bradley suit. I was in the last batch of examinees before lunch. As always, the big item was the long case. Mine was a bricklayer, diagnosed with tuberculosis of the right shoulder joint years earlier. This was treated with drugs and an operation called an arthrodesis, which was meant to fuse the bones together, stiffening the joint permanently. All was well until he'd recently developed a large, almost painless shoulder swelling. I'd never seen TB of the shoulder, and never have since – of all the joints affected by TB this must be the rarest – but the swelling had to be tuberculous pus. This meant that the arthrodesis had failed in the first place or, alternatively, heavy work had disrupted a weak union.

I examined him with great care, trying to find movement at the joint. Eventually I was satisfied that it was a little loose, at least in one plane. I noted the other abnormal features and was ready for the bell. Sir Reginald Watson-Jones, one of the world's best-known orthopaedic surgeons, conducted my viva. I gave the history and described my findings, and when I reported slight joint movement the eyes of both examiners lit up so gleefully that I suspected I was the first candidate that day to detect this absolutely key finding.

The session flowed smoothly from then on. After desultory talk about other forms of tuberculosis requiring surgical treatment they showed me a series of short cases. The only one I remember was a man with a femoral hernia, which I identified correctly. The second examiner, Mr Hosford, asked if a truss worked for this variety of groin hernia, and I said no, as I'd been taught. He told me there was one situation in which a truss controlled a femoral hernia; what was that? I was speechless so he looked at Watson-Jones, but he didn't know either. With boyish triumph Hosford said a truss would control a femoral hernia if the hip on that side had been arthrodesed. 'Of course,' said the great man. If anyone might have been expected to know this it was Watson-Jones, which shows that whatever our eminence in a specialty, some trivia will beat us. I've never met anyone who has seen a patient with such a combination, but this useless info will stick in my brain forever.

Not knowing this detail in such exalted company perhaps should have bolstered my confidence, but it didn't. The remaining segments of the examination are a blur, and when I joined the others to hear our results I wasn't at all hopeful. We knew that only eight to ten of 32 examinees passed each day. As our names were read out we walked over to the uniformed clerk, standing like a guard at the foot of the grand staircase, to hear our results. A pass meant a trip upstairs to sign the fellows' roll. Failures turned and slunk out the side door. A dozen had passed before my name was called, and I felt sure that the day's quota (if there was such a thing) would be reached before they got to me. Mine was the seventeenth name, and despite having sat the exam as an exercise to see how it was conducted, seeing all those happy chaps flying up the stairs had its effect, and I now felt much more like a player than an onlooker. I stumbled across the carpet with my heart pounding. The clerk beamed as he told me I'd passed.

I took my seat in the Billericay train and surveyed my fellow passengers in rather a daze, and with something like pity. Theirs had been one more humdrum day at the office, like thousands before it; with this mighty hurdle behind me so unexpectedly, mine had been momentous almost beyond belief. I ran the half-mile from the station to our house. Gwen wasn't surprised, precious supporter that she was. Then I hurried to the telephone exchange to book the only call we made home in our three years away. My proud parents weren't surprised either, having little conception of the treacherous nature of the FRCS examination, despite my repeated warnings.

Overnight the news flashed around the hospital and next morning I suddenly became Mr Clezy. The switchboard girl congratulated me as I came in the gate, and Gwen was given the deference due to a surgeon's wife when she was admitted for the birth of our third daughter, Kathleen Ruth, on 20 December 1958.

I was now in a position to apply for RSO posts for which the FRCS was a prerequisite. In early 1959 Mr Martin gave up Billericay work, with his position filled on a locum basis by Peter Philip, later a well-known urologist at the Charing Cross, a great London teaching hospital. We were to become lifelong friends, but despite the obvious value of working for him I knew he wasn't aiming to be appointed to Billericay. It was time to look elsewhere.

In mid-1959 the RSO position at the Chelmsford and Essex Hospital, London Road, Chelmsford, was to become vacant. Peter Martin was Chelmsford's senior surgeon and had much more to teach me, so I applied, and was successful. The city's two hospitals were busy, with plenty of operative and management experience for the registrars. Both PM and the second surgeon, Bruce Pender, who majored in urology, had a system whereby the registrar ordinarily operated in one theatre while they and the intern were next door. I assisted the boss only when he had something specific to teach me. Otherwise I operated with supervision and help immediately available if required, which was an excellent training arrangement.

Another Australian, John Fisher, was registrar at St John's, and we were on call for both hospitals on alternate nights. We gained experience rapidly, and got on well together. Married accommodation went with both jobs. The rent for our hospital flat was so low that we overlooked the flaws in the grotty secondhand carpet in the lounge. It was much too long, with one end rolled up against the wall. Our only real problem was the snooty spinster in the next unit who reprimanded Gwen for hanging washing on our outside line.

PM was too busy to arrange operation lists, which was the RSO's duty, and I met with his secretary on Mondays to construct the next week's program. I remember only one real error, in which I called in for myself a man with a swelling of a submandibular salivary gland. Scarring from recurrent inflammation made its removal unexpectedly difficult, and the patient awoke with evidence of at least partial injury to all three important nerves in the operative field. This was bad enough, but next time I saw our secretary she asked astringently if I knew that Mr Martin had seen the chap in private and had intended doing his operation himself. I was horrified, but when I went to apologise the boss was unperturbed. Fortunately the nerves were showing signs of recovery at our last review.

Vascular surgery was in its infancy, and until late in my time Peter still used freeze-dried irradiated homografts as replacements for aortic aneurysms and blocked femoral arteries. It was the RSO's duty to keep an eye on supplies, which were selected in the autopsy room by our pathologists and sent away for processing. With patients referred from as far afield as Melbourne we didn't want them waiting around for operation, so grafts had to be always available. Life became simpler when PM visited Michael DeBakey in Houston, Texas, and brought back artificial grafts. He didn't much enjoy this trip, and told us America was a terrible place where it cost ten cents to spend a penny.

When a consultant was away he left the RSO in charge of his unit, with the other surgeon available if required. I was seeing Bruce Pender's outpatients in his absence when the nurse asked in a loud whisper if I'd heard of a certain famous English novelist. I had. ('We're not all peasants in Australia, sister.') The next patient was his brother. The referral letter gave his full style and title, which included two orders of knighthood well up the table of precedence. The trouble seemed to be with his prostate. I watched in awe as a finely dressed eighty-year-old walked in, straight as the proverbial ramrod, his perfectly knotted regimental tie glowing. I took his history and did a general examination, but couldn't bring myself to feel his prostate. I ordered routine investigations and gave him an appointment to see Mr Pender in a week.

Years later I found that young PNG doctors sometimes fumbled the management of Europeans with problems that they'd have approached perfectly correctly if the patient had been a fellow Papua New Guinean. I always sympathised with them. If I with my FRCS (admittedly fairly recent) felt unable to put my finger into Sir What's-his-name's rectum …?

As in Adelaide, appendicectomy was the intern's prerogative. One duffer habitually arrived late in theatre and towards the end of his time he missed a couple for this reason. Again I promised him the next appendix, and again the anaesthetist had the patient asleep and was pressing me to get on with it. My intern was nowhere in sight, so rather than risk him accusing me of theft I had the theatre nurse do it. She'd been scrubbing since I was in school and undoubtedly was competent to remove an appendix, which she did with aplomb. This caused no comment, but years later a surgeon elsewhere in England was punished severely for doing the same thing, and suffered the indignity of having an account of his misdemeanour published worldwide.

As well as giving excellent general surgical, vascular and urological experience, the Chelmsford hospitals provided a certain amount of orthopaedic work under Mr Harris, an elderly general surgeon who was also an almost self-trained orthopod. Major trauma rarely came to us because ambulances took serious accident cases to the regional orthopaedic centre some miles away (as happened at Billericay, too). Management realised that my exposure to trauma was inadequate so allowed me to attend a superb course at the Birmingham Accident Hospital, the first institution of its kind in England. I'd been attracted there by a lecture given by Ruscoe Clarke, the BAH's high-profile surgeon with all the attributes recognised as *sine qua non* for a trauma surgeon, plus one – he was the best-known card-carrying communist in the medical profession. Such was his eminence that few held this against him.

If Mr Harris's elegant home was a tad less than a mansion, it boasted a sumptuous music room displaying a splendid nested pair of grand pianos. Music was not his only touch of couth; he was the proud owner of a fabulous collection of Georgian silver. Surgically he was not wildly venturesome, to put it mildly, but as well as operating on hernias, piles and bunions we managed almost all the fracture work that came our way, highly selected as it was by the regional trauma arrangements. He had the annoying habit of doing his routine ward round at 9 am on Sunday, when the appearance of his gleaming black Armstrong-Siddeley drop-head coupe was the signal for the telephonist to buzz the duty RSO to come running.

But I remember him most vividly for something else entirely. Towards the end of my time we had five or six admissions following an accident in which a car pool driver ferrying children to school hit another vehicle. The youngsters' injuries were minor, but the mother on roster that morning sustained a punctured lung and two broken wrists. She needed an urgent chest tube to drain air, and Mr Harris said, 'You know all about that side of it, Clezy, so you put the chest tube in while I do the fractures.' We got on with it, and all was well. As we stripped off our gowns Mr H said the insurers would pay, and he would claim ten guineas for my part of it. Compared with my meagre salary this seemed an unbelievably generous reward for so little work, but I had to believe it because he pulled out a bulging wallet and gave me the money on the spot.

Several months after I began in Rabaul a letter arrived on his deckle-edged, embossed letterhead. After expressing his hope that all was well with us and so on, he was terribly sorry to inform me that our lady's insurers had been through the accounts with exceptional care and objected to paying me for inserting the chest tube. This was because junior National Health Service doctors were full-time, and thus weren't entitled to private fees of any kind. So he'd be glad to have my cheque for ten guineas at my convenience. I dutifully paid up, to the great amusement of all who have heard this story. One wag thought I should have sent him interest too.

In Chelmsford we enjoyed the London Road Congregational Church where the minister, A.E. Gould, was amongst the denomination's finest preachers. We made good friends there, most memorably with the Rider Blanks family who were dairy farmers. We visited them regularly for almost 40 years.

Rail services between London and both Billericay and Chelmsford were excellent, so Gwen and I took opportunity, singly or together, depending on the availability of babysitters, to attend concerts at easily accessible venues. Tchaikovsky's first piano concerto was on the program somewhere every year, but the performance I heard was exceptional. Three horns played that opening bar of four descending notes with one instrument so woefully off pitch that the conductor propped momentarily, but he kept going. The poor perpetrator's instantly bright red face identified him to the packed house. Otherwise it was a great performance, with Emil Gilels the soloist.

Another time I heard a blind organist, the great Helmut Walcha, strut his stuff on the Festival Hall instrument. His wife led him onto the stage, helped him onto the organ stool and controlled the stops throughout his virtuoso performance, a brilliant display far beyond the capacity of most organists with all their faculties. How blind musicians memorise a complicated score has always been a mystery to me, and a blind man playing music, difficult by any standards, on a foreign organ is a breathtaking achievement. Piano keyboards are all the same but organs are individuals, with the relationship between each instrument's several manuals close, but certainly not identical. A flawless performance at the console of a strange organ must be a special challenge for the blind.

Our first holiday, motoring in Scotland, was in midsummer 1958. We soaked up the history and saw Edinburgh at its best, understanding why the cognoscenti rate it as one of the three most beautiful cities on earth (with Salzburg and Rio). Grandma Schinckel had been a McLeod, so we visited Skye to see the clan's ancient fortress, Dunvegan, propping up the western sky. We found that the further from London the lower the B&B tariff and the larger the breakfast.

We had plenty to see closer to home too, and as well as visiting Adelaide friends Joan and Allan Day in Oxford we made trips to Cambridge and its surrounds, once with Allan Burrow, Gwen's cousin who had married us, when we went to evensong in the packed King's College Chapel. All was well until Kathy, then about a year old, added her barely audible obbligato to the first anthem. It was happy, harmless chortling but in no time a grim black-gowned beadle (or something) appeared with a long stick and thumbed us a peremptory 'Out!' We crept away like burglars, barely refraining from quoting the verse that begins 'Suffer the little children …'

The most perfect family memory I have of this time is of a visit to Ely, an otherwise undistinguished fenland town that boasts one of England's most renowned cathedrals, an enormous building set on a rise and visible for miles around, like a great ship tied up at a small wharf. After viewing the cavernous interior and seeing the sculpted memorials to numerous long-dead worthies, Gwen joined the party waiting to climb up to the octagon, from which most of Cambridgeshire is visible. This ascent was not for children, so while she puffed her way up the steep stairs I took Meredith and Robyn across the cobblestones to the cathedral park, a soft and gently sloping lawn dotted with ancient oaks. It was a perfect summer afternoon, with barely a cloud in the sky. In rare serenity I lay on my back, head in the shade, staring lazily at the jet trails streaking the heavens far above me, sharp and spiky at one end, fading and feathery at the other. For background music I had the gleeful squeals of our daughters, who had found the thick grass soft enough, and the slope steep enough, for them to curl up and roll downhill effortlessly. Thrilled at discovering something like perpetual motion, they were still at it when Gwen reappeared. For me to be free to mind them was almost unheard of, and this brief experience of their limpid, unalloyed delight on the grass of the Ely cathedral park remains, by a huge margin, my most precious memory of their childhood.

In the summer of 1960 Alethe, who had been studying at the London Bible College, house-sat with the children while Gwen and I spent three weeks camping on the Continent. It was an unusually wet year and soon we were experts at erecting our tent in the dark and in the rain. We took one of the great tourist routes, through Belgium to Heidelberg, down the Romantische Strasse to Munich, years before the Marienplatz became a mall, and to Schloss Neuschwanstein long before its acres of priceless parquetry were covered to shield it from the millions of feet that tramp through this fairyland castle nowadays.

After driving east to Vienna we turned south into drab and poverty-stricken Yugoslavia. Roads had been prettied up with flags and bunting for the visit of some African president, and the army was everywhere. I photographed a tank, bringing shouts and threatening gestures from its crew. Poor Gwen thought we'd land in gaol. Then to Postojna where the world-famous caves were no better than those at Naracoorte.

We reached Italy feeling happier and safer, and while we rated Venice a cross between chocolate-box kitsch and smelly aquatic slum we were enthralled by the wonders of Florence, where we bought Meredith and Robyn linen dresses at a smart boutique in the shadow of the duomo. They seemed expensive but, as so often happens, we got what we paid for. They were to survive fresh and unfading in the tropical sun, to pass down the family as Sunday dresses for years.

Chapter 8

Rabaul

Early in 1960 Mother sent the long-awaited ad for a surgeon in New Guinea, at Nonga Base Hospital, Rabaul, the recent replacement for the ramshackle hospital I saw in 1952. I phoned Australia House for application papers and filled them in immediately. Nothing happened for months until I was asked to appear in London a few days later, when they gave me another form to fill out. All went well until I came to a question about fits or epilepsy. I had to tick the 'yes' box.

When I was about 20 I'd suffered several strange episodes, like daytime sleepwalking, from which I could be aroused in a confused and agitated state. Our GP referred me to an Adelaide psychiatrist who said the problem wasn't psychiatric, but toxic, whatever that meant. (A pre-war European migrant, perhaps he brought heterodox Continental nosology with him.) Months later a convulsion left me unconscious on the floor, and the sleepwalking now made sense; it was a non-convulsive manifestation of epilepsy. A physician ordered the primitive electroencephalogram (EEG) then available in Adelaide. It was normal, but in view of the fit he prescribed Dilantin, then the anchor drug for most forms of epilepsy.

All was well for months until I had more strange turns. Example: after working all hours I took a tram to the Adelaide Oval to see the test cricket, but instead of hopping off at the oval I stayed aboard until a mile or so later the conductor noticed his freeloader. I was in a daze, and presumably he got no sense out of me, but I remember him angrily ejecting me. Unconcerned, I walked back to the cricket ground, bought my ticket and found a spot on the grass.

Some time later I realised something was wrong, and after replaying the incident in my mind I took a cab home, where I was vague and dreamy for the rest of the day. There were a few more non-convulsive episodes, months apart, usually when I'd been very busy. When I was on with Jim Dinning in 1955 they became more frequent, so I saw John Gordon, Adelaide's sole neurologist, who found nothing wrong, and after an EEG on his new machine was normal he added phenobarb to the Dilantin.

I'd been at Billericay for about a year when I had a convulsion while sitting in the theatre tearoom. A physician admitted me for observation but nothing else happened, so I took myself home next day. This was slightly improper, and meant that I was in what is called post-ictal confusion. My unauthorised departure miffed the physician but everyone else took it in their stride, and I carried on without my problem being of apparent concern to anyone.

I don't remember how much of this I disgorged at Australia House, but the doctor gave me the thumbs down without hesitation. They wanted A1 fit staff only, as no risks could be taken with superannuation funds, so another candidate was appointed. I was downcast. The law of diminishing returns was setting in at Chelmsford, and it was high time I went somewhere else. For years I'd been preparing to go to New Guinea, where God had called me. What now? Next, the TPNG Director of Health, Dr Roy Scragg, wrote saying he'd be in England shortly and wanted to see me. I'd met Roy briefly on Bougainville in 1952, where his research took him to count children's teeth, and I came to know him better when he was on study leave at the RAH in 1956. Gwen and I spruced ourselves up, took the train to London, and met the Scraggs at their Mayfair hotel. After hearing my story Roy said the Rabaul appointee had pulled out because his wife wouldn't go to New Guinea. He suggested I consult a neurologist, the more eminent the better, in the hope that he would pass me for employment.

Denis Williams was a big name in British neurology, especially in epilepsy. He saw me at Queen Square remarkably promptly and admitted me for investigation, which began with medication withdrawal to see if this precipitated a fit, but nothing happened. I had another EEG with needle electrodes inserted deep beneath my skull, under Pentothal anaesthetic, and was horrified to see no sucker, oxygen, or emergency equipment of any kind in the room, which I knew should always be available when anaesthetics, especially Pentothal, were given.

This EEG was normal, so they performed a left carotid angiogram in another attempt to identify an organic abnormality. I barely felt the radiologist's needle puncturing the artery in my neck, but for a few seconds the injected dye felt like boiling water coursing through the left side of my head. The films were normal, but coloured lights flashed in one corner of my visual field for hours afterwards. Things moved slowly so once again I discharged myself. I was to see Dr Williams in a fortnight, and it was pointless being in hospital while they re-stabilised my Dilantin dosage.

Dr Williams was supportive and saw no reason why I shouldn't enjoy a surgical career, although he'd have advised against it if I had consulted him years previously. Rabaul was desperate for a surgeon and Dr Scragg knew I'd had no serious problems at the RAH, so the Department accepted me, but not as a permanent officer. I wasn't eligible to join the regular superannuation fund but this didn't matter; my only concern was to go to New Guinea. Later Roy suggested that I apply for permanency, but when my application was eventually processed Canberra had ceased appointing permanent staff in TPNG. I ended up being the longest serving so-called 'exempt' officer, so that at independence I didn't qualify for the level of payout showered on others with comparable seniority.

Few know I have a form of epilepsy. Apart from one more convulsion in my sleep in Rabaul, I've been free of them for over 40 years, although I've had hundreds of brief absences in which I'm unable to speak for a few seconds. If they are heralded by tingling of the upper lip I can disguise them, but Gwen says there have been more than I know of, which may have puzzled other people occasionally.

The most extraordinary non-convulsive episode occurred in Yemen in 2001. I'd been frantically busy, and was up for hours in the night before a visiting English nurse came to tea. At table he told us not to worry if he had a fit; he was a well-controlled epileptic who still had very occasional seizures. I wondered about telling him he was in good company, but decided against it. An hour later I was showing him around the hospital, feeling dog-tired, and in the male ward office apparently decided to change into theatre clothes. I remember coming to on a chair, asking for my trousers. Somebody said, 'You've taken them off.' I responded by pointing at my socks, which were green. I was trying to say I wanted my green trousers – my theatre garb – but couldn't find the word 'green'.

Someone persuaded me to put my trousers on, and we resumed the tour. A worried-looking Australian doctor followed me to the female ward and asked that chilling and ominous question, 'Are you feeling alright?' When I said yes, he said I'd been acting strangely, which gave me an inkling of what had happened. I replied tersely that if he'd been on Dilantin and phenobarb for 50 years he might sometimes act strangely too.

Then it all sank in and I slunk home, greatly embarrassed. I slept soundly, and appeared next morning to hear that an elderly Indian nurse who had expressed shock at my behaviour had herself fallen in a fit shortly afterwards, her only convulsion since a few in childhood. She was admitted for observation, and was gracious enough to laugh when I dropped in to say I hoped she hadn't been trying to change her uniform. Somebody suggested that a biblical evil spirit, brought by our English visitor, was doing the rounds. Happily our Yemeni workers weren't put off, being only too familiar with epilepsy in its many forms.

So, apart from that glitch at Australia House, my life has been affected very little. When I sent him Dr Williams's report Dr Scragg pushed buttons and things moved quickly. We booked to Sydney on 3 December 1960 with Canadian Pacific, the only airline that simplified returning to Australia with children by stopping at night in Vancouver and Hawaii.

The Australia House people had booked us to Sydney by ship and straight on to Port Moresby, but the clerk handling our travel agreed that after three years away it was only proper that we fly home and spend time with our families. As a sea voyage would take a month he allowed us that as holiday, on full pay. He offered us first-class tickets too, as befitted public servants in those gilded times, but I was bonded for our travel costs for my first term and couldn't be sure of making the grade, so I refused. We'd planned to carry Kathy, who was almost two, so accepted a ticket for her. This was wise, given that the journey took five days, including two nights in a hotel on Waikiki Beach. We chugged across the Pacific in a lumbering old DC-6 the week before they put on their first 707.

I spent January 1961 as locum for Frank Smyth, the Port Moresby surgeon, so I went up alone and lodged at the Boroko Hotel, a raucous joint within walking distance of the hospital, variously called the POM General or the PMGH. Its main section was the spreading pavilion-style native hospital down on Taurama Road. The smaller, smarter

European hospital was on the hill, with X-ray and pathology departments alongside it, despite most of their work being for native patients.

I remember little of that month, but hours after removing a Papuan girl's gallbladder I decided she no longer needed IV fluids so removed the drip. That night the duty doctor for the whole hospital, Bill Symes, an Assistant Director of Public Health, was called in because her blood pressure had dropped a little. Re-inserting her drip was difficult and he told me all about it next morning. I don't know how much longer admin people did after-hours hospital duties; it ceased long before we moved to Port Moresby in 1970.

Another memorable operation was on a lad who had cut the flexor tendons of two fingers months earlier and, unusually for these cases, had kept his hand supple. With no operative experience of this injury I followed the book to perform tendon grafts, which impressed the theatre sister because she'd never seen it done either. We had a good physiotherapist, and the hand did well.

On the due date Gwen and the girls arrived from Sydney at 6 am, and we flew on to Rabaul in a DC-3. I still remember the buzz I felt as we circled Simpson Harbour and swooped in over Matupit volcano to land softly on the grassy airstrip. The RMO, Charlie Haszler, the Hungarian I remembered from Ela Beach in 1952, met us. He drove us up Tunnel Hill with dense clouds of suffocating white *coranus* dust flying behind us, and along the western side of the Gazelle Peninsula to our new Nonga house. The evening sea breeze made life there much more comfortable than inside the steaming crater of Rabaul town. The hospital was built in a clearing in an old coconut plantation, on a slope above the beach. A central covered way ran between long pavilion-style wards, each with outbuildings, so that from the air the place looked like an organisation chart. The Region's referral centre, Nonga had over 300 beds.

With his basic qualifications bolstered with diplomas in paediatrics and tropical medicine, Len Champness was medical superintendent, physician and paediatrician, and greeted us as old friends, even though we'd never met. Nonga had five other doctors (a Lithuanian GP, a Hungarian couple, an English eye specialist, and a bonded Queensland graduate) and about a dozen European sisters. These ladies and/or their husbands were adventurous types, or they wouldn't have been in New Guinea. Xavier Herbert's brother ran the boiler-house and his wife ran outpatients. Nonga had a nursing school with an excellent New Guinean principal, but its graduates were thought to be not yet ready for charge positions, so foreigners managed all wards and departments.

Although Rabaul's main product in German times was copra (the dried meat of the coconut), the Gazelle was now noted chiefly for its much more profitable cocoa. As well as large foreign-owned plantations there were numerous village smallholdings operated by the Tolai, one of the Territory's largest tribes. Their mellifluous language is Kuanua, but few foreigners learnt it as almost every male spoke pidgin English (now known as Tok Pisin). I struggled to learn a little Kuanua for medical purposes, which pleased and perhaps amused my patients. The letter 'r' has a Scots burr, and the soft 'v,' unlike any sound in English, is pronounced with the bottom lip pulled in over the teeth. Otherwise I now remember little more than the body language for Yes and No. A faint upward flicker of the eyebrows is Yes, and the suggestion of a pout of the bottom lip (for *pata*) means No.

Since the 1880s German Catholics and Polynesian and other Methodists had evangelised the Tolai, and there were well-attended churches in most villages. Missions had been running schools for many years, and early Tolai politicians, like those elsewhere in the Territory (as in most colonies the world over) had attended them. It was largely for this reason that PNG's constitution describes the country as Christian.

After a hospital tour I was shown my spacious office. The single letter in my in-tray, addressed to The Surgeon, Government Hospital, Rabaul, New Guinea, was from Denis Burkitt, a surgeon in Uganda. He enclosed a pamphlet illustrating an apparently newly discovered tumour of the jaws in children that he'd identified in several parts of Africa. He was asking surgeons all over the tropical world if they'd seen it. I hadn't even heard of it, and failed to do him the courtesy of answering his letter. Burkitt's tumour did occur in New Guinea, as was proven about this time by Rolf ten Seldam, an ex-East Indies pathologist in Perth, and a tropical expert if our local pathologist needed help. Burkitt went on to blaze a new trail in the understanding of cancer, and became one of a tiny handful of practising surgeons elected a Fellow of the Royal Society in modern times.

My ward sister was Phyllis Hodges, a fat and jolly Englishwoman who had trained at the Royal Northern, Hamilton Bailey's hospital, against her father's will, because he saw the makings of a concert pianist in her. (Hamilton Bailey's two books were the most widely used British surgical texts for half a century. A manic-depressive, most of his output occurred during his manic phases.) Phyl interrupted her course to nurse at the siege of Madrid, and married instead of going back for her final year. The Hodges migrated to Australia after World War II and ended up in Rabaul, where the nursing shortage led to Phyl, who had no certificate, being made the only female EMA in the service. She was a superb charge nurse, and knew the exact score with each of our 50-plus patients, spread throughout three long wards. She inserted the drips and took the blood. After a day in theatre I could call her and ask if she had any problems. The answer no meant I could go home for dinner and leave my post-operative round until later.

One morning Phyl walked into the ward and sniffed. 'Gas gangrene,' she announced, having seen it in Spain. She was right, and the man eventually lost his leg. She made many other shrewd diagnoses. As well as being the ideal clinical nurse for our situation, and a born manager, she spoke better Kuanua than any other foreigner apart from a few old missionaries. She was a fine artist in both pencil and paint, and an excellent chess player who once gave visiting Russian scientists a brisk run for their money. This great lady's nursing career came to a halt when a Rabaul-born Chinese returned from Sydney with her SRN certificate, and had to be employed. SRNs had precedence over EMAs, however experienced the latter might be, so Phyl became a clerk in the X-ray department, where she was wasted. And from then on I had to keep a much closer eye on the ward.

The surgeon was expected to perform caesarian sections. I'd done no obstetrics since graduation but Len had, so he soon taught me the essentials, and until Nonga's first obstetrician arrived in 1963 I did most of the caesars, except for private cases.

One of three private practitioners in town was an elderly New Zealander, Marion Radcliffe-Taylor. She must have been the first woman in the world to have formal orthopaedic training, in Vienna and other fountainheads of the specialty. How she became a Rabaul GP I do not know, but she did almost everything. Her caesar fee was £70, which seemed a large sum. She was away one weekend when two of her ladies went into labour, and when her assistant failed with the forceps in both he had to refer them to me for caesarean section. I felt a certain amount of *Schadenfreude* in depriving Raddy of her fees that weekend, more than I was paid for a week's work. Government doctors had no right of private practice and the Department didn't charge for our services when we treated Europeans, who nevertheless were classified as private patients.

Morris Willis, a fine Melbourne physician who served with distinction with the Red Cross during the bloody Congo debacle, arrived in Rabaul a month after us. We soon found that the town's GPs weren't referring patients to us. Many people were barely able to afford Raddy's fees, and had problems that in Australia would have been referred to specialists, so we held open clinics at the Town Clinic run by Betty Fenwick, another outstanding nurse. (Her husband was master of the chronically overloaded *Pollurian,* which sank in a 1963 storm, somewhere between Bougainville and Rabaul, drowning him and many others.) Betty ran an outpatient service for town natives and anyone else who cared to use it. With wide experience and abundant common sense, she didn't err in sending us cases that should have been managed by their GPs. Morris and I were happy with this arrangement but it soon caused ripples. The Assistant Administrator, Dr Gunther, the Director of Public Health before Roy Scragg, came to Nonga and leant on us unpleasantly firmly, but although we dutifully mouthed yes, yes, we went on much as before.

One patient who didn't come via Betty Fenwick was a lady who phoned during a Tuesday operating list, demanding to see me. I mentioned Friday's clinic but she insisted on consulting me immediately. Her desperate tone made me agree to see her between cases if she cared to come out to Nonga, which she did. The wife of a prominent businessman, she had seen Raddy on Monday after missing a couple of periods. This alarmed her because when her only child was born 19 years previously her obstetrician had said she'd never have another. (Why he was so sure remains a mystery.) She had taken him at his word until now. Raddy gave her a hormonal injection, a then fashionable pregnancy test that produced the equivalent of intense premenstrual tension, and she was close to boiling point when I saw her. I found enough evidence to diagnose pregnancy, and suggested a toad test, in which a sample of urine injected into a female toad produced massive ovarian swelling within 48 hours in positive cases. The lady's stiletto heels stabbed the terrazzo as she departed. 'I suppose it'd be worse if it was cancer,' she muttered. I had to agree. Sure enough, the toad test was positive, but this wasn't the end of it. She flew to Sydney and fronted her old obstetrician who did a mouse test that was likewise positive, so she called her husband to drop everything and head south, which he did. After coming to terms with everything they bought a grand layette, as became people who never did anything by halves. She intended keeping mum until her bump required explanation, but calling her a secretive sort would be reckless with the truth, so within days of her return all in Rabaul who cared, and doubtless many who didn't, heard the happy news.

Weeks later she miscarried. This was a sad end to what had had the makings of a lovely Indian summer of motherhood, but before long she called me again because she'd missed another period. Again the toad test was positive, and this time she felt no compulsion to go south. All was well for about three months until she couldn't empty her bladder, due to an uncommon situation in which the enlarging uterus becomes jammed in the pelvis instead of rising like the sun, and compresses the bladder outlet. We stood her on her head, almost, and did various other things to bounce the uterus clear, without result. Betty F passed a catheter each day while nature righted things, but no dice.

Ordinarily the treatment would have been to anaesthetise her and push the uterus upwards but I was afraid she'd miscarry again, an extremely disappointing outcome because she very much wanted this baby. After a week of catheter life she was fed up and agreed to an anaesthetic. We gave the uterus a nudge and she awoke with her pregnancy advanced by about three months. We all sighed in relief until she announced that I'd be caesaring her. Nowadays a lady in her forties having her second child 20 years after the first would be offered an operative delivery but we believed in *via naturalis* then. A Sydney obstetrician who happened to be visiting Rabaul saw her, and after a long interview he came out with a hangdog look and said, 'Caesar.'

So the pregnancy proceeded to term, when I delivered a fine girl through a transverse, skin-crease incision below the bikini line. This became an item of some note around town, as Raddy's caesars all had ugly vertical scars from pubis to navel. Somebody said my lady had to be restrained from exhibiting her wound the first time she went shopping, but this sounded like Rabaul-type exaggeration. At follow-up she said that in view of her trying experiences it was only proper that her husband have his operation too. I thought she meant vasectomy, but oh no: she wanted an operation for his piles. I said that would be OK if he wanted it done. He'd have it done all right, she assured me firmly, but there was one minor problem: he was terrified of hospitals, so I'd have to manage him as an outpatient. I said the operation was painful, and most patients needed several days' hospitalisation for pain relief. She was a jump ahead of me and had already arranged for her neighbour, a nurse, to give any needed injections.

Reluctantly I agreed to perform my first, and for about 40 years my last, outpatient haemorrhoidectomy. We gave him a post-operative shot and sent him home by ambulance. Next morning his bladder was full; he couldn't pass a drop. Wearily I drove the six dusty miles to town, drained a litre or so of urine by catheter, which I then removed. He had the same trouble that evening, and I catheterised him twice a day until things were normal again. Nowadays we'd leave the catheter in place, but in the early 1960s that was regarded as second-rate management. They knew I'd gone some way beyond the call of duty, so had Gwen and me to dinner in style, waited on by their starched servants.

Usually surgical life was much simpler than this, at least in respect of the decisions I had to make. The Tolai had great faith in Western medicine, partly because of the miraculous effect of a single dose of penicillin on yaws. This disease was endemic in much of the tropics, but after a morning shot the messy skin lesions dried by mid-afternoon and disappeared within days. Power was perceived to lie in the needle so New Guineans often asked for injections when they felt unwell, and were disappointed by refusal. Explanations that not every condition was appropriately treated with intramuscular penicillin cut no ice, so pliant village aid post orderlies gave large numbers of injections.

If I said an operation was necessary there was rarely any debate. *'Samting bilong dokta'* was the usual response in Rabaul. Elsewhere it wasn't always so straightforward. In about 1970 I went ashore at Losuia, in the Trobriand Islands, to find the medical assistant vainly attempting to re-establish an IV line in an old lady with intestinal obstruction. Her belly was distended and tender, and clearly she needed an emergency operation. Her skinny little husband, clad solely in a tatty woven grass jockstrap, wrung his hands at the bedside, and as

I turned to him the MA said he couldn't give permission for operation; we needed to consult the lady's brother.

His village was miles away but at least it was on the main road. The Land Cruiser's starter motor was out (for months no government vehicle in Losuia had had a functional starter motor) so the MA let out a shrill two-finger whistle that brought a bunch of youths running through the coconut palms to push until the engine fired. An hour later he returned with 20 men of all ages in and on the vehicle, looking exactly as they must have done when Malinowski made them famous so long ago, apart from several wearing plastic combs in their hair instead of the traditional intricately carved bamboo model favoured in the Trobriands.

The patient's eldest brother came to the sickbed and I began my explanation, translated by the MA, but as soon as he caught my drift he cut us short. Without so much as a glance at his sister or her husband, both terrified because they knew what was coming, he said peremptorily that under no circumstances would there be an operation. The MA told him his sister would die without it, but he was unmoved and said they'd take her home. So we gave her a pain shot for the road and left it at that.

Trobriand islanders had had prolonged European contact and had seen penicillin's effect on yaws, but remained persistently suspicious of European medicine. In Rabaul things were different, even amongst people from truly primitive areas. In 1961 we admitted a shipload of patients from Kandrian, a patrol post on New Britain's south coast. Some were from the interior, from an area recently patrolled for the first time. It was scarcely believable that New Britain, a long narrow island less than 100 kilometres across, held inhabitants who had never seen white men until 1961, but I was assured that this was so. The Kandrian EMA sent the usual letter, referring in particular to a young man with an enormous jaw tumour. He said that effective treatment would be a great advertisement for government services, but if there was any risk of the man dying in Rabaul we should do nothing but repatriate him on the next boat.

The poor man eyed me suspiciously. He had the biggest lower jaw tumour that I've ever seen, spreading in every direction so that chewing was impossible. The diagnosis was obvious. He had an ameloblastoma, a rare tumour that grows very slowly. Once surgical services are introduced anywhere, patients suddenly appear with tumours that have been enlarging for ten years or more, giving the impression of an epidemic. Pioneer surgeons collect them in considerable numbers. I saw them regularly in Rabaul, once admitting two Manus women with it on the same day.

This man knew no pidgin, and no local spoke his language. (Tolai women rarely spoke pidgin, but otherwise communication problems were rare at Nonga. Should a patient not understand us we sought help from our 100 or so nursing students, who had about 35 mother tongues between them.) I admitted him, knowing that other patients would teach him pidgin soon enough, and three weeks later I obtained as informed consent as one could hope for. I told him we'd put a tube into his windpipe under local anaesthesia, and put him to sleep while we removed his tumour. He would have a breathing tube in his neck for two or three weeks, but this wouldn't worry him. He agreed, and the operation to remove almost the entire lower jaw was uneventful. Under our circumstances reconstruction was impossible, and we settled for giving him a knife, fork and spoon. As with so many other bushies, not only in New Guinea, the bright lights got to him. He found work in Rabaul as a *hausboi*, and rapid increase in weight confirmed that his cutlery was more than making up for his inability to chew. As far as he was concerned this was a good result, but we never found out if his *wantoks* knew why he didn't come home.

For months I met new diseases almost daily. Spinal tuberculosis was a common problem that I'd never seen. An orthopaedic surgeon at a TB hospital near Chelmsford had made an international reputation with its management but it hadn't occurred to me to visit him. Our TB patients were confined at Bitapaka, a sanatorium run by the nursing order that worked at Vunapope. Triple drug therapy was given, and heavy plaster of Paris jackets were applied according to almost universal practice, in the erroneous belief that they restricted spinal movement enough to promote healing, and minimised the hunchback deformity characteristic of advanced spinal TB.

In the late 1950s a Hong Kong team introduced a new operation for it, consisting of excision of the diseased parts of the affected vertebrae, with the defect being filled with a bone graft that soon joined up with healthy bone above and below. In theory, and in good hands, this was fine. The Hong Kong surgeons were highly skilled, and when treating early cases they avoided deformity. In addition, the duration of drug treatment and the incidence of late relapse were reduced.

Most spinal TB patients complain of mild backache, sometimes with weakness of the legs, and have disease localised to a few lower thoracic vertebrae, although it can occur anywhere in the spinal column. Performing the Hong Kong operation, anterior spinal fusion, usually meant opening the lower left chest to allow wide exposure of the affected area. It seemed a marvellous operation, and I did many in Rabaul. Some patients had been on drug treatment for months and I found little disease worth excising. I had doubts about the operation as routine treatment, and eventually decided that its worth was exaggerated. The Hong Kong specialists operated early, as I saw when I visited them in 1966. Early in the disease process there was plenty of pus and little scar tissue, so that approaching the affected area was much easier than it was many months later. But I thought most cases needed no operation at all, and decided that if surgery was indicated, less radical procedures would suffice. Years later this view was vindicated by elaborate international clinical trials.

A Milne Bay lady seen by a Port Moresby surgeon in 1973 exemplified the success of the conservative approach. She had paraplegia due to pressure on the spinal cord from an enormous tuberculous abscess, with several vertebrae affected. Urgent operation was advised but she refused. Threats of permanent paralysis didn't budge her so she was shipped back to the TB/leprosy hospital at Ubuya, an island in Milne Bay, where I saw her eighteen months later, almost completely recovered on drugs alone. Mild but unimportant spasticity in both legs was evidence of previous spinal cord compression. She had surprisingly little deformity, and the result was almost as good as if she'd had a perfect operation.

Cancer of the mouth was another disease new to me. This occurs in the West, mostly in tobacco users, but is much commoner wherever betel nut is chewed, and has been blamed on tobacco mixed with the betel, lime and whatever else is fashionable locally. Papua New Guineans don't chew tobacco, and it seems likely that lime is the real culprit. Our cases usually presented late, with ulceration right through the cheek, or of much of the tongue. Except in the tongue this isn't a particularly aggressive cancer and often it can be excised widely, with expectation of cure. The main problem is in reconstructing the defect left by such radical surgery. Frank Smyth, Port Moresby's senior surgeon, was interested in this cancer and became such an expert that Australian surgeons visited him to see his technique. It was impossible to ship all our cases to Frank so the rest of us had to learn his methods.

Chemotherapy as part of advanced mouth cancer treatment was introduced in the USA in about 1960, the preferred method being infusion of the drug methotrexate into the main artery supplying the tumour. With no pumps to deliver the infusion against arterial pressure we had to rely on gravity. I used this treatment in 1963, with the patients' beds in the centre of the ward, with drip bottles hung from the ridgepole. Management was difficult and dangerous but the tumour shrivelled and dropped out in a matter of days. After a patient who might have been cured by surgery alone died of an air embolus to the brain I abandoned this treatment, relying instead on methotrexate tablets that worked almost as well, if more slowly.

Why didn't we try to discourage the betel habit? Officially the reason was that it was a deeply ingrained cultural marker, and foreigners had no business pointing the finger when the ills of alcohol and tobacco were well known in European society but were tolerated nonetheless. Sir Burton Burton-Bradley, an influential member of the Department and honoured internationally for his contributions to transcultural psychiatry, denied that there was sound evidence betel chewing did harm, but some saw his view as doctrinaire sanctification of Culture. Sociologists of many stripes have approved harmful traditional practices or have denied evidence that screamed at everyone else, simply because of their philosophical positions.

Other kinds of cancer were common, but with a different pattern from that seen in the West. Apart from mouth tumours the big three were primary liver cancer, cervical cancer, and squamous cancer in old tropical ulcers. In theory these are now almost entirely preventable. Melanoma was rare because dark skin provides protection against the sun's rays, and the few we saw were on the sole, under a nail, or in the mouth.

Tropical ulcer was (and is) a common problem, and begins as a painful oval septic area on the shin, almost invariably in the lower third. The patch of skin becomes gangrenous, and eventually drops off leaving a raw area that heals slowly unless it is grafted. Even then the leg is permanently vulnerable, because a skin graft lacks protective sensation, so its host may ignore further injuries, resulting in more sores. Some patients, whether or not they have been treated well, wear leg bandages all their lives. Some legs scarred from repeated injury never heal, and sooner or later sores become cancerous. Most such patients recognise a change in their sore's appearance and come to hospital. Amputation was the standard treatment, but few of these tumours are aggressive, and sometimes it is possible to widely excise them, including a wedge of underlying bone, and graft the wound with expectation of cure. I didn't realise this when I went to Rabaul, and took off many legs believing that nothing less would do. It was my friend Bert Wilken, an Englishman who spent what he describes as the three best years of his surgical life in the Solomon Islands, who taught me about radical excision without amputation. Even so, most patients came too late, and preservation of their legs was impossible.

Many surgical patients were anaemic, from malaria or hookworm infestation if not from their primary illness, and needed blood transfusion. Kath Tweedy, a Queensland nurse, managed Rabaul's excellent Australian Red Cross Blood Transfusion Service. She maintained good relations with the Tolai, and visited a different village each week. Radio Rabaul announced the number of units collected, together with the information that next week Sister Tweedy's team would visit such and such a village. The Tolai took pride in donating blood in quantity, and each village aimed to out-do the last. Such generosity meant that I rarely postponed operations for want of blood. It was a boon that Rhesus negativity was almost non-existent. Occasionally we were caught short and had to ask nursing students, who lived on site, to donate. Sometimes enough people with the right blood group came with the patient, and we always encouraged healthy relatives to donate.

In 1961 we admitted a road accident victim with a liver injury that I thought would need more blood than was available. When I asked the accompanying crowd for a few pints it was like throwing gravel at the chooks, but somehow we found enough donors and took the man to the theatre. The liver injury was massive, I was helpless, and we saw him bleed to death on the table, which was a first for me and for the young Queensland doctor giving the anaesthetic. I wrote a report for the coroner, and that was that.

My first appearance before the Rabaul coroner was about a death from a ruptured spleen. The deceased was a plantation labourer on a distant island, and the *wantoks* insisted that their boss had kneed him in the belly for being slow loading copra onto a boat. The worker collapsed, and died that night. It seemed an open and shut case. The coroner took me through the allegations, and I agreed that a knee to the left upper abdomen could have ruptured the spleen. The plantation owner's rather dim lawyer asked many questions about the kidney, while the coroner and I struggled to persuade him that this was a different organ with no bearing on the case.

Another expert witness was called – old Raddy, whose profile in the town was much higher than this newcomer's. The dim lawyer put it to her that the labourer's physical exertion in throwing the bag of copra off his shoulders, backward into the boat, had caused the rupture. She supported this ingenious but absurd proposition with such vigour and authority that the coroner allowed himself to be convinced that any contribution from the planter's knee, an action he denied absolutely, was immaterial. But he didn't get off scot-free. Later, in another court, he was fined two pounds for common assault.

I'd removed several ruptured spleens in England, enough to prepare me for Rabaul, where I saw them regularly. Some resulted from motor accidents or falls from trees but the commonest cause was personal violence. If the patient came in with an abdominal injury and signs of blood loss the diagnosis was usually obvious, and because the standard treatment was splenectomy, every surgeon did this straightforward but rather dramatically bloody operation, and the sooner the better. But the diagnosis wasn't always obvious. A labourer from Ulu plantation, a Methodist Church property in the Duke of York Islands, beyond Kokopo, came with a note from the mission sister saying he had a ruptured spleen. He'd been fighting a few days earlier, was slightly tender below his left ribs and moderately anaemic but not acutely ill, and didn't seem to need an operation. We kept him on a drip for a couple of days, his pain lessening all the time, and fed him for a little longer before sending him back to Ulu along the bumpy Kokopo road. A week or so later the nurse sent him back, certain he had a ruptured spleen. I felt a firm tender lump under his left ribs, and at exploration I found buckets of thin old blood in the abdominal cavity, but no active bleeding. The spleen was encased in the greater omentum, the fatty caul we all have, which wraps itself around inflamed or bleeding areas. After prolonged dissection I found that the Ulu sister was right, with the spleen torn widely. The tear was sealed by the omentum, but my scratching about caused more bleeding so I removed the spleen, but with much more difficulty than in a fresh case. This incident should have taught me that some ruptured spleens will heal, but I went on blindly following standard teaching.

We all saw cases with a history of injury days previously, their only complaints being mild abdominal pain and distension, and sometimes shortness of breath due to acute anaemia. At exploration we found much old blood and the spleen healing, often encased in omentum. A surgeon in Madang, where on-call theatre nurses were notoriously difficult to locate after hours, regularly transfused even acutely ill patients overnight and operated next morning when his staff surfaced.

Two young Canadian paediatric surgeons published a landmark paper describing the experience of a retired senior colleague at the Toronto Hospital for Sick Children. He'd figured that it could be bad to remove ruptured spleens from children, so transfused them instead. This was remarkably prescient, when surgical cavaliers elsewhere were gaily removing thymus glands on their way to children's hearts to see if anything much happened, which they supposed would be unlikely. The Toronto surgeon found he could avoid operating in most cases, with the injury healing just as other body parts do. This paper was read at an important meeting, and like so many new ideas it was scoffed at by bigshots in the audience. The presenters felt compelled to back-pedal, and respectfully assured their betters that they spoke merely for the record, rather than seriously recommending this line of treatment. But children's specialists everywhere took notice, and non-operative management of the ruptured spleen became their standard practice, long before it was tried seriously in adults.

Several of us knew that New Guineans sometimes died suddenly, months or years after splenectomy. This was unexplained until we read American reports describing rare instances of children suffering late overwhelming sepsis after removal of their spleens. The commonest germ responsible was the *Pneumococcus*, which causes what was once called lobar pneumonia. Pneumococcal infection was widespread in PNG, killing both children and adults. In addition, we read of suggestions that people without spleens were more susceptible to the most dangerous form of malaria.

At long last the penny dropped. We were gaily removing ruptured spleens in an environment rich (if that's the right word) in two organisms known to kill some people without spleens. Should we try avoiding splenectomy? Several surgeons agreed to trial it, unless the patient was clearly bleeding to death. The first to collect a substantial series was David Hamilton, who was my locum at the PMGH in 1973 before he moved to Rabaul, where he saw many cases. His registrar worked for more than two years without seeing a ruptured spleen that needed removal. This may have been sad in respect of his operative training, but undoubtedly the Hamilton policy saved many lives. The Rabaul team even treated a haemophiliac successfully without operation. In 1982 they published a good paper describing their experiences. Paediatric surgeons already preferred non-operative management when possible, but Hamilton and Pikatcha made the point, for the first time, that this method was applicable to adults.

We had an ideal situation in which to explore the question further, and at a surgeons' meeting we agreed to try avoiding operation. As only eight or nine hospitals had trained surgeons this meant encouraging doctors with less experience, but enough to do an emergency splenectomy, to try our non-operative method. We found that, even when the patient showed signs of acute blood loss, the first litre of IV fluid usually produced obvious improvement, in which case we carried on, with careful observation. In those occasional patients that were unimproved we proceeded to splenectomy without delay. Sometimes there was a real possibility of injury to organs for which operation was essential, but most patients suffered low velocity injuries and could be observed safely. There was good cooperation for this study and we collected over 200 cases from all over the country. Just on 80 per cent were managed non-operatively, and others were under doctors without strong commitment to the idea of non-operative management, or who had little blood available. Without doubt more spleens could have been spared. An account of this experience was published in 1987, shortly after a similar report from Europe.

Many conditions familiar to Western-trained surgeons were oddities in Rabaul. I saw one or two cases of gallstones a year, very little appendicitis, and the bowel cancer so common in the West was almost non-existent. Ideas about the influence of diet on bowel cancer (and many other cancers, for that matter) were about, but didn't really impinge on surgeons' thinking. Then Denis Burkitt, great salesman that he was, began promoting the notion that a high-fibre diet was protective against bowel cancer. In my three years at Nonga I saw only three cases, two of them in a husband and wife who came to hospital together. 'I wonder what they've been eating' was my remark when we operated on them. We may have lost a great opportunity by not pursuing this matter.

A safe view is that Burkitt was about half right. The appearance of bowel cancer as a major problem in young Africans, and in other parts of the world including PNG, has been rapid, and has occurred whether or not there have been substantial changes in diet. Some ubiquitous feature of Western ways may be the culprit, rather than inadequate dietary fibre. At one time I wondered if it was detergent, but it may be something simpler, such as some component of ordinary soap. Something out there awaits discovery.

Before Rabaul I hadn't met primary liver cancer (hepatoma). The liver cancer so common in the West is usually secondary from bowel, stomach, pancreas, breast or other tumours, but while we often saw stomach cancer in PNG, most liver tumours were primary. It is now known that these follow hepatitis B or C infection. A tumour in one side of the liver was sometimes suitable for wide excision, but our patients almost always had widespread disease for which we could do nothing.

We had some high profile cases. I saw a girl in her twenties, the wife of a departmental head, who died rapidly of hepatoma. Sir Iambakey Okuk, a highlands politician who was deputy prime minister in the 1980s, developed it, and was assessed as inoperable in Brisbane. By this time I was known to be operating on liver tumours in Goroka. Lady Okuk phoned me, at the instigation of their Simbu *wantoks*, telling me what the Brisbane doctors said, and asking if I'd go to Port Moresby to see her husband. I asked the name of their doctor there, and suggested that I phone him first to hear the details. He had CT evidence of hopelessly widespread tumour. I rang Lady Okuk back and explained this, as others had done, and said that as her husband's condition was inoperable I didn't feel my travelling to Port Moresby would be of help to them. She seemed to understand the situation perfectly, but I've often wondered if the *wantoks* did. Goroka was frantically busy and a visit to Port Moresby to see a hopeless case seemed pointless, but it may well have been sensible, and diplomatic, for me to have made the trip.

My interest in cancer of the oesophagus began in Rabaul with a man Len Champness admitted one evening in 1961 on account of sudden inability to swallow after he'd bolted down sweet potato. He recovered by morning, but Len was a sharp clinician, so arranged a barium swallow X-ray that demonstrated the smallest oesophageal tumour I had (and have) ever seen, in the middle third. I'd assisted Peter Martin with oesophagectomy, which involved mobilising the stomach through an abdominal incision, after which the patient was turned right side up to allow the chest to be opened and most of the gullet excised. The stomach was then hauled up and joined to the top end of the gullet high in the chest. Some patients died after operation, and even those who seemed to be cured had little chance of surviving five years.

Like most Tolai, the man was thin, which usually makes for easier surgery and recovery, and everything went well. None of the well-known complications of oesophagectomy ensued so I thought I'd won, but he was back in eighteen months or so with widespread disease. I saw more cases over the years, but although some seemed curable I doubt that any were.

At first I had no surgical intern, which was one reason why Phyl Hodges was so valuable. Later, when it was obvious that the workload would only increase, young national doctors were rostered to the ward. One of the earliest was Ako Toua, a Fiji School of Medicine graduate, long afterwards to become the first local departmental head, when he was made Director of Health. (The incumbent director, Bill Symes, heard about it on the breakfast show.) Ako later became High Commissioner to Fiji where he did well, partly because he had married a Fijian. I once dined with them at their fine house on the hill in Suva. In the late 1990s a son lived half an hour from us, doing paediatrics at the Mersey Hospital in Tasmania.

General surgeons had to treat fractures of all sorts. In Rabaul I inherited several men with broken tibias (shin bones) that were unduly slow in healing. Usually these injuries were managed in thickly padded plaster casts until the swelling subsided, after which new casts were applied. It could be many months before healing was sufficiently advanced for weightbearing to be safe. More aggressive surgeons operated fairly freely, lining up the bony fragments to perfection and holding them with plates and screws. Unless performed by experts, an apparently good result at the end of the operation was about as secure as a house held together with tintacks. And healing was delayed, sometimes for years, if the wound became infected.

I read a paper from a US Army hospital stating that open operation could usually be avoided. The writers pulled the leg straight and applied a layer of stockingette with no padding, apart from wisps around the kneecap and over the fracture site. A cast was applied and the patient made to walk from day one. The feared swelling didn't occur because walking pumped excess fluid out of the leg as fast as it formed. The virtually skin-tight cast meant that the leg was a closed hydraulic system, which prevented the broken bones telescoping. And fractures healed in double-quick time.

This was good enough for me. If energetic, sometimes knife-happy young American surgeons with the best ironmongery on earth at their disposal could treat broken legs without operation, so could I. Applying perfectly moulded casts required something approaching artistry, but the method worked. I allowed my patients two crutches for a week and one for the next, after which they were on their own. I changed plasters at intervals of about three weeks. I treated tibial fractures this way in all patients without other injuries that prevented walking, never needing to remove a cast because of swelling and never encountering seriously delayed union.

In Madang a young conventionally treated Australian had such delayed healing that her doctor sent her to Sydney, where non-weight-bearing was advised until the fracture united. Somehow she came to me and I had her walking in a skin-tight cast immediately. Within weeks her fracture was solidly united, and she had leg muscles that had been working instead of wasting away.

I tried to interest Dr Radcliffe-Taylor in treating delayed union this way but she preferred to stick with what Boehler taught her in Vienna long before, when he criss-crossed the fracture site with five or six drill holes to hasten union by scattering healthy new bone cells throughout the area. For all I know this works, but it seems never to have been properly tested. We'll never know, as the need to try it has passed, at least in the West.

Longstanding goitre was another frequent problem. Operation was usually trouble-free, but one morning the patient couldn't breathe when the anaesthetist removed the endotracheal tube. He re-intubated her and waited until she was fully awake before trying again, with the same result. I reopened the wound and found her trachea so soft that it collapsed when unsupported by the tube. I'd never heard of this complication of goitre surgery, for which the treatment had to be tracheostomy. But how long would she need the tube? I left the theatre to collect the morning's mail, which included a fat new book entitled *Complications in Surgery and Their Management* edited by two eminent Americans, Artz and Hardy. I ripped off the packaging and turned to the long chapter on complications of thyroid surgery, but found no mention of this morning's problem.

The tome had cost me close to a week's wages, so I was disappointed that it failed the taste test, and wrote to Professor Hardy asking for advice. He replied saying that no surgeon in his unit had met this complication of goitre surgery, but judging from recent experience with an aortic aneurysm causing similar airway softening, in which a tracheostomy for three weeks had allowed it to firm up again, he expected me to find the same. By the time his letter arrived I'd discovered this for myself and had removed the tube. While the lady was in hospital I mentioned her to Charlie Haszler, who told me that Kocher's surgical textbook, a standard German work two generations back, described the problem.

Years later a visiting professor, an acknowledged goitre expert, lectured in Port Moresby on the myriad complications of thyroidectomy, but failed to mention this one. Frank Smith was present, and I knew he'd met it in Goroka, so at question time I asked about it. This brought a tortuous reply that, stripped of the waffle, amounted to: 'I haven't seen it. Therefore it doesn't happen.'

Frank and I exchanged wicked grins. 'Pompous old goat,' we told ourselves. I knew that one day I too would be old and at risk of supposing I'd seen absolutely everything to do with various diseases in which I had a special interest. Sure enough, I was to find myself displaying occasional traces of this unseemly oracular trait, but human nature being what it is, it never seemed remotely as objectionable as it did from the mouth of our illustrious visitor in Port Moresby.

Rabaul offered such challenge and interest that we'd have been content to live there indefinitely, but we knew this was unlikely. The first suggestion that we move to Port Moresby came in 1962, when there was to be a vacancy at the Papuan Medical College, the PHD school providing training for nurses, health educators, dental assistants and, at long last, doctors. Papuan doctors had been trained in Fiji for many years, but the problems students faced far from home were serious enough to make the Department decide to shoulder the burden of running a medical school. The college was in the hands of Eric Wright, originally a general practitioner in Rabaul, where he allegedly removed every Chinese appendix. Undoubtedly he was that community's preferred doctor, and the lady the Department insisted he dignify with a marriage ceremony before he became Assistant Director of Health (Medical Training) was a Rabaul Chinese. Eric had abundant imagination and drive, but chronic waspishness made him almost friendless, and few were prepared to admit how pivotal his vision and energy were in the development of education right across PNG's health sector.

I expected to move to Port Moresby early in 1963, but was stymied by the non-availability of housing, which was in very short supply, and transfers in (apart from replacements) were possible only for people declared to be key personnel. The PHD had played this card too often, and the first free house in many months went to another Rabaul public servant who'd been appointed manager of the Philatelic Bureau. Even though I was a keen stamp collector I failed to see how he was more important in the overall scheme of things than I was.

Eric put me to rights when he came to Nonga and made it clear that the PMC didn't need me. He wasn't simply making a virtue of necessity; he didn't want me. He must have had a reason, but I never learnt what it was. We got on well when work threw us together years later, and had a long-running friendly dispute about management skills. Naturally enough, he believed and taught that leaders could be made, but I stuck to the view that in the last analysis they're born.

I managed to be free most Sunday mornings, when we worshipped at the Methodist Church in town, a mixed congregation of Chinese, European and other foreigners as well as a few English-speaking natives. Rabaul also had a small Anglican congregation, but the biggest Christian presence was Roman Catholic. The town boasted a cathedral, served by Father Franke, a warm-hearted German and the most popular priest in the country, who visited his flock at Nonga every evening. Despite our denominational differences we became good friends, and he invited me to play the church's aging Hammond instrument whenever I liked. This was rarely, because I was so busy. When Pope John XXIII died Father Franke asked me to provide music for the Rabaul memorial service. I was in two minds about it, but felt that it would be churlish to refuse, and would serve no good purpose. The plainsong was unaccompanied, and I merely had to play something suitable at each end of the service. The bishop of Rabaul preached the most mournful sermon I've ever heard. The doctrine of purgatory wasn't mentioned, but came through clearly enough. He said Pope John lived on in the memories of those who had known him, in the changes he brought to Catholic life and worship at Vatican II, and in the memory of every faithful Catholic; nothing about his having departed 'to be with Christ, which is far better', to quote the apostle Paul. Having come to know the Christian hope and assurance that triumphs over death, and that can turn mourning into celebration, I found the service extremely disappointing. Pope John Paul II's obsequies in 2005 were a striking contrast.

I had no political antennae, but even I sensed changes afoot. When the UN's 1962 team assessing Australia's performance as trustee of a UN-mandated territory visited Rabaul I attended their packed public meeting. There was a scattering of businessmen and planters, a crowd of Tolai villagers, and Administration personnel who in general resented what they perceived as egregious and ill-informed outside interference. Sir Hugh Foot, the mission's leader, told the New Guineans they shouldn't fear independence. If they thought the country was too poor or otherwise unable to support itself, no matter; the rest of the world would line up to provide whatever they needed. The sooner New Guineans moved into self-governing mode the better.

We knew about Harold Macmillan's wind of change in Africa and something of the proactive anti-colonial stance of the UN, but all that was on another planet. We heard Sir Hugh out silently, except for unrestrained belly laughs from a few planters and murmurs of approval from the New Guineans. Decolonisation was going mad, or so we thought. If any of the government people thought Foot was talking sense they kept it to themselves. Now it is difficult to see how events could have unfolded differently.

There were few other memorable non-medical events, but one afternoon in 1962 a keen golfer managed to drag me onto the lovely Rabaul course in the lee of the Mother and Daughter volcanoes. We'd played two holes when I was called to the clubhouse phone. I've never been back.

When a Nonga baseball team joined the Gazelle competition I tried to help as coach. The match I remember best was at Kokopo one Sunday afternoon, when I was called to a phone towards the end of play. The doctor at Kavieng, the New Ireland HQ, was on the fuzzy line saying a US warship had come in the previous evening with a sailor vomiting blood, due to a bleeding duodenal ulcer. He was A-negative, still bleeding, and they were fast running out of suitable blood. An emergency operation seemed necessary, so he asked me to charter a DC-3 and bring my theatre sister plus any special instruments. So while others arranged things I rushed back to the Rabaul airport and off we went. Near the equator night falls with a thud at about 6 pm, and we made Kavieng right on last light. Every vehicle in town was at the airstrip in case we needed their headlights to illumine the runway, but we managed on our own. What the locals made of a surgeon arriving in a baseball uniform I do not know. I saw the sailor and agreed that under the circumstances there was nothing for it but an operation. We took him to the tiny flywired theatre where the Kavieng doctor put him to sleep. Sure enough he had a bleeding duodenal ulcer, for which the usual treatment at that time included removal of most of the stomach. All went well, and we took him back to Nonga on the same aircraft next morning. He made an excellent recovery, and being American, was astonished that his treatment was free.

Len Champness delivered our fourth daughter, Shirley, on 5 May 1961. We left Rabaul before she reached school age, but the others took the hospital bus to the Kamerere Street Primary School. Our experience of schooling there and elsewhere in PNG was entirely satisfactory. Standards were high, perhaps partly due to the qualities found in most public servants, whose children made up most of the population in international schools. This was particularly obvious at the Port Moresby International High School, where students sat the NSW examinations, turning in averages well above those in schools there.

Specialists at base hospitals had responsibilities for their whole region. For me this entailed occasional visits to the three other main stations in the Islands Region, at Sohano, Kavieng and Manus, to see problem patients, talk to doctors about their difficulties, and to operate on straightforward cases, ideally assisting the local doctor. Patients for major surgery came back to Nonga. Kavieng presented me with a problem I've never seen again. An old Lihir lady had intestinal contents discharging from a hole in her right groin. She had developed a painful groin swelling, abdominal distension and vomiting some weeks before. Days later the groin swelling burst, discharging pus and food. In general she had recovered, but she was fed up, or maybe down, with semidigested dinner trickling all over her leg.

The Kavieng doctors made no sense of this self-healed strangulated hernia. I said that in the bad old days the best hernia surgeons were those who knew when to lance a strangulated hernia and sometimes have a patient survive. This lady had survived with no treatment whatever. It was a fairly simple matter to unscramble her.

The first duty of any government servant visiting another district on business was to call on the District Commissioner. DCs had almost total power, and some carried on like medieval monarchs. Most were pleased to see officers from elsewhere, and I was amazed at the deference some showed to doctors junior to them in every way. Courtesy calls could extend to half an hour or more of wide-ranging conversation, occasionally followed by an invitation to the residency in the evening.

We were living in Madang when I visited Bougainville on leprosy business in about 1966, and as usual called on the DC. Surveying for the venture that was to become the world's biggest open-cut gold and copper mine had halted because village women were lying on the ground, obstructing the surveyors. Bougainvilleans had long protested that taking their land was much the same as taking their skin, and they didn't want the promised benefits at any price. The police could handle men but female protestors bested them, so work stopped.

The DC's reputation was at stake, and he was about to inspect the scene by helicopter. Would I like to come? Inwardly I answered, 'Not really,' but I lacked the gumption to say so, and so made my first and only helicopter trip. I doubt that his inspection contributed to the DC's decision-making process, but at least he was seen to be doing something.

The women lost, as did Bougainvilleans in general, but it took millions of dollars, ruined land, poisoned rivers and much bloodshed to prove this to the world. The jungle has reclaimed the Panguna mine, but my prediction is that the second autonomous Bougainville government, if not the first, will find ways and means of re-opening it. Those prepared to leave all that money in the ground must buckle eventually.

When I asked Les Johnson, a notable Director of Education who succeeded Gunther as Assistant Administrator, how it was that the government had initially settled for such derisory Panguna royalties, his answer was that the administration was unaware of how rich the mine was, which still seems a weak excuse for such poor and naïve resource management. Panguna, and Ok Tedi on the upper Fly River in Papua, provide sorry object lessons in the dealings of mining companies with Third World governments.

Chapter 9

To India

In late 1963 I was visiting Manus in the Admiralty Islands when I received a yard-long telegram from PHD headquarters. WHO was offering a year's fellowship for a surgeon to go to Vellore in south India to train in the reconstructive surgery of leprosy with Dr Paul Brand. Was I interested? Terms and conditions were spelt out in great detail and, as usual, an immediate reply was expected.

Nonga was too busy, with no satisfactory solution in sight, and having met Dr Brand in England when he spoke at a 1959 Christian Medical Fellowship meeting, I was fully primed. The prospect of working with one of the most original and exciting thinkers in Third World surgery was instantly attractive, and we had no difficulty in deciding to go to India, even though I had little knowledge of, nor particular interest in, leprosy. Doug Russell, TPNG's leprologist, had persuaded me to perform a few minor procedures, but I was quite ignorant and basically had to follow his directions. I knew the leprosy germ was in the same genus as the TB bacillus, that it wasn't highly infectious, and that an individual's immune response determined the extent and effects of the infection. Those with total immunity (specific to this organism) never got leprosy, those with moderate immunity could suffer mild, localised disease, with a few numb and discoloured skin patches, and those with poor immunity could become riddled with it. In all cases the effect of dapsone, the only drug known to be effective, was slow. Patients suffered a bewildering variety of deformities. This was about my limit, scarcely enough to ignite my interest had I not already met Dr Brand at the only CMF conference we attended during our time in England.

For years Russell had wanted someone to train at Vellore, but the Department was prepared to release a surgeon for a maximum of four months, which didn't suit Brand, who insisted on a year. This stalemate was resolved at a Western Pacific Regional WHO meeting in

Port Moresby in 1963 when many dusty pigeonholes were cleared out. Of course the Department would release a surgeon for a year. With WHO applying pressure and offering funds the only problem was to find a candidate. Doug Russell, who had taken part in important research at Vellore, knew that many Christian doctors were attracted to leprosy work, which was why the opportunity came my way. Brand stipulated that a whole team should be trained – a surgeon, nurse and physiotherapist as a minimum. W.R. McKeown, a retired-early Melbourne businessman who was the CEO of the Australian office of The Mission to Lepers, as it was then called, wanted to establish work in New Guinea, and agreed to look for a physiotherapist and a nurse.

Madang, on the north coast, was chosen as the site of the new unit because there was a long-established leprosy control program in the district, with many deformed patients, and because the government hospital had many empty beds. This unusual situation arose because the American Lutheran Mission hospital at Yagaum, a few miles out, had an excellent and well-deserved reputation nationwide, largely due to Theo Braun, a shy man of immense surgical ability. The Brauns had been in New Guinea since before the war, and survived Japanese internment. For as long as Dr Braun was at Yagaum the government hospital in Madang was bound to be quiet.

A third reason for the choice of Madang was because it was the hub of the aircraft network serving the highlands, where there was a large, well-managed leprosy control program. In terms of aircraft movements its airport was one of the busiest in Australasia, because until the Highlands Highway was completed in the '70s all cargo to and from the rapidly developing interior passed through Madang. We could fly to or from almost anywhere in the highlands, any day of the week, on government charters.

Madang is no ordinary town. As Friedrich-Wilhelmshafen it was the German colony's mainland headquarters. From the beginning malaria was a major problem, and killed many admin personnel. One of the greatest medical scientists of all time, Robert Koch, spent two years in Madang at his government's behest, trying to unravel malaria's mysteries. Earlier he'd identified the TB germ, still sometimes called Koch's bacillus, and had described the organism responsible for cholera. Amongst his other notable achievements was working out the pathology of the serious South African veterinary problem rinderpest.

But malaria bested him, and he returned to Berlin with little to show for his time in New Guinea. A century later scientists at the Madang branch of the PNG Institute for Medical Research worked on various aspects of malaria, still far from being a beaten disease.

A high rainfall keeps Madang lush and green almost all year around. The town occupies a narrow peninsula, which means good nocturnal sea breezes that make up for the enervating daytime heat and humidity. Until a few years after our time foreign residents delighted in their gardens and took pride in the town's appearance, so that it was a tropical Eden, only Rabaul rivalling it for beauty. Now a more appropriate description might be 'decayed Dutch', were it over the Indonesian border rather than in PNG. *Sic transit...*

Peter Martin was to visit us in 1969, and as he was an avid blue-water sailor we arranged a trip on our picture-postcard harbour for him. He said it was as wonderful a sight as any he'd ever seen, and this without him sampling the scuba diving, another superlative Madang attraction.

On his way back to India from Rio de Janeiro in late 1963 Paul Brand visited TPNG, and I had the task of showing him the highlands, where much of our best leprosy fieldwork was established. We flew to many out-of-the-way places in bright yellow single-engine Cessnas of the Missionary Aviation Fellowship (MAF). Highlands flying can be hazardous, especially in the afternoons when cloud often descends suddenly. Paul always remembered this trip, and even I, after scores of similar journeys in later years, will never forget one sudden detour our pilot made through what only he knew was a safe hole in the clouds. I still don't know whether we went up, down or sideways. It was all in a day's work for the pilot, who giggled as he apologised for frightening us.

At a leprosy colony outside Wabag, in Enga country, Paul saw what he always described thereafter as the most foul-smelling feet he had met anywhere on earth. His ideas about managing ulcerated feet hadn't percolated to New Guinea, and his visit to Wabag convinced him I needed to come to India.

My time there was the richest professional experience of my life. Personal tuition by Paul Brand in what turned out to be his last class in India was not only uniquely instructive, but gave me an insight into the life of a truly great man. Totally unspoiled by his fame, he was a convincing model of mature spiritual equipoise. He was so open and unassuming that it was easy for us to forget we were in the presence of a paradigmatic pioneer, the man almost solely responsible for our understanding of leprous nerve damage and how to treat it.

Paul was alone because Margaret (herself a major contributor to the management of leprosy's eye complications) had left for England with their children, so we saw more of him than we might have. He led the weekly staff Bible study, in St Mark's gospel. He was a Christian leader unlike any I have ever met, and although I got to know him well I never saw feet of clay. Gwen hosted his 50th birthday party, and we still have a paper table napkin that was decorated for the occasion. All this seemed but yesterday when we heard in July 2003 of his death in Seattle.

WHO assumed that I'd go to India solo, and it was weeks before we knew that family housing was available. Only dimly aware of the richness of the experience ahead, we packed up and flew off to India in February 1964. I was shocked and amused when I was offered powdered betel nut after dinner on the Air India flight. We arrived to find that Paul's course had already begun, with several other foreign doctors with some surgical training in the class. We had a fine stone house at the Schieffelin Leprosy Research and Training Centre, one of the most important and productive institutions in the leprosy world, set on a barren plain at Karigiri, a few miles outside Vellore, the city famous for its Christian Medical College and Hospital (CMC). The staff surgeon at Karigiri was Bill Lennox, a friendly and innovative young English orthopaedist. Ernest Fritschi, son of Swiss missionaries, and an Indian citizen, returned from the UK in mid-year, and was most helpful. He was followed by Saku Karat, a surgeon whose physician husband Benty was one of the bright lights in clinical leprosy. But the star, as a clinician, as a teacher, and as a person, was Paul Brand.

He was born in south India, where his parents were pioneer missionaries. His father died young but his mother worked as an evangelist until she was over 80, riding around remote hills on her pony. Paul came to prominence shortly after being appointed to the CMC, where he majored in orthopaedic surgery. Bob Cochrane, a leading British leprologist, and the then dean of the Vellore medical school, challenged him to do something for leprosy victims. He showed Paul people cured in the bacteriological sense but who remained outcasts from work and family because of easily recognisable deformities. The commonest and most obvious problem was the claw hand. But for it many ex-patients would be socially acceptable. Surely a surgeon could devise a way to correct it?

Brand took up the challenge and after prolonged experimentation arrived at a modification of a previously described, but rarely performed, tendon transfer that produced excellent results, exciting both his patients and experienced leprosy workers.

He was persuaded to present his researches as a Hunterian lecture at the Royal College of Surgeons in London. He was a polished and articulate speaker, with a unique and engaging blend of earnestness, infectious enthusiasm, authority and humility, and his hearers perceived that a new chapter had opened in the history of an aspect of the disease that had seen no striking advances in living memory. Soon he was famous right across the leprosy world, and amongst surgeons with an interest in hand problems.

Before Brand, leprosy was a disease apart in every sense, and was left to the leprosy doctors. Now a magnetic mainstream specialist was providing, for the first time, dramatic relief for the claw hand, the bane of thousands of so-called 'cured' patients. It mattered not that by the time he was famous this first tendon transfer had been shown to be too powerful, causing yet another progressive deformity. Brand was appalled but his patients were unconcerned, because the new claw looked nothing like leprosy, so they remained socially safe and confident. Professor T.N. Jagadisan, an early patient and a leading activist in the Hind Kusht Nivaran Sangh (Indian Leprosy Association), had what we now regard as a very unsatisfactory result, but to the end of his life his speeches were accompanied by gestures proving that, as far as he was concerned, his spidery hands were no longer terrifying badges of leprosy.

After studying thousands of patients Brand identified standard patterns of nerve thickening and dysfunction, with certain hand and arm muscles regularly paralysed and others preserved, some of which could have their tendons re-routed surgically so that they pulled in new directions. After his first dramatically successful procedure turned out to be generally unsatisfactory in the longer term because the motor was too powerful, he devised transfers of tendons controlled by weaker muscles, with superior results. It was then possible to convert a claw hand into an extremity that looked good and functioned well, provided that skilled physiotherapy was available to teach the patient to use the muscles pulling on his/her re-arranged tendons in a new way. A partner in developing his best operation was Mary Verghese, a Vellore graduate paraplegic after a road accident. Mary took up hand surgery because she could do it from a wheelchair, and later trained in New York to become a pioneer Indian rehabilitation specialist.

As well as operating on hands the team explored other problems, especially footdrop and ulcers on the sole. Although he performed the first operations to improve the appearance of hands and feet, Brand soon discovered an even more important reason for his work. Before he studied nerve damage some experts believed loss of digits and the appearance of non-healing ulcers, particularly common on the feet, were due to local destruction of tissues by the leprosy bacillus. Others saw this destruction as evidence of depressed immunity to germs that ordinarily were harmless. Some said digits simply dropped off, despite this phenomenon having never been witnessed.

Brand proved that the real cause of loss of tissue was repeated unrecognised trauma to numb parts. Normally pain protects us, so that after suffering a bruise or other injury we instinctively nurse the part until it recovers. A patient with a numb hand may find his tools beginning to slip because he doesn't know how firmly to grasp them. Having had this happen repeatedly he adjusts automatically and grips everything far too tightly, sustaining pressure injuries that wouldn't occur if sensation were present. Or if he has a numb foot he continues walking despite bruises, blisters or lacerations. Continued overuse and injury of a part that needs rest if it is to heal interferes with its blood supply, and sooner or later it dies.

In the hand this tissue death can be slow and silent because tissue may be absorbed as quickly as it is destroyed, so that no sore ever appears unless a patient burns or cuts himself. Pressures applied to the feet are much higher, with skin and deeper structures crushed to death in greater volume. Dead tissue flakes off or finds its way out, and a raw area, or ulcer, is formed. The patient goes on working, or walking, and nature has no chance to heal the injury, which worsens inexorably. Secondary infection of open wounds may play a part, but usually this isn't a major problem.

This effect of injury to anaesthetic parts is bad enough, but in the hand the claw compounds it, because loss of power in certain muscles means that the sufferer grips with the tips rather than the fingers' whole surfaces. High pressure slowly destroys them, and after some years a patient may be left with nail remnants on the knuckles, but no fingers. Somewhat similar muscle imbalance in numb feet results in them being highly vulnerable. So, in the long run, the most important reason for the hand operations was to improve muscle balance so that, provided the patient understood that s/he must always guard against injury, the numb hand could be used without inevitable damage.

In the feet it was important to correct muscle imbalance, but even more so to find a way of avoiding injury to the sole. Ordinary footwear provided little protection and could even do harm, with what we call shoe-bites being common. Brand experimented with many substances, and with help from a Madras industrialist developed microcellular rubber insoles. Ordinary sponge rubber didn't protect the foot because a person's weight squeezed the air out of it, but rubber with tiny closed air-cells incorporated during manufacture didn't compress so far, so that the patient in effect walked on air. Provided that he never takes steps without appropriate footwear, a leprosy patient with a numb foot needn't develop an ulcer on the sole. Unfortunately most numb feet were already ulcerated by the time Brand saw them. At first the treatment was complete rest, but at Fritschi's suggestion they tried walking plaster casts, which they found allowed ulcers to heal. These innovations transformed the management of plantar ulcer.

It is scarcely possible to exaggerate the importance of the discovery that trauma to anaesthetic parts is the cause of loss of tissue in leprosy, and that its prevention requires unflagging, lifelong effort, almost amounting to an obsession. Diabetics and their physicians face a somewhat similar problem with anaesthetic feet, and despite wide publication of Brand's work the same fundamental discovery had to be made all over again in that disease.

Brand's ideas were readily accepted in the English-speaking world but were disregarded by francophone leprologists, largely because their understanding of neurology included the mistaken belief that we have nerves with vital nutritional responsibilities. If such nerves are damaged in leprosy, as they believed, the resulting impaired nutrition means that the part is degenerate and fragile, regardless of protection from injury. Such an attitude leads to therapeutic nihilism. It is difficult enough to maintain momentum in the fight against deformity without the added impediment of philosophical brakes of this kind.

All this was unknown to me when we went to Karigiri. I soon realised that besides mastering the surgical techniques to correct its deformities, and the management of plantar ulcer, I needed a rounded knowledge of the disease. I'd come to the right place, because it provided experience in the treatment of every imaginable medical and surgical complication of leprosy.

Paul saw outpatients twice a week, and watching him examine a new patient was a revelation of how to assess the disease in general, and nerve damage in particular. We saw none of the rubber gloves all too often used elsewhere, which were psychological even more than physical barriers. Paul took the lowliest patient's bare hands in his as if they were family. Many problems seemed identical, but he didn't work on this assumption, and approached each deformity, and each apparently normal limb, as if there was something to be discovered. Many patients went on the surgical waiting list, so that I had ample opportunity to see the various procedures performed, and in due course do them myself.

We operated three days a week in the luxury of an air-conditioned theatre, a unique experience under the supervision of world experts. Karigiri offered unparalleled training opportunities, and I will always treasure the fact that I was there in its heyday. The commonest operation was to correct finger clawing due to paralysis of the ulnar nerve, but many patients also had a damaged median nerve at the wrist, so that they were unable to lift the thumb away from the palm, and had a 'key' pinch only. First we corrected the fingers, and when they functioned satisfactorily we did a second operation to allow something like proper use of the thumb. With experience, and for highly motivated patients, it became possible to combine these procedures at a single session in a little over an hour. Some hands were so contracted that restoration to anything like normality was impossible, but many could be significantly improved if we fused the finger joints in a functional position and held them with fine wires until the bones were solidly united. As well as these operations, we learnt other procedures on hands, feet and face.

Most patients were Tamil and spoke a difficult language with a bewildering script, but I learnt a few medical phrases. I thought I was going well until I tested an outpatient's hand for sensation. I told her to shut her eyes (which she understood) and then asked if she felt the cotton wool I drew across her fingertips. Her reply was incomprehensible, so I asked the nurse to translate. 'Sir,' he said, 'she says to tell you that she doesn't speak English.' Clunk.

Julie Christie, a New Zealand physiotherapist recruited by The Mission to Lepers there, arrived in April, so we had the beginnings of the team. She rapidly gained experience and put it into practice for over 40 years in several countries. The problem of finding a nursing sister was solved when Valerie Taylor, a Bristol nurse, turned up at Karigiri unexpectedly, after hearing Paul in Canada. She had ability, enthusiasm and initiative, and Dick McKeown agreed to pay her fare to PNG, where she worked for more than 25 years.

Karigiri provided an unmatched breadth and depth of experience in virtually every clinical aspect of leprosy, and had other attractions. We had visitors from all over, so met many of the big names in leprosy. There was an excellent library. Our children attended school in Vellore with other mission kids, travelling on the hospital bus. Most Saturdays were free, but as we had no private vehicle, the institution was a mile off the road and bus services were infrequent and unpredictable, we were in no position to go far. We occasionally walked three miles across the paddy fields to a swimming pool, once with Jona Senilagakali, a Fijian studying reconstructive surgery in at CMC, where the orthopaedic service treated leprosy patients in the course of their ordinary work. Jona swam the length of the pool under water, frightening and then fascinating the children.

On Thursdays we were bussed to Vellore for the hand meeting, Paul's major teaching session, when difficult problems were demonstrated and discussed. The stream of overseas surgeons in town on Thursdays sometimes provided valuable input. One day a stubborn ulcer on the sole was shown because routine treatment in a walking plaster should have healed it weeks before. A Melbourne surgeon at the back of the room said laconically that where he came from they'd feel the pulses. This was done. The patient had leprosy and seriously blocked arteries.

While I was at the meeting Gwen did her marketing, largely for fruit and vegetables that came down from Ootacamund by train. The Vellore bazaar was typical of thousands all over India, with scrawny coolies competing to carry madam's bag when not scavenging individual grains of rice. Gwen had been fully occupied managing the guesthouse since shortly after we arrived, because Trixie McKay, an Australian nurse who was Karigiri's matron, was transferred to another Mission to Lepers hospital. The Indian cook and his helpers coped with routine matters, but Gwen had to approve some purchases and keep an eye on things generally.

Food was scarce in India in 1964, with cereals in particularly short supply. White sugar was rationed but there was plenty of crude brown, liberally sprinkled with cane remnants, gravel and rat dung. For breakfast Gwen prepared a coarse porridge by soaking *sooji*, a variety of millet, overnight before boiling it hard. It was sweetened with *jaggery*, a molasses-like sugarcane derivative. Meat was mostly buffalo, brought around by an old man on a bike. Another chap brought eggs, which Gwen always tested in water; if they floated they were bad.

In mid-year a rat-fall in Vellore heralded bubonic plague, so we were inoculated against this fearful disease. The injection often had unpleasant side effects so children had the next day off school, but our girls were untroubled by it. On Sundays we attended the Church of South India service in Vellore. As in many united churches, in India and elsewhere, individual congregations carried on more or less as they had done before union. The CSI prayer book was Anglican in layout, with a distinctive feature of communion being the richly expressive passing of the peace.

We marvelled at CMCH Vellore, the great hospital begun by Dr Ida Scudder, the dynamic American who pioneered medical work amongst Indian women. It had about 1000 beds in our time and remains the world's most famous missionary medical institution, a fine example of cooperation between many organisations. The original all-India training centre for neurosurgery and cardiac surgery, it provides quality care in every area of medicine for a local clientele and for patients from all over India and abroad. The medical school attracts students from all over the nation. Most Karigiri doctors were Vellore graduates.

We had no car because they were in short supply, with waiting lists of up to 20 years in some states. There were two common models: the black Hindustan Ambassador, essentially a 1950s Morris Oxford, and a grey version of a small Triumph. These were reliable squarish no-frills vehicles with plenty of screws visible and no obvious design changes from one year to the next. Foreign cars were rare because India's economic policies deemed that, in general, what couldn't be produced locally was unnecessary. This tight embargo on imports, barely comprehensible in this era of so-called free trade, was the key to India's successful industrial development and maturity.

We made few trips away, but one excursion to Madras was to see the Simpson/Lawry team play India. I wouldn't have mustered the enthusiasm but for a Yorkshire physiotherapist, down from the Green Pastures Leprosy Hospital at Pokhara, Nepal, wistfully remarking that she'd love to go to the cricket on Saturday if only she had someone to go with. It wasn't too difficult to discern a *cri de coeur*, so we caught a bus before daylight and reached the ground shortly after play commenced. Our tickets were for flimsy wooden folding chairs out in the blazing sun, but someone took pity on us and put us in the grandstand for no extra charge.

The Nawab of Pataudi captained India and batted all day. His father had captained India too, and had made a century in his first test against Australia. The son was intent on doing the same and by late afternoon was in the 90s, waiting patiently for the rare loose ball. After 25 minutes without a run scored I lifted up my voice in Sydney hill fashion and told him to have a go. There wasn't a flicker from the ground, not even from the Australians, but pandemonium broke out behind us.

'What is wrong, sir?' a man asked.

'English I am understanding it, but what is this "Have a go"?' asked another.

Somebody wondered if the heat was getting to me. Small boys pelted me with paper aeroplanes. The demure Yorkshire physio went scarlet and tried to look inconspicuous, or at least not with this uncouth Australian. Pataudi got his century, next day.

Another trip was to the bonesetters of Chittoor in Andhra Pradesh, the next state north. Vellore orthopaedic surgeons took many visitors there, to a clinic run by two brothers who had inherited skills from their father. We missed the more famous of them because he was away treating the chief minister of another state. They worked without anaesthesia and were said to treat almost any fracture with good results. After bone fragments were realigned a secret mixture of leaves and eggwhite was applied before bamboo and other splints were carefully moulded to the part. We saw a badly displaced fracture of a collarbone slowly and carefully reduced, with the jagged ends restored to a normal relationship. Treatment of a broken ankle followed, with the immediate result less obvious to the naked eye. The Vellore doctors couldn't fault the bonesetters' work, but a Madras orthopaedic surgeon told me all their mismanaged cases bypassed Vellore and came to his unit. The truth is probably somewhere in between – it isn't credible that such a business could thrive for generations if it regularly produced bad results.

Another Hunterian lecturer on the surgery of leprosy was Noshir Antia, the head of the Tata Department of Plastic Surgery at the JJ Hospital in Bombay, and widely regarded as India's premier plastic surgeon. Trained under Sir Harold Gillies, the father of the specialty in Britain, he was a superb operator. Although he did hand work he was best known for his method of dealing with collapsed noses, a common problem in Indian leprosy patients but, as I was to find, rare in PNG. There were other areas of surgery in leprosy for which he was well known, so I visited him for three weeks around Christmas. It was well worth the effort.

We planned to take the midnight train to Miraj, south of Poona, where Gwen and the children would stay with Trixie McKay while I was in Bombay. I'd booked seats weeks earlier as Christmas trains were even more crowded than usual. Shortly before we were to leave Karigiri Gwen developed dengue. Delirious and with a high fever, she lay in bed confused and listless. I have never seen her so ill. Some thought I was reckless, or worse, to expect her to travel, but I saw little difference between a bed at home and a sleeping berth on a train. If we cancelled our bookings there was no telling when we'd reach Bombay, so we pushed on. It was a cold windy night and I was trying to make Gwen comfortable in the waiting room when the potbellied stationmaster waddled up with worry written all over him.

'Doctor,' he puffed, waving a fistful of papers, 'we are having problems, it seems. For you I booked six berths, but Madras is giving two only. I am boarding the train immediately it arrives and will see what to do. Leave it with me, doctor.'

We had a journey of more than 24 hours ahead of us. The night seemed suddenly colder, if that were possible. The children were even more concerned than I was, and mentioned it. Perhaps I should have listened to that overcautious Karigiri mob. The train pulled in and would-be passengers milled around like cattle at a trough in midsummer. Eventually the stationmaster reappeared, beaming. 'I've done it, doctor. They are not together; you have a four-berth compartment and another two seats next to it. Come, I will show you.'

Gratefully we clambered aboard and claimed our berths. The stationmaster coughed behind me and murmured hopefully, 'I will take my leave now, doctor.' His kindness and concern warranted significant recompense, so I pressed a healthy bundle of rupees into his waiting hand. He thanked me profusely and disappeared into the night. Within minutes the train let out a whistle to wake the dead and pulled out. Next, the conductor appeared with his clipboard, and ticked off the 'Clezy x 6' as entered on his passenger list weeks before. I wondered, but not for long, how many others the wily stationmaster duped each night.

After a weekend in Miraj I took yet another night train to Bombay and put up at Church Mission House, memorable for the African mahogany tree planted in the front yard by David Livingstone a century earlier.

Antia was a Parsi, and when we first met he had the austere patrician demeanour characteristic of his community's upper strata, and terrified his staff beyond anything I've ever seen. Like many Parsis, he had a strong social conscience, which was partly responsible for his interest in leprosy. Late in life he was to mellow dramatically. After ceasing surgical practice he forsook expensive suiting for the clothes of the common man, and spent his time encouraging poor villagers to organise their own health care according to their perceived needs, thus promoting independence amongst people who were being left behind by their betters. He founded the Association of Rural Surgeons of India, a body striving to provide affordable, quality surgical care for the masses. He was bitingly critical of airy metropolitan theorists who felt able to state how health services for the Indian poor should be organised, but with unrealistic, sometimes absurd, conceptions of what was practicable. Like many high achievers, Antia had an intangible and effortless capacity to spark enthusiasm in those around him.

After Bombay we had a fortnight in Nepal, partly to visit the Shining Hospital at Pokhara, whose surgeon Ruth Watson had trained at Karigiri alongside me, and whose physiotherapist had triggered the trip to the Madras test match. We spent a couple of days in the United Mission to Nepal guesthouse and saw the sights of the city. We drove past the gaol, where the first Nepali Christian pastor was doing seven years for changing his religion.

Towards dusk I suggested to ten-year-old Meredith that she come outside to see the sun set on Mount Everest, which I didn't know was invisible from Kathmandu. 'Can't you see I'm reading a book?' she replied tersely. This came to encapsulate my experience of travelling with children.

A DC-3 took us to Pokhara, a long thin village three miles down a dusty track, with Machapuchere (fishtail mountain) the most striking of the many Himalayan peaks in the backdrop. Four-star hotels were far in the future. I'll never forget my first visit to the Shining Hospital, so named because the glint of its aluminium roof was the signal to weary travellers entering Pokhara Valley that they were nearing their journey's end. A young woman was being carried away in a four-man sedan chair.

'How long before they get home?' I asked.

'About a fortnight,' they said. Such travel times weren't unusual, and were no great problem for Nepalis. Porters were paid by weight, and few looked at a load of less than 40 kilograms, even for a journey of a week or more. Heaving the cargo up was the main problem, so stone structures along the mountain tracks were designed so that a porter needing to rest had a raised seat for himself and another, a step above, for the load. So carrying a loved one home for a fortnight was all in a day's work.

Despite being largely self-taught, Ruth Watson was a fine surgeon, and became a Fellow of the Royal College of Surgeons of England by election rather than examination. Her commonest abdominal emergency was small bowel volvulus, a condition very rarely seen in the West.

From Pokhara we flew on to Gorkha, where Howard and Betty Barclay ran a mission high school two hours' walk from the airstrip. They were very fit and happily hiked down to meet guests. Shirley flagged towards the end of our struggle up the mountain, so Howard took her on his back and sprinted, with the rest of us breathless in his wake. He carried her again days later when we climbed even higher to Amp Pipal, where the mission ran the beginnings of a hospital, where

I performed the first hare-lip correction in this part of Nepal, for a sixteen-year-old girl. As always, I used Millard's technique.

The Barclays were pioneers, gladly enduring difficult conditions. Apart from chicken, meat was rare, the only available variety being buffalo. Nothing was wasted and Betty even made a sort of stew from diced hide. This became unnecessary after their transfer to Kathmandu a few years later, when Howard became Executive Director of the United Mission and served with great distinction. The Barclays finished their time abroad as much loved leaders of Joint Christian Services in Mongolia.

Chapter 10

Madang

Nepal enthralled us, but we were more than ready to return to PNG. This we did to some fanfare, as the Department wished to capitalise on its new venture. Doug Russell at PHD headquarters and Laurence Malcolm, DMO Madang, couldn't have been more helpful. We admitted local patients from Laurence's list and the highlands leprosy team sent us many more.

As usual, the worst cases were presented first, but if anything useful could be done they were pathetically grateful. Soon we saw that I had to visit the various leprosy colonies to explain our aims and select candidates for transfer to Madang – well-motivated patients with permanent paralyses but with little tissue loss. Our first patients displayed an odd mixture of pleasure and timidity at being guineapigs, as they perceived themselves to be. Everything about our methods seemed new. Instead of using anaesthesia for major hand surgery we relied on massive sedation, which was perfectly adequate for cases with substantial sensory loss. And rather than using the so-called functional position after operation (that is, with each finger joint gently flexed), we splinted the hand in what is called the lumbrical position. Brand introduced this posture, in which the fingers are held straight but are fully flexed on the metacarpals, so that from side-on the cast looks like an L (without serifs). Fingers were rather stiff and a little puffy after three weeks in plaster. This frightened many patients but Julie explained that it was normal. She took them through the re-education process twice a day, and slowly they learnt to use the motor muscle(s) in a different way so that they could straighten their fingers and flex them normally. This physiotherapy took three weeks or so, and those a week ahead of others would encourage them, demonstrating their own progress, and doubtless explaining some aspects better than we could. Our ward was the happiest in the hospital.

Christian missions managed about a dozen leprosy colonies

scattered across the country, some in sadly and symbolically isolated places. The best known and the busiest was on Gemo Island in Port Moresby's harbour, and was my first peripheral centre. Audrey Davey, its dynamic English physiotherapist who had worked with Ron Huckstep's polio patients in Uganda, already had some experience in leprosy following a brief 1964 visit by Dr Grace Warren of Hong Kong. Grace had begun as a general duties medical officer with The Mission to Lepers, and became the leading surgical authority after Paul Brand, travelling and working incessantly for over 40 years, with cases anywhere from Seoul to Jerusalem.

By 1965 she was demonstrating how satisfactory itinerant surgery could be, which I felt was the only way to go in PNG. Paul still much preferred a centralised service, knowing that without a physiotherapist with specialised training the best-performed operation would produce a poor result. As well as being discouraging for patients and their providers, this could only bring reconstructive surgery in leprosy into disrepute. Some in high places, especially at WHO headquarters in Geneva, believed that too much money was being lavished on the correction of deformities. Critics ignored the fact that we all regarded prevention of deformity as even more important than its surgical correction, and ignored the enormous boost to morale that well-performed surgery brought to all concerned.

Serious post-operative complications such as swelling in plaster and wound infection were extremely uncommon, so that close supervision by the surgeon was unnecessary. Working out of Karigiri, Bill Lennox and Ernest Fritschi had found that a surgeon could operate far from home, provided that competent physiotherapy was available. And visiting surgeons could reinforce whatever was being done locally in the way of foot care, exercises to prevent contractures, and health education generally. It seemed that without onsite input and encouragement from a surgeon it was unlikely that patients would ever practise the obsessive care needed if damage to numb parts was to be minimised.

Another reason for making Port Moresby the first place on this program was to introduce medical students and doctors to modern surgical methods in leprosy. Valerie and I flew over every six weeks or so for five years, first visiting Gemo to select candidates who were brought over to the mainland on the next available launch. The PMGH gave generous blocks of theatre time and we operated on about a dozen patients in three mornings. Three weeks after our first session Julie went to Gemo to help Audrey, who soon became fully competent.

Extending this approach elsewhere was more problematic, but we saw that if a leprosarium staff member could be taught the specific physiotherapy we could add that institution to the program. In Madang we had patients at every pre- and post-operative stage, so were able to hold effective three-week courses for staff from elsewhere. We taught the relevant anatomy and the students came to theatre to see what was done. Julie took them through the essential exercises and Valerie taught general management details. We all made every effort to instil a preventive approach to injury and deformity. As in Port Moresby, after the first session at one of these peripheral places Julie visited to take staff through their cases.

As Paul Brand and his students always found, introduction of corrective surgery was a great encouragement for patients, even though the stigma that went with leprosy in most parts of the world was less obvious in New Guinea. Staff were enthused by the striking improvement in the appearance and function of hands and feet, and the walking plaster method of treating plantar ulcers proved that this bane of leprosy work no longer had to be a hopeless problem.

Eventually we handled large numbers of cases in each week away, partly because a high-volume program makes for speed, and also because we pre-packed and sterilised all our suture material and other items in Madang. Local nursing staff provided the extra hands needed to minimise changeover time. We became highly efficient, and with a full week at home and the next at one or two other institutions it often happened that I had around 100 limbs in plaster at the one time, many for treatment of plantar ulcers but most after tendon transfers.

I don't know how many hands we did in December 1965, but I recall logging 35 footdrop corrections, more than the total experience of the authors of the chapter on footdrop in the only textbook on the surgery of leprosy available then. In French, it came from the Institut Marchoux, a research and training centre in Bamako, Mali, that I was to visit in 1968. Paul B had refused to write such a book because there was no substitute for experience. He feared a book would lead people to operate without proper training, bringing this work into disrepute, but I thought there was a need for a comprehensive text, and as we were amassing a large experience I felt able to write one. I was well on with it when I revisited India in 1968 and found Fritschi ready to go to press, so I abandoned mine.

Paul had found that an intelligent and motivated patient who'd had an operation or two made an excellent physiotherapist, regardless of his educational background. We found likely candidates, and two became expert enough to be taken on staff. Both were almost illiterate. They were Simi, a highlander who had operations on both hands, and Trugam Amos, a youth from inland Madang whose footdrop I corrected. Simi worked in Madang for about two years before we sent him to Ubuya, the island leprosy/TB institution in Milne Bay Province where we spent a week every three months. He selected patients, prepared them, and managed them after operation to my complete satisfaction. Following Julie's example he did his best to encourage all patients to care for numb parts. Even though we only saw him at quarterly intervals he was always busy.

Trugam had the additional advantage of administrative skill. Some time after we moved to Port Moresby in 1970 I brought him over to do the physiotherapy (Audrey Davey having married and left the country), look after footwear, and be useful in other ways. If he ever knew what a key team member he was, it didn't spoil him.

The Mission to Lepers (or The Leprosy Mission, as it was renamed, to avoid the objectionable word 'leper') had long wanted to have its own unit in New Guinea. Shortly after we began in Madang Dick McKeown recruited a team, trained at Karigiri, and led by young Melbourne surgeon Bill Ramsay. They had a purpose-built unit at Tari in the Southern Highlands, and eventually took over much of the highlands work. When I moved to Port Moresby in 1970 Bill transferred Madang as a general surgeon with leprosy work as part of his duties. Dr Braun had retired from Yagaum, so the government hospital was much busier.

Being out of town every second week meant that it was just as well that I was rarely required to do major surgery in Madang, apart from emergencies. Even so, my first elective craniotomy in New Guinea was in Madang, on a child who had suffered meningitis nine times over several years, after an attack by a cassowary, a vicious bird rather like an emu. Its dagger-like middle claw went up her nose and holed the floor of her skull. This didn't heal, and bare brain sat in it like a loose plug. CSF dribbled out almost constantly and sooner or later germs got in. Eventually a doctor realised that the chronic wet patch below one nostril indicated a CSF leak, and knew that meningitis would keep recurring until the breach was repaired. X-rays revealed a hole in the bone, but when I opened her skull the defect was much larger than I'd expected. I repaired it with local material and a sheet of gristle from the thigh. Leakage stopped immediately and she went home happy.

My second Madang craniotomy was on an aggressive old lady whose children were at their wits' end because she'd burnt down several copra dryers in a few months. Village solidarity coped with most aberrant behaviour, but this expensive arson was intolerable. Medication was impracticable, so I suggested that prefrontal leucotomy might solve the problem. I'd assisted Jim Dinning with it in 1955, when it was fashionable. The relatives reckoned anything was worth trying, so I bored two holes in her forehead and passed an instrument back and forth across her frontal lobes in the approved manner. She awoke with an agreeably flattened emotional state and the family was delighted with her tractability. All was OK for about a year, when some worm must have turned, because she fired another copra dryer.

I arrived home at midday on a Saturday and was asked to see a businessman with severe nose bleeding. Our doctors' simple treatment had failed so I decided to insert packs behind his nose, under anaesthesia. We have an easier method now but I was unaware of it then. My anaesthetist was Neville Henry, the doctor rostered for that week's European outpatient session, where he saw a distraught young woman said to have been in tears since her marriage three weeks previously. There were depths here that couldn't be plumbed during a brief clinic visit so he admitted her, much to the family's relief, planning to sit and talk with her after lunch.

It was almost 3 pm by the time we'd dealt with the nosebleed and the patient was awake enough for Neville to leave for the ward, which was just as the miserable bride's mother charged into the nurse's office complaining about their dilatory doctor. The nurse apologised and said he was very busy. In fact, he was in theatre. 'What?' the lady screeched. 'Operating on a Saturday afternoon! A likely story.' Neville arrived in time to hear this outburst, which he handled with his usual restraint. At times like this I was glad to be the leprosy doctor.

Because we had so many patients at every stage of the rehabilitation process, instructive 'before and after' examples of most procedures were almost always available for demonstration to anyone interested, which was one reason why our unit was on the circuit for official visitors, whether medical or not. Lord and Lady Casey showed informed interest when they visited Madang in his capacity as governor-general of Australia, because they'd seen leprosy work in West Bengal when he was G-G there. I remember their visit best for another reason. Lady Casey, a renowned pioneer airwoman, knew the only female pilot working in New Guinea. She flew for Talair, was based in Madang, and had become a friend of ours. She was invited to a grand reception for the Caseys, and being a qualified dressmaking teacher she ran up a fetching garment for the occasion that would have been the envy of other guests. But they never saw it, because the Talair roster manager disdained female pilots and made sure she overnighted in a town far from the great event.

Visitors who came by the busload included a bunch of diplomatic trainees from Canberra, seeing government facilities. About two years later I was in Lagos, Nigeria, wanting a visa for Mali, a country with sparse consular services. I walked into the Australian High Commission hoping that if they couldn't solve my problem they would at least help a fellow countryman far from home. Having heard my story the Third Secretary asked if I remembered where we'd met. I suggested that perhaps he'd been among the diplomatic trainees who'd visited Madang. He was, and pointed me in the right direction. On that African trip I ran into two other people previously unknown to me who had recently been in Madang. How many others in Africa had so much as heard of our small town I cannot guess.

As well as entertaining visitors at the home base we had plenty of interesting experiences on trips around the Territory. Surgical visits to the leprosarium managed by the Seventh Day Adventist Church at Togoba meant calling on the nearby Mount Hagen government hospital, which often had no resident surgeon for months at a time, despite Hagen being the capital of the densely populated Western Highlands Province.

No doubt I had failures too, but I remember making two correct spot diagnoses there on one day, the first in an elderly woman in bed with incapacitating backache. A serious cause was usual when a New Guinean complained of backache. TB was nonexistent in the highlands in the 1960s, and in any case her pain was much worse than expected in spinal TB. I plumped for metastatic malignancy, the commonest primary being breast. 'On which side is the breast cancer?' I asked, pulling up her *meri* blouse. There it was, one breast puckered by a hard little lump. The junior doctor whose name was over the bed was most embarrassed.

The next bed contained a young woman admitted with a sinus on her back, just below her right ribs, that had leaked pus intermittently for months. She gave no history of injury and denied having an operation. (In some parts of the highlands traditional practitioners were remarkably adventurous with sharpened pieces of bamboo.) I'd never seen or heard of spontaneous drainage of a kidney abscess, but this was the most likely diagnosis. We X-rayed her and found a big kidney stone, a rarity in New Guinea. There was so much gristle between the kidney and the skin that it seemed impossible for pus to find its way out unaided, but clearly it had done so. Years later I saw hundreds of people in Yemen with kidney stones, and many kidney abscesses, but none like this.

Once a quarter I operated at the Missouri Synod Lutheran Hospital at Wapenamanda in the Western Highlands, and they regularly provided something out of the ordinary. I was in the middle of the fourth hand operation that day when a MAF plane buzzed us. Jim Macarthur, an American paediatrician, was my surgical assistant, and said it was a signal for a vehicle to rush to the airstrip to pick up an emergency. Within minutes a nurse brought news of a woman at the point of death from a presumed ruptured uterus, after labouring at home for days. I found her barely conscious on the emergency room table, and agreed with the nurse. Saline drips were running well with little effect and it was obvious that I had to stop the bleeding without delay, so I opened her then and there under local anaesthetic and had the uterus out by the time the lab brought blood.

Often I flew with Max Meyers, amongst the best known of MAF's many legendary pilots, and later the president of the parent organisation in the USA. He was gaining altitude while lifting me out of Wapenamanda, his home base, when the Cessna engine coughed a couple of octaves too low, and then picked up again. For an instant I wondered if we were about to end up in the treetops or on the rocks in the gorge far below, but Max explained that he'd flicked the throttle as a signal for Jo to come to the radio and take a message.

Wives were very much part of the MAF team and must have lived under some strain, knowing that sooner or later a pilot would not come home. MAF recruited only experienced flyers, and maintenance standards were faultless, but weather and other conditions made small plane work hazardous. There is a widespread belief that twin-engine planes are intrinsically safer, but this must be only marginally so. The disasters I remember most clearly happened to twins, belonging to other companies. A single-engine Cessna at least had the advantage that if it ran out of noise an aircraft with a legal load could glide for many miles. Several pilots made successful crash landings on the sand of dried-up riverbeds or other comparatively safe places. One MAF flyer did it twice in the course of a couple of years, which led to a gentle mandatory retirement process, no doubt to his wife's relief.

A century and more ago Christian workers in tropical countries were aware of the hazards involved and accepted them, just as did commercial adventurers. Some took their coffins with them. Nowadays being a missionary rarely poses risk to life. It is much less dangerous than being a journalist in a war zone, for example, but those who help mission work by using their skills as pilots still face substantial dangers in terrain such as the New Guinea highlands, even when obeying all the rules. They accept that God is in control, and that they are in His hands. Only those who are Christian believers are able to see the distinction between this confidence in God and the fatalism that is a feature of some other religions.

I was in Mendi in the Southern Highlands and expecting to be stuck there all weekend, but the work went even more smoothly than usual. We began well by doing six footdrop corrections after lunch on the day we arrived, and the list rolled on without a hitch. At midday Saturday I told the local doctor that if there was a plane to Mt Hagen after about 2 pm we'd be able to get away. He shrugged and pointed out the window to the fog and drizzle, meaning that further flying that day was unlikely, but within minutes we heard a Cessna on its landing approach.

I asked the doctor to head for the airstrip and tell the pilot, who was with a commercial airline, that we'd be done in half an hour. If he was bound for Hagen we'd pay waiting time if necessary. Minutes later we heard the plane take off and thought this meant a rare Sunday away from home, but the doctor returned saying that, after a short flight to a Mendi outstation, the pilot would gladly take us to Mt Hagen. As so often happens, a little operating took longer than I'd estimated, and the plane returned when I still had one small case to go. The doctor drove back to make sure the pilot waited, and minutes later they both appeared at the theatre door. The doctor said that capturing the pilot was the only sure way of having him stay until we finished, and as a sort of bonus he wanted to give him the pleasant experience of seeing a surgeon in action, so they both entered the room. I was removing a piece of dead bone from a foot, which I wouldn't have regarded as too disturbing a sight, but I was wrong. In no time at all the pilot hit the floor with a mighty thump. Nurses dragged him outside and found that he'd had nothing whatever to eat or drink since his cup of black coffee in Port Moresby at 5 am. It was now 3 pm, so they steered him to their house and filled him up with glucose. Soon afterwards we took off for Mt Hagen in blinding rain, with me wondering if I had the skill to take us down if our pilot fainted again. We arrived just in time to catch another plane back to Madang.

I have another unforgettable memory of an outstation visit. Years later, when I was based in Port Moresby, we were about to rush off to the airstrip when the young (well, 30-something) nurse looking after our leprosy patients asked if she could see me. We stepped into the doctor's office where she reported a tender breast lump that worried her. Shyly she half undid her shirt and exposed part of a breast, where I felt a tiny firm smooth tender lump just under the skin. I said I thought it had to be innocent, and we left it at that.

Months later she phoned saying that the lump had become painful, so she'd asked the local doctor to remove it. The pathologist reported it as cancer, this in the days when the standard treatment was modified radical mastectomy. She wanted to come to Port Moresby for me to do her operation. Aghast at my error, I agreed to admit her as soon as she arrived. The tumour was said to be of a slow-growing type but this was little comfort, and I approached the procedure at the end of a long operating list with less than my usual equanimity. At the time I had a foreign registrar with a much higher opinion of his own competence than did the Port Moresby surgeons, and none of us enjoyed having him on our unit. He was most annoyed that I intended performing the mastectomy myself rather than taking him through it, and assisted me with bad grace and less than the required attention. It was an afternoon session, and his breath carried a disagreeable odour that I foolishly took to be booze.

I was repositioning his retractor in the armpit for the third or fourth time when I lost my cool and asked if he'd been drinking. He exploded, stormed out, and drove to Konedobu where he demanded to see the Director of Health, Bill Symes, with whom I'd been on good terms for years. He told Bill I'd insulted him and his religion, and threatened to pursue the matter at the highest level if he didn't take disciplinary action. A simple personal apology wouldn't do. I had apparently mistaken garlic breath for beer. Bill called me in for an interview that was most embarrassing for us both and followed it with a stiff and formal letter of rebuke, copied to the complainant. Its tone must have been convincing, because I heard no more.

All this the result of a kerbside consultation! My patient was fortunate in having an uncommonly low-grade tumour for her age, and it is unlikely that the nonetheless unforgivable delay in diagnosis and treatment did her harm.

Nowadays a well-standardised protocol for investigation of breast lumps should protect women and their surgeons from flagrant errors, but pitfalls remain, largely but not solely over what was said and when it was said. Two sensational Australian court cases a few years ago brought some of the problems in breast surgery to the attention of almost everyone in the land.

By comparison with such things the surgery of leprosy was straightforward. Our unit had clear guidelines and the results of operations were predictable. Conversion of an ugly claw hand into one that looked almost normal and functioned well always provided great pleasure, and even after operating on hundreds of cases a year I never lost the enjoyment of what I was doing. Repetition can be boring, but this didn't happen to me, partly because however standardised a procedure may be there are enough subtle differences between cases to keep one alert. And many patients became my friends, and would stop me in the street, even 20 years later, to show me how their surgery was holding up.

A Catholic order ran a leprosy colony at Aitape in the far north of the country, and did it well, so that it was always a pleasure to visit them. As usual, I saw their general surgical problems too. A schoolgirl about fifteen had a very tight Achilles tendon, for no obvious reason, and had put up with walking on her toes since infancy until she began to suffer disabling pain in the fore foot, which looked like a ballerina's pointe. I suggested that I cut her Achilles and attempt to manipulate the foot into something like a normal position. The mission doctor thought this sounded rash but I said it should work well, with the tendon reforming at a proper length. Sure enough, after cutting the Achilles I was able to position the ankle at a right angle, with the tendon ends five or six centimetres apart. She was in plaster for six weeks, and some months later won the 100-metre dash at the school sports, proving that a severed Achilles tendon will grow and rejoin spontaneously.

The Aitape trade store belonged to brothers named Parer, a family with notable members, including a world-class pioneer pilot and a renowned photographer. Otherwise Aitape's chief claim to fame was St Anna, the large house that served as a base for Catholic priests and lay workers of several nationalities. The bishop of the Sepik lived nearby. We often flew out of Aitape on a Saturday, which meant invitations to Friday night excitement at St Anna – the regular get-togethers for workers in town from lonely outstations, at which some let their hair down a bit. I have a vivid memory of tipsy priests singing Irish love songs under the stars at midnight, which for truly excruciating pathos must be hard to beat. At one such party I went to the loo. It was of commercial proportions, as befitted the institution, and on a shelf at eye level was a large bottle of oestrogen tablets. It had to be there for one reason only, to provide chemical support for anyone struggling with celibacy.

Years later a Port Moresby monsignor set out to correct someone who had written an angry letter to the national newspaper making intemperate accusations about the Catholic Church and sexuality. In his detailed rebuttal the priest said it wasn't church policy to use drugs to help deal with what were essentially moral problems. It was sad to see him go out on a limb in this way, and I wrote him a private letter describing what I'd seen at St Anna. He wrote a courteous and slightly apologetic reply, so I felt sure his letter to the paper was written in ignorance.

When Peter and Mimosa Martin visited Madang in 1969 the work was thinning out, and he asked what I would do next. I'd been telling him for years how busy I was, but the present reality was rather different. We'd cut through the backlog of deformed patients, and most cases were now being diagnosed and treated early enough to avoid deformities. The pace of life was almost leisurely. I even had time to escort the Martins around the highlands, which would have been impossible the previous year. I didn't know what was ahead, but as so often in the past, the next door opened at exactly the right time.

Chapter 11

Port Moresby

As 1970 approached I was invited to go to Port Moresby as a hospital surgeon with a view to becoming a lecturer at the medical school when the position became available. Such was the relaxed and cordial arrangement between the university and the government that I would be PHD staff and simultaneously fill a university position.

We left our jungle-green town for the grinding aridity of Port Moresby with some reluctance because we'd made many friends in Madang, where we had a new four-bedroom house with a fine garden, close to an ideal beach for children. Our last child John was born there in October 1965, and for long after we left it he called Madang home. But it was time.

The University of Papua New Guinea was in the process of taking over medical training from the PHD, with most teaching in the clinical years being done by the specialists on the PMGH staff. Later the university appointed its own staff, who also worked as hospital specialists. In practice there was little difference in our duties.

I took over the lectureship from Carl Castellino, a Goanese who had done much of his surgical training in Hobart. I was one of his referees when he applied for a post in Burnie, Tasmania, and many years later our warm association at PMGH was to prove very useful.

The undergraduate syllabus was already in place. Before he left Carl and I formulated a training syllabus for several PMC graduates with apparent aptitude and interest, and proposed a four-year program towards a Master of Surgery degree, as had been done in other developing countries. We aimed to prepare trainees for old-fashioned general surgery, so that they would know how to cope with almost anything that was likely to confront them. There was the usual criticism that we aimed too high (and wide), but narrow specialisation was inappropriate. The trainees saw themselves as our replacements, and broad skills were required. Over the years our Master's graduates have tended to develop their own interests and a number have gone on to specialise, with advanced training in Australia and elsewhere.

PMGH had over 600 beds crammed with an amazing variety of cases, and our students had an enviable exposure to a breathtaking range of conditions. Some only came to realise how fortunate they were in this respect when they visited Australian teaching hospitals, where the quality of care was often higher and more advanced than anything we could offer, but the caseload and variety were much less.

The hospital was no architectural triumph and was irritatingly inconvenient, with its sprawling layout responsible for delays of many kinds that often made a day's work longer than it should have been. The long dusty dry season in Port Moresby and its hinterland didn't help, and after a couple of years I began to have regrets that I'd accepted the transfer. The upside was that our eldest daughter Meredith, who had lived with my sister Ailsa and attended high school in Naracoorte, was in the UPNG medical school and living at home. Had she trained as a vet, as she'd originally intended, she would have been far away.

Leaving the hospital at the end of an exceptionally tedious Saturday morning, chewing over a slew of petty irritations, I collected my mail and found a brightly stamped Ethiopian aerogram from David Ward, an English physiotherapist who had worked at Karigiri in our time. He was now at the All Africa Leprosy Research and Training Centre (ALERT) in Addis Ababa, and wrote because they were looking for an experienced leprosy surgeon. Was I interested?

I was excited, knowing ALERT's reputation. It had recovered from the slump I'd seen in 1968, described in a later chapter. At about 2500 m ASL its climate was vastly superior to Port Moresby's. Perhaps Addis was the answer to my problems. Rereading David's letter I noticed that it had taken three months to reach me, which seemed odd. I composed an enthusiastic reply in my head while walking home, but by the time I got there I was ready to telephone ALERT straightaway. I found that the next available slot in the London–Addis sked was on Tuesday, so I settled for a telegram and soon learnt that having heard nothing from me they'd assumed I wasn't interested, and had found another surgeon.

Quite apart from the upheaval that moving the family to Ethiopia would have entailed, subsequent events in that land probably meant that we were better off well out of it. So I can thank God that the clerk handling the aerogram was half asleep, and stamped it as surface mail. And I soon recovered from my Port Moresby blues.

For years I'd taken an interest in the surgery of head injuries and brain abscess, and did regular elective neurosurgery at PMGH, usually for brain or spinal tumours. Conscious of a need for further training, and eligible for study leave in 1973, I asked Jim Dinning how to go about it. His answer was predictable: 'Come to us for six months.' By taking leave on half pay I was able to stretch it out for twelve months bar one day – this in order to avoid releasing our government house into the pool. We rented in Adelaide and I spent the six months in the RAH neurosurgical unit, where the staff went out of their way to make my time worthwhile. One surgeon was a recent FRACS in neurosurgery and another was preparing for it, so there was an active teaching program that was to my lasting benefit. As well as taking part in ward and clinic work I assisted in theatre and did some solo operating. On the basis of our prolonged if intermittent association since my neurosurgical residency in 1955 Jim Dinning and Donald Simpson put me up for corresponding membership of the Neurosurgical Society of Australasia, and on the initiative of John Liddell, Hobart's senior neurosurgeon, this was converted to honorary membership in 1998, to my great satisfaction.

After that enjoyable six months I headed for the New Hebrides for a month to operate on leprosy patients at the only institution caring for them there, an Anglican Mission general hospital with a leprosy annexe, on the northern island of Aoba that I'd visited two or three years previously. An American physiotherapist came over from the leprosy hospital in Fiji. I found plenty of patients with deformities ideal for correction, and also undertook the usual education about the care of anaesthetic parts.

We had a hospital chapel service each evening, and as the islands were still an Anglo–French condominium this resulted in a curious twist to the liturgy. When the rubric came to prayers for the sovereign, one night we prayed for the Queen of England first and the next night the President of France. This even-handedness pervaded the whole of life, except for the road where it was agreed that everyone would drive on the same side. I was told that when the Supreme Court was set up in 1910 the constitution specified that one judge be chosen by the British, another by the French, and the third by the King of Spain.

Eventually a judge died, by which time Spain was a republic. Trilateral fiddling with the constitution was too difficult, so the court functioned with two judges.

I was waiting for my flight out of Aoba when the clerk at the bush-materials waiting room approached another traveller, a British civil servant. The clerk and his brother wished to open an airstrip kiosk to serve passengers who often had to wait in the heat for hours. When he asked about a trading licence the Brit said he'd need to discuss it with his French counterpart, and would then be in a position to advise him. If such minor matters required bilateral approval it is remarkable that the condominium's administrative machinery turned over at all.

Port Vila, the capital, had both British and French hospitals. I only saw the former, the Paton Memorial Hospital, named for a distant relative and built long ago by Australian Presbyterians on an island in the harbour. The matron was a Miss Trudinger, a member of a well-known missionary family, some from our home church in Adelaide. She and another Australian nurse were run ragged by their midwifery service. Often they needed to check patients in the night, and had found that the only reliable way of waking to do so was to drink a litre of water before retiring. Medical staffing was also a problem, and there was no surgeon either time I visited the British hospital, once just in time to remove a prostate from an old man with acute retention of urine.

It was on an earlier Vila visit that I met Carleton Gajdusek for the second time in a week. After an introduction in Port Moresby on a Tuesday I saw him again in the British hospital on Saturday, when he was charting the family histories of two nurses who had babies with phocomelia, the devastating limb deficiencies resulting from mothers taking thalidomide in early pregnancy. As far as was known the drug had never been imported into the New Hebrides, so was there, perhaps, another cause?

This was the kind of challenge that interested Gajdusek, who ran research projects worldwide on an extraordinary variety of topics. A polymath from the National Institutes of Health in Bethesda, Maryland, he had been in and out of PNG for years, but our paths had never crossed until now. He first visited the country shortly after arriving in Melbourne to work in paediatric immunology with Sir Macfarlane Burnet. He was the kind of voluble gadfly that got up

Burnet's nose, so when he needed to send somebody to New Guinea to look into kuru, a recently described disease of the nervous system, he knew who to send. But Gajdusek was already there, and although it has been stated that Burnet tried to call him back so as to leave the field open for Australian researchers, there may be doubt about this version of events. If Burnet gladly accepted his refusal to return to Melbourne, little did he know that Gajdusek was on a journey that would lead to a Nobel Prize in 1976. (Years later, in a privately published diary, Gajdusek seems to have alleged that the clonal selection theory that won Burnet his Nobel laurels had in fact been hatched in *his* brain. Perhaps we will never know.)

Kuru was an apparently new disease, restricted to the South Fore people in the Okapa sub-district of the Eastern Highlands. Women, in particular, were affected in large numbers, and developed a rapidly progressive in-coordination that began with minor clumsiness and stumbling, and soon rendered them bedridden. Within months increasing difficulty in swallowing saliva and food resulted in fatal inhalation pneumonia. There were many theories about the cause of kuru, and the big break came when Gajdusek injected brain tissue from post-mortem specimens into the brains of chimpanzees who too came down with it.

It was known that the South Fore people ate the brains of their recently departed. Women harvested this material with children tagging along. Here was a transmissible neurological disease, and the causative agent was eventually recognised as a new type of almost indestructible infectious material called a prion, amounting to skinny protein fragments much smaller than a virus. Scrapie in sheep and somewhat similar diseases in various other animals are caused by related agents. Another human disease in this class is Creutzfelt-Jacob disease, and it is the rapid onset variant of CJD that is transmitted from so-called mad cows to humans.

Kuru has disappeared, and in recent times each new case was a year or so older than the previous year's cases. Although many scientists earned doctorates while working on aspects of kuru, and Dr Michael Alpers, the longtime key man on the ground, was elected FRS, the kingpin of it all was Gajdusek, who had the admirable quality of never forgetting those who helped him, even in minor respects, along the way. He must have hiked through more jungles than any other biological scientist, and patrol officers and others in the remotest parts of PNG, Irian Jaya, Patagonia and anywhere from Reunion to the Marianas were amongst those who cheerfully provided accommodation for him when necessary. He was unfailingly and memorably hospitable to acquaintances visiting Bethesda.

Gajdusek adopted small boys from many different tribes, raising them in some style in the US, and those who even half-knew him were not exactly astonished when at the height of his fame *Time* magazine told the world of his trial and gaol sentence for pederasty.

All this was far in the future when he asked me to join his party for dinner in Vila. As the soup arrived I asked, 'Carleton, what were you doing in Paraguay?' As I'd expected, I was the only member of his audience who knew he had a research project there. He rose to the bait, and was still in full flood at eleven o'clock. He could, and would, talk for hours on almost any subject.

My next stop was Bergen, Norway, where Gwen, Kathy, Shirley and John met me for the 10th International Leprosy Congress. In 1873 Hansen had suggested that leprosy was caused by the microscopic rods he had discovered in the skin lesions of many of his patients. He was a native of Bergen, and the Norwegian government made this centenary meeting an occasion of national pride. The king opened proceedings, standing in the shadow of Hansen's statue in the city gardens. The scientific presentations were excellent and the social program made the most of what Bergen had to offer. We were shown a hospital, preserved as a museum, which had contained 600 patients in Hansen's time, and visited Grieg's house where a young lady played 'Wedding day at Troldhaugen' on the composer's piano.

That day the piercing late afternoon light of autumn in high latitudes was softened and dappled and even picked up a golden tinge as it passed through the thinning woodland surrounding the house, giving an exquisite ambience that seemed to make the music yet more brilliantly evocative. As the pianist lifted her hands from the keyboard after the last chord there was total silence for a second or two, as if we were waiting for Grieg himself to appear. Then came the applause. If ever there was *tristesse* this was it, and I will remember it until the day I die.

Despite my misgivings about travelling with children I have to say that on balance we then enjoyed, rather than endured, a three weeks' tour of Europe in the campervan I'd brought over from England. But all those comfortable campsites and perfect weather don't guarantee a perfect holiday, and I let out the occasional threat to make straight for Frankfurt and put them on the next plane home. Little else about this trip sticks in my memory apart from our visit to Linderhof, mad King Ludwig's smallest but most beautiful castle, where we arrived just after the last admission to the house for the day. The fabulous formal garden with those statues lining the stairway up the hill was still open, and the rest of us were admiring it from every angle when John disappeared behind a hedge and found the switch that turned on the fountain. Not just on, but into overdrive, spewing water halfway to heaven, which drew a blast of *Donner und Blitzen* from a management type somewhere in the distance. We weren't into tangling with Bavarian officialdom, so the rest of the family skedaddled while I found the switch and hit it. When John took us, with his own family, to revisit Linderhof in 2002 he had no recollection of his escapade of 30 years before.

Gwen and the children returned to Adelaide while I spent three months in Indonesia helping TLM establish surgical services for their patients in Medan, North Sumatra. This was Dick McKeown's baby, and he had two excellent nurses working under the general direction of the Indonesian government doctor responsible for leprosy work in the province. Clinics functioned well over a wide area but no surgical treatment was on offer, although TLM surgeons had been working intermittently for several years at the national leprosarium at Tangerang, outside Jakarta.

Like many others, Indonesian culture was permeated by age-old misconceptions about leprosy, and most general hospitals shunned those with it. Our base was in a church-owned hospital some miles from Medan, where the plan was for me to demonstrate the various operations and take an Indonesian doctor from Tangerang through them for six weeks before going back with him to his own hospital. I didn't manage to teach him to operate independently, so as a training exercise this trip was something of a failure, but we performed many operations, and as is always the case with introduction of surgical services, morale of both staff and patients was boosted.

Bishop Nommensen, a German Lutheran, first evangelised the Batak, the major tribe of North Sumatra, and such was his influence that churches and schools he founded continued to prosper. Other denominations were represented in Medan, and the TLM staff worshipped at an English-speaking Methodist church that grew out of the work of the famous Chinese evangelist John Sung, who left his mark in many parts of the world and can be said to have spiritual descendants to this day.

One Saturday we drove north to Lake Toba, Sumatra's greatest tourist attraction, but didn't have time to take a boat out to the island in the middle. There was talk of visiting Aceh, but this province was out of bounds and dangerous, because the Acinese were fiercely anti-government as they had been since earliest Dutch times.

There were several lonely leprosaria in North Sumatra, run-down relics from the old days. Down rough and muddy tracks, far from any main road, they were effectively prisons from which escape was all but impossible. Lifelong incarceration was still common. I saw an ancient Chinese who clearly had never had leprosy, but having been admitted more than 40 years previously he had nowhere to go. Many others were suitable for outpatient treatment, but having lost all family contact and any real possibility of independent living they expected to be inside forever.

A few months before my visit a leprosarium inmate with a strangulated hernia had been taken to the university hospital in Medan. Whether or not his leprosy was active I do not know (not that it should have mattered) but when the ER staff heard the word 'leprosy' they threw up their hands and refused to admit him, so he was taken back to the leprosarium where he vomited until he died.

In PNG this degree of ostracism of leprosy patients was all but unknown. In parts of the country they were sometimes shunned, but usually this was because someone else wanted their land, wives, or other property. For all practical purposes the only social disruption caused by a diagnosis of leprosy was incarceration in a leprosy colony for an inconvenient number of years. This was bad enough, but at least the disease didn't render patients outcasts for life. With the use of better drugs in the 1970s we didn't have the huge hurdle, common elsewhere, of having to overcome deeply ingrained community prejudice before outpatient management could become the norm.

I remember little of my time at Tangerang, apart from the heat of Jakarta, the stench and squalor right alongside obscenely flaunted wealth, and the necessity to pay urchins to guard cars in the street to avoid tyres being let down or slashed. I then spent a welcome week in Irian Jaya before flying back to Port Moresby. We knew missionaries in that primitive province, and some had been my patients in Madang, with general surgical problems. Like everyone else in PNG, I was aware of the tensions that had followed UN Trusteeship Council transfer of this remnant of the Dutch empire to Indonesia, a betrayal driven by *Realpolitik* and masterminded by Ellsworth Bunker, an American diplomat. The inhabitants were Melanesian, like most Papua New Guineans, with whom they felt a strong affinity. They regarded their Javanese rulers as alien in the extreme, and fiercely resented the transmigration policy that even then was depriving them of their ancestral lands. At Sorong, the district HQ on the western tip of the bird's head, the doctor proudly showed me the hospital he was building. When I commented on the brickie's labourer's straight hair that marked him as a Javanese immigrant the doctor said, 'Papuans are unemployable. They simply won't work.' White Australians in Darwin sang a similar tune.

I was in the provincial capital, the former Hollandia, on the day of the monthly flag-raising ceremony, and like everyone else I dutifully went to the parade ground at noon. Indonesian troops formed a square in front of their commanding officer's dais and an unlucky Papuan soldier had the task of marching to the middle of the ground and saluting the flag on behalf of all those present, while the band squeezed out the national anthem. The last note had barely died away before the CO stomped to the middle, grabbed the Papuan by the shoulders and screamed abuse as he pushed and pulled the terrified man into what he regarded as a more martial stance, and had him salute the flag again. A more inappropriate attitudinal display by a senior member of the occupying power would be hard to imagine.

The city's doctors entertained me at a harbourside restaurant where the specialty was soup. One item was highly recommended, and I had to agree until my spoon picked up a loop of what I took to be sliced duodenum. As I was deciding what to do I noticed that all eyes were on me. Recognising the challenge, I battled on to the last drop and the last slice. Having passed the test I was told that their last foreign visitor had failed it.

Cenderawasi University had few buildings in 1973 but its museum was well established, with an enthusiastic young curator, Arnold Ap, trained at the Bishop Museum, Hawaii. His encyclopaedic knowledge of his country's cultural heritage, together with good English, made him a fine guide. Like many West Papuans he had strong separatist sympathies that eventually brought him trouble, and it is widely believed that his 'accidental' death was really an assassination, making him yet another in a long line of Papuan nationalists ruthlessly extinguished by the authorities. It is unlikely that the halfway house of limited autonomy, with a name change from Irian Jaya to Papua, will satisfy Papuan aspirations. In this regard, sooner or later Australia will be called upon yet again to choose between expediency and honesty, as the Whitlam government did with East Timor in 1975, to their everlasting disgrace.

Chapter 12

Dean and professor of surgery

I came full circle to find changes afoot in Port Moresby. David Hamilton had looked after my unit well, and with his wife, the former Julie Christie who had been our physiotherapist on the leprosy team in Madang, moved on to the surgeon's post in Rabaul, where their exceptional skills and personalities endeared them to the Tolai.

On the leprosy scene members of an Apex Club in Port Moresby were the driving force behind an international Apexian fundraising campaign to construct a leprosy ward and associated facilities at PMGH. Following the recent closure of the Gemo hospital, and with our general wards chronically full, we needed space for operative or other leprosy patients needing hospitalisation. We already ran an outpatient clinic in rather cramped and otherwise unsatisfactory quarters, so the welcome self-contained new building allowed us to concentrate all our activities under one roof. Valerie Taylor was nurse in charge, and Trugam Amos, our ex-patient from Madang, managed the physiotherapy and footwear, looked after the garden, and served as a useful conduit for information that might otherwise have passed us by.

After Doug Russell retired a university physician with an interest in leprosy (successively Ian Riley, Iain Aitken and Hugo Ree) dealt with the medical aspects of our patients' disease. We made rounds together, and between us ran a lively Wednesday morning clinic that saw new patients every week, many from villages known for 50 years to have an unusually high incidence of leprosy. I've seen similar clinics in many parts of the world, but rarely such a variety of clinical material as came to us at the Apex Ward. Our patients liked the arrangement as much as we did, and tended to come straight to us whatever their problems, be they leprosy-related or not. The bonhomie and social solidarity of Apex Ward made working there a particular pleasure, and provided an ideal atmosphere in which to instruct our medical students.

And I had returned to find changes in the medical school, where various personality conflicts and minor imperfections of teamwork were making unpleasant ripples. Even in our small faculty we had fair copies of the irresistible force and the immovable object. The dean, a Sudanese professor of pathology, was taking up a position in Australia, and there appeared to be no suitable replacement available. Those otherwise well qualified also had their own very visible barrows to push, and undoubtedly this would have made them generally unacceptable. It was a part-time position and had to be filled internally. To my great surprise somebody suggested that I allow my name to go forward.

The notion that someone who was Health Department rather than academic staff might be acceptable to the university was novel, but Ken Inglis, the vice-chancellor, had no difficulty with the idea, so more or less by default I became dean in 1974. I didn't pretend to bring any particularly appropriate skills to the position, and wouldn't have accepted the appointment had I not known that the dean's secretary was a self-starter and well able to think outside the square. This made her fully competent to handle or at least suggest solutions for most of the problems that came our way. I still had a full clinical load and had little time to devote to the deanship. It was while holding this position that I learnt that one of the most useful administrative attributes is the ability to say no to harebrained schemes. And being dean provided me with a rare experience when I presented Meredith to UPNG's chancellor, Sir Alkan Tololo, for him to confer her MBBS degrees after her graduation in 1975. There must be few who have had this particular pleasure.

Years before, Dr Gunther had made a trip to Africa as Assistant Administrator of the Territory and came back with the conclusion that Africa had nothing to teach us. How wrong he was, in so many ways. We all tried to learn from Africa, and PNG is still doing it, for good or ill. One of my first tasks as dean was to receive a visitor from Nigeria, Professor Grillo from the University of Ife, who had been invited to examine the medical school. He was a senior medical scientist with three well-earned doctorates and was said to be an expert on medical education in Africa, but whether that fitted him to tell us what we should be doing in PNG is still open to question. He curtly refused to have me in the lecture theatre when he met the student body, clearly branding me a colonial relic.

The day I took him home for lunch he made straight for the piano, his tribal robes flying behind him, and dashed off a rather smudged

Debussy prelude. Apart from the time taken for this performance he talked non-stop. Whether or not he had pearls to offer us about the medical school I do not know, because his report to the vice-chancellor was a very long time coming, and if it arrived in my time I never saw it.

But things seemed to be going well for me, with the next surprise being an invitation to accept appointment as professor of surgery. I owe this to Ian Maddocks, who after a long and productive career in the medical school, culminating in successful occupation of the chair of medicine, was about to leave the country for Adelaide, where he was to distinguish himself as a leader in palliative care. There was a single professorial position in our Department of Clinical Sciences, and although we assumed that another physician would be found to fill it, this was not to be. Once again, the university was desperate to avoid employing a misfit or a loose cannon.

My problem was that I lacked some of the usual qualities sought in professors, with next to nothing that could be called research experience. The university's problem was that a string of senior appointments had been made in other faculties on the basis of fine CVs, glowing references, and promising interviews by the most discerning committees, but with much less than satisfactory outcomes. At least I was a known quantity, committed to the country, and with a good track record as far as it went.

I filled out application papers and in due course was appointed without so much as an interview. I still have the warm welcome note that Ken Inglis wrote me, anticipating a long and agreeable association in the university. Unfortunately for me he left shortly afterwards for a chair in history at the Australian National University in Canberra. I styled myself professor of clinical surgery in an effort to indicate that whatever skills I had were practical rather than academic.

UPNG was a highly and (in my opinion at that time) an absurdly democratic institution, which meant meetings galore. It soon became clear that we needed an extra surgeon to help carry my clinical and teaching load, and we were fortunate in recruiting Hamish Foster for a year. This well-trained young Australian so enjoyed his introduction to PNG that he came back to work at Arawa on Bougainville until the forced closure of the Panguna copper mine, after which medical services in the province fell apart. His innovative work on Bougainville was to provide his entrée to the star-studded list of authors of the *Oxford Textbook of Surgery*.

When I began as Frank Smyth's locum in January 1961 the surgical staff at PMGH consisted of two surgeons, their interns, and a registrar on rotation from the Royal Melbourne Hospital. Members of this cadre were almost always highly energetic, the cream of the crop, and spent four exciting months in Port Moresby, with more hands-on experience than was available in Melbourne for trainees at their level. In the course of a day they might drain bigger abscesses than they'd ever seen, set fractures, remove an inflamed appendix (a condition that was becoming more common), bore a hole in the skull to let out a blood clot on the brain, and operate on a strangulated hernia or some similar emergency, as well as assisting us with a wide variety of complicated cases.

These positions were much sought after until increasing lawlessness in Port Moresby terrified young doctors, their wives, and the Royal Melbourne Hospital management, not necessarily in that order, so that the rotations ceased. Another issue was that some Papua New Guinean registrars felt that one or two of the visitors hogged more than their fair share of the most interesting work.

The occasional Melbourne registrar broke the mould, like the chap whose first plane trip ever was to Port Moresby, and who went home four months later with a private pilot's licence, a singular achievement that meant he was unavailable late in the afternoons more often than usual, whether or not he was on call. Another I left in charge of my unit for a few days while I visited the highlands, and returned to find that he'd felt able to refer two post-operative cases to Australia for more expert management than he believed I had been providing, without even discussing them with other Port Moresby surgeons. I was not amused, but in general these relationships were of great mutual benefit.

There were three surgeons in the late 1960s, and four in the '70s, each with his registrar and intern. Teaching medical students is always labour-intensive, and we were all fully occupied. Each surgeon made regular visits to other hospitals in Papua, and I continued to travel in connection with leprosy. In addition, I was being referred increasing numbers of neurosurgical cases, notably brain abscesses and tuberculomas.

Brain abscess has all but disappeared from the West, but in

under-developed countries where middle-ear disease is common it remains a well-known complication of chronic mastoid infection. I saw many children with headache, vomiting, fever, a depressed level of consciousness and a long history of discharge from one or both ears. It was usually simple enough to determine which ear was responsible. Shortly after arriving in Rabaul I found that the absence of an ENT surgeon was in some respects an advantage – sometimes a committee of even two can be awkward. It seemed simpler to have no need to coordinate treatment with somebody else. First I drained the brain abscess through a burr hole just above the ear, and then proceeded to perform radical mastoidectomy. In the cases I saw there was almost always extensive destruction of middle-ear structures, and attempts to conserve them to improve hearing were pointless.

Well over half those referred as suspected brain tumours turned out to be tuberculomas, solid masses of tuberculous tissue. Unless the mass is large enough to cause raised intracranial pressure needing urgent decompression, this condition responds well to anti-TB drugs without any operation, and it was therefore important to be sure of the diagnosis as soon as possible. It was rare to find evidence of TB elsewhere in the body, but the standard skin test for TB would be intensely positive. In such cases we aimed to give three weeks of anti-TB treatment before re-assessing the situation, and almost always found that the signs and symptoms of disease were clearly improved after this time. It was important to avoid the use of cortisone or other steroids at this stage, as these drugs could produce striking improvement whatever the cause of the raised intracranial pressure. I once treated a man with an ordinary brain abscess, mistakenly diagnosed as tumour, whose symptoms responded well to steroids while transfer to my care was being arranged.

Twice I removed tuberculomas because before operation I believed them to be malignant tumours, but set out to do it deliberately only once. This patient was a teenage lad from Daru, in the Western Province, with severe headache and vomiting due to a huge mass in one frontal lobe, and a strongly positive TB skin test. He made no progress on drug treatment and decompression became urgent, but this was delayed because his uncle, a leading politician and the most influential member of the family, was out of the country. He was called back and gave permission, and for the only time in my life I removed an egg-like tuberculoma that instead of being solid had a thin shell and a liquid centre, a variant well recognised in some other countries.

Some neurological cases bypassed specialists in PNG and went directly to Australia, not always to their benefit. Years later, in Goroka, we admitted a senior public servant for the night, together with his distraught wife, on his way home to die of what was said to be an untreatable malignancy of the brainstem. The onset of fits in adult life, plus headache, had made his Port Moresby GP suspect a brain tumour, and in view of the man's seniority he had no difficulty in having the government pay his fare to Australia. He turned up at the Goroka hospital complete with his case notes, the CT scan from Australia and plain X-ray films taken in Port Moresby. Our astute physician noticed that the plain films showed faint speckles of calcification deep in the brain, of the kind sometimes seen in tuberculoma. The CT report made no mention of TB as a candidate diagnosis so I phoned the radiologist concerned, who admitted that this possibility hadn't entered his head. The strongly positive skin test persuaded us that this man's problem was tuberculoma of the brainstem, and he proved it by making rapid improvement on anti-TB treatment. He was left with mild intellectual deficit that would have interfered with him resuming his previous position, so he was happy to accept his pension and go home to the village. When I last heard of him he was trying to sue somebody.

With air travel between Australia and PNG becoming easier every year we found that many people who could be treated perfectly satisfactorily in Port Moresby, or further afield for that matter, wished to go south for their second opinions and/or operations. We sometimes had to refuse certificates stating that such trips were essential, which naturally annoyed patients, their relatives, and sometimes their employers. Marginal cases could cause awkward problems. For example, a long-distance foot race was organised so brilliantly that it crossed one of Port Moresby's busiest road junctions at peak period, and at dusk, on a Friday afternoon. The lead runner was knocked down by a car and was brought to hospital unconscious. The only injury was to his head, and at first there was little to indicate that anything life-threatenng had occurred. Instead of waking up properly his improvement was doubtful at best, but I could find nothing to suggest that he needed his head opened, and was happy to watch him. Next morning he was more restless and irritable but was unchanged otherwise. The chairman of the athletic club and his henchmen were in and out of the ward and eventually asked for a second opinion. It happened that the only other surgeon in town that weekend was notoriously inactive when managing head injuries, so there was no point in consulting him. The physician on duty had more grey hairs than I did and an interest in neurology as well, so I called him in. He pondered the problem and decided on lumbar puncture as a useful investigation. I was horrified, believing that this was absolutely contra-indicated, but I was fast losing control of the case and decided against objecting. He put a needle into the spinal canal and was rewarded, unsurprisingly, with a vigorous jet of very bloodstained cerebrospinal fluid. The bystanders ahhhed as if this was the clue they'd been waiting for.

With an eye to flight times the athletics people demanded that the man be prepared for transfer to Brisbane forthwith, but I objected, saying that if he was to be flown out I would need to make burr-holes first to be sure that I wasn't missing a clot that could cause fatal deterioration on the way. The clubmen could then do what they liked with him. Somebody signed permission and we took him to theatre. I was doing a preliminary head shave in the corridor, an activity that aroused the patient a little so that he spoke for the first time since admission, screaming abuse and complaining of headache, when the athletics boss appeared at the door.

'My wife used to be a ward sister at St Vincent's, and she says these things can be very tricky,' he said without demur. 'Are you sure you have the facilities for it here?' – code for 'Do you really know what you're doing?'

I told him we had everything we were likely to need, and got on with it. I found a substantial extradural haematoma (clot between the skull and the brain) and after removing it the brain was quite slack, which satisfied me that there was no other major problem. He went off to Brisbane with a much-improved level of consciousness, and some days later a further small blood clot was removed and the bone defect I'd made filled with plastic. When he returned to Port Moresby the athletics club put in a request for a refund of his airfare, on the grounds that I'd referred him to Brisbane. Headquarters asked me about it, to which I replied that the club had taken him south rather than me referring him. In view of everything the Department paid up.

On another occasion an Australian employed in Port Moresby

wanted a referral letter and his fares paid to Australia for repair of his simple hernia. The locum surgeon said this wasn't necessary, so against his will the chap agreed to operation at PMGH, and suffered two complications, a moderately severe wound infection and a mild iodine burn. A fortnight later he took himself to Sydney where a surgeon immediately removed the nylon used in the repair, and apparently said that this should have been done even earlier.

Naturally enough, the patient felt that his initial reluctance to have surgery in Port Moresby was fully justified, and quickly put in a compensation claim for loss of wages, his airfare, the cost of his Sydney treatment, suffering, and anything else his lawyer could think of. Eventually the file came to me for an opinion. I said that wound infection could occur anywhere, and despite common gossip it wasn't notably frequent in Port Moresby. On the face of it there was no reason at all why he should have rushed off to Sydney, and I wouldn't have been in any hurry to remove the nylon. I happened to know that the first surgeon was a commendably careful operator, and having suffered a nasty iodine burn when having my own hernia repaired in Port Moresby I couldn't see why this was a matter for compensation. Surgeons are likely to be very careful indeed when operating on a colleague, and if my surgeon (not the same one) could accidentally burn me with iodine it might well happen to anyone. I don't know what action the Department took, but a threatened lawsuit against the surgeon fizzled out.

Several young Papua New Guinean graduates wanted to become surgeons, and we put serious effort into training them. The first three that I predicted would do well all failed to make the grade. One simply didn't have the self-discipline to study, another might have done well but for a total inability to make a management decision, and the third was a genial spiv who hoodwinked us all. I've often wondered if these failures also indicated my own lack of perspicacity, and later I became much more cautious in predicting trainees' success or failure. One wonders if the so-called objective criteria now in vogue almost everywhere will be any better in selecting the most suitable candidates for higher training.

A full clinical load, under- and post-graduate teaching, never-ending university meetings, the leprosy ward and various other things meant that the day was too full. The dean's position had already been localised, but towards the end of 1976 I decided that I still had too many irons in the fire, and that the medical school would be better served by some other surgeon. We were able to attract Sankar Sinha, an Indian who'd been a gold medallist all through his training. He had gained his master's degree at the All-India Institute of Medical Sciences, and subsequently had worked in Zambia. I retired from the chair and he came in at lecturer level, and eventually rose to the associate professorship. His warm, open personality and his all-round clinical expertise were only a few of his many outstanding qualities, and we could not have made a better appointment. A long-time friend of the medical school, Scotty Macleish, a leading Melbourne surgeon and sometime PRACS, recognised Sankar's worth early and arranged for him to prepare for the FRACS examination in Melbourne, which he passed with ease. Their association led to a long line of Australian surgeons making valuable short-term teaching visits to the medical school, an exceptionally useful form of overseas aid that has continued to the present.

Leprosy work continued to absorb me, and in that connection I made WHO-funded teaching visits to the Solomon Islands and Western Samoa. Pacific travel was idyllic in those days, with absence from home being the only drawback. On my second trip to Samoa Gwen came down for a fortnight, just in time to comfort me in the middle of an agonising dental experience, the condition called dry socket, which came on after an extraction. We stayed at Aggie Grey's, the less formal but more famous and livable of the two hotels in Apia, widely known for the smorgasbord and cultural performance put on every Friday night that culminated in a stirring four-part rendition of R.L. Stevenson's *The hunter home from the hill*. Aggie was still doing the hula at 80, and enjoyed these evenings as much as anybody.

This second trip included a three-day visit to the larger of the main islands, Savai'i, to review leprosy patients and their management. A team of doctors, nurses and assorted public health officials travelled in a bus driven by a Canadian lay brother. Shortly before we pulled into a village where we were to spend the night I noticed a large residential building with church attached, an unmistakably Roman Catholic property. Our hosts were about to call us to the table when a Samoan nurse asked me anxiously if I'd seen Brother John. 'He's gone off to see his priest,' I said. Quick as a flash this doctrinally sound Methodist lady replied, 'We're all priests, doctor.' I had to agree.

In 1978 the 11th International Leprosy Congress was held in Mexico City. Hugo Ree and I attended as the PNG delegation, at our own expense. The government of the Northern Territory, which had a much smaller leprosy problem, found the money to send five people. Neither Hugo nor I had been south of LA before, and as well as enjoying the meetings we had a great time visiting the sights in and around the city. Rivera murals lined the concert hall where a visiting pianist played the Tchaikovsky number one, and museums displayed massive Mayan carvings and other treasures from the great civilisations that once thrived in Central America.

On Sunday afternoon we decided we had to see the bullfight, so joined an enormous and noisy crowd in the sweaty Plaza de Toros, the biggest bullring in the world, a huge theatre seating 45,000. After watching picadors taunting a series of none-too-clever bulls into rage before they were dispatched disgustingly slowly, painfully and bloodily by only slightly cleverer matadors, we decided that one such dose of death in the afternoon was definitely enough. The locals around us looked aghast and growled nastily in Spanish when Hugo and I applauded one canny bull that refused to play. We upset them still further by cheering the renegade as he was whipped out of the ring in disgrace.

Back in Port Moresby life was becoming busier, and in many ways more interesting, with the post-independence political processes developing around us. But the city was a dangerous place and many people suffered repeated housebreaking, which made for plenty of party talk. I once remarked that our place seemed strangely inviolate, at which another guest assured us that the explanation was that I had once treated, I must suppose successfully, the leader of the *raskol* gang holding the franchise on our part of Boroko.

Despite the growing unrest and increasing management problems in the hospital that meant that few days went according to plan, we may well have stayed on indefinitely but for a family disaster that came to a head early in 1980. Our second daughter Robyn was a nurse in Adelaide, and unbeknown to us had been sliding into a combination of anorexia and suicidal depression. A colleague's daughter had recently committed suicide far from home, which I took as a warning. We decided that we needed to return to Australia to look after Robyn, and it seemed to me that she would only believe we were serious if I were to resign rather than take extended leave.

The Secretary for Health, Dr Allan Tarutia, was generous enough to suggest that I take up to two years' leave on full pay, without obligation. He said he had the Public Service Commissioner's approval for this unusual offer, but I foresaw a string of potential problems and felt unable to accept it, so I resigned. While this was going on Gwen and John, our only remaining child in PNG, had packed and gone to Adelaide. Not long before this we had bought a house from a friend in College Park with part of the proceeds from my share of the recent sale of Clezy land, which Dad had put on the market because he judged correctly that it was a good time to sell. So Gwen had a home to go to while I tidied up in Port Moresby and followed six weeks later.

Much of the next four years is too painful to describe, with our highly disturbed daughter apparently able to escape at will from maximally secure psychiatric facilities. She was missing from the doubly locked and guarded ward of the Glenside Hospital the day I arrived in Adelaide, which I took to be some sort of message. I went to the hospital and heard the staff's feebly apologetic account of her escape. I was so disgusted that I phoned the medical superintendent, who was a medical student in my time, and asked politely if they couldn't do better. The shrug of the shoulders was palpable. 'It's a big hospital' was the best he could come up with.

As time went by Robyn's repeated admissions to numerous hospitals alternated with longer or shorter periods at home. Many hours spent in psychiatrists' offices seemed to do nothing, and to this day I believe that such recovery as she made had little to do with her doctors' care, consistently empathic and unstinting as it was. While we were at a leprosy meeting in India she managed to persuade a surgeon to repair her hiatus hernia, which she (and I suppose, he) thought made it easier for her to vomit. This crude attempt to find a mechanical solution for a psychiatric problem was bound to fail and, worse than that, over the next few years she suffered almost every known late complication of surgery for hiatus hernia, and had repeated major operations to deal with them.

Eventually there was some improvement and she was able to marry another recurrent depressive she met in hospital, a delightful man who had become a Christian because of her influence. Michael Mortlock-Verne looked after her wonderfully well until her death during an emergency abdominal operation at an Adelaide hospital in 1997 under worrying circumstances that were never adequately explained. We delayed her funeral to allow time for the coronial autopsy that we assumed would be mandatory, only to find that the coroner had issued a death certificate without one. I wrote to the attorney-general of South Australia complaining that even in New Guinea we could do better than that. I pointed out the obvious, that the label of mental illness was apparently a millstone around the neck in death, as it so often is in life.

During those four years in Adelaide I conducted a small private surgical practice and made several trips to PNG, filling holiday vacancies for surgeons in Goroka and Mt Hagen. I also served for several weeks at a mission-run general hospital I knew well at Balimo in the Western Province, where I'd operated on leprosy patients since 1966. After Robyn and Michael married it slowly became clear that she needed encouragement to lean on him rather than on Gwen, so we looked into the possibility of returning to PNG. There was a vacancy at the Goroka Base Hospital (GBH), and as I had enjoyed my recent locum period there, and had visited it many times over the years, we had no difficulty in accepting an appointment in 1984.

Chapter 13

Goroka

In German times the interior of New Guinea was a blank on the map, with the occasional, usually punitive, expedition into the foothills uncovering no hint of the wonders in the mountains beyond them. When Australia took the Territory of New Guinea as a League of Nations mandate after the Great War the few personnel in the fledgling colonial service were fully occupied on the coast, and scanty budgets meant that officially sponsored pure exploration was out of the question.

Europeans first saw Goroka in October 1929. Privateers in search of gold, they came upon a large and highly organised stone-age culture where the wheel had never been seen. Indeed, the first wheels in Goroka were on planes bringing supplies to the airstrips that explorers hacked out of the jungle. An old theatre orderly told me he remembered the first plane landing, but this seems doubtful.

Goroka became the original highlands administrative centre for several reasons. The locals were as friendly as could be expected, the area was well watered, appeared readily defensible, and had adequate more or less level ground for a commercial airstrip and other possible developments. At a little under 2000 m ASL it lies towards the western end of a broad deforested valley bounded by sharp, smoky blue-green mountains, with six or seven more ranges rising behind them. Fainter and fainter as they stretch into the distance, the farthest pastel-toned peaks merge imperceptibly with the sky.

Goroka was a rough and ready frontier station when I first saw it at Easter 1961, when Roy Scragg had me escort a Brisbane ENT surgeon around the Territory. The hospital consisted of modified highland longhouses with thatched roofs, except for the operating theatre, which was a simple wooden shed. The ENT man and I found Goroka's (and the whole highlands') Hungarian surgeon Lajos Roth expertly draining an abscess deep in the back of a warrior's neck, one thin layer outside the junction of the brain and spinal cord.

We arrived just in time to see him extract triumphantly a long-buried arrow tip, the cause of the problem. This operation would have been neurosurgeon's work in Australia, but was little more than an interesting but unremarkable item on the sort of list Roth dealt with every day. He was notably neat and gentle, with an enviable ability to cope with almost any surgically treatable problem that came his way.

As more of the highlands came under control its enormous area was broken up for administrative convenience. Goroka became the headquarters of the Eastern Highlands District (later, Province), but remained the regional centre for many purposes, including health. When the two-storey hospital was erected it proved to be the most functional in the country. I visited it often when I worked out of Madang, and always saw interesting cases. Frank Smith (not to be confused with Frank Smyth, Port Moresby's mouth cancer expert) and Alan Shepherd each worked there as solo surgeons for long periods and attracted difficult cases from all over the highlands. They and the trainees fortunate enough to work with them dealt with a referral population of over a million in addition to the 200,000 or so Eastern Highlanders. Most nursing aides and a few sisters were Eastern Highlanders, with vigour and initiative that was less common on the coast. The near-perfect climate must have helped, but the highlanders were, and are, in many ways a different people, tough and resilient almost beyond belief.

By 1984 Goroka was officially a two-surgeon station, and when I arrived my colleague was Fe'ao Takitaki, a Tongan UPNG graduate who had been my student. He was a sound and level-headed clinician and a quick, expert operator. His laid-back Polynesian style was an excellent foil for the more volatile and impetuous of our juniors, who saw him as a natural leader and role model. He was greatly missed when he followed many other postgraduates into general practice, where the money was ten or more times better than in government service as a specialist.

Repeated efforts were made to persuade the Public Service Commission (PSC) to allow UPNG medical graduates to combine public and private practice, a concession that would have been a logical way to keep them in the government system as part-timers for long enough to pay back some of their training costs. The idea had always been anathema to the PSC, and before independence the argument went that if doctors were allowed private practice other public servants would want it too. The only exempt cadre was the small number of licensed marine surveyors. Insurers required foreign-going vessels, and for all I know, local ones too, to be inspected after even the most minor accident. Time was money, and ships couldn't lie idle for days while inspectors flew up from Brisbane to do what might be a few minutes work. Thus big business could exert irresistible pressure on the PSC, but government departments could not.

So it often happened that I was the only surgeon in town, but at least I had good trainees, usually two at a time. We were all kept busy. We spent Monday and Thursday mornings in the wards, and with about 60 adult patients and a swag in the children's ward we had abundant teaching material for medical students and surgeons-in-training. The Goroka surgical unit provided me with the greatest variety of challenging experiences I've ever had. Its only rival was my last workplace, in the Yemen highlands. We kept three theatres busy on Tuesdays and Fridays, and on many Wednesdays too, with emergencies in between. A gynaecologist and an eye specialist had the place humming at other times. On Monday afternoons I saw outpatients, and if weekend admissions provided less than a full day's operating on Tuesday this clinic filled the gaps.

GBH had long been known for peptic ulcer cases. This problem was uncommon on the coast but we saw hundreds, usually in thin old men complaining of chronic upper abdominal pain and vomiting. Typically they came in rubbing their thumbnails up and down their midriffs, indicating that they knew what they needed. Almost all were well beyond drug treatment, even if this had been practicable. Our registrars learnt to cut the vagus nerves to the stomach and perform the bypass operation favoured by most surgeons in PNG. Just as in other countries with a large ulcer burden, many cases really had stomach cancer, and I remember a session in which we operated on three before morning tea, all incurable.

A more famous highlands problem was a peculiar gastro-enteritis known as pigbel. In Roth's time this was the commonest abdominal emergency, but it had almost disappeared by the late '80s. It followed the infrequent pig feasts that were a central feature of highland culture, and at first the doctors assumed it to be somehow due to eating improperly cooked meat. Gregor Lawrence, Tim Murrell and others took years to prove that it followed a massive protein, not necessarily porcine, meal in people who ordinarily ate little protein. Starving Germans had the same disease in 1945.

The highlanders' staple was sweet potato that has so small a protein content that we were amazed at their physique. Their digestive processes were so adapted to this monotonous fare that they couldn't cope with a massive protein load. Sudden alteration of the contents of the gut after the gorging of pig meat encouraged enormous overgrowth of certain bacteria that were harmless in small numbers. These germs produced toxins that clotted blood vessels in variable lengths of the small bowel. Minor cases suffered mild colic and diarrhoea, but at the other end of the scale enough gut went rotten to kill the patient unless the diseased segment was removed.

Frank Smith has a photo of five children whose pigbel he operated on, all having been guests at the funeral of another child who had died of pigbel. Pig feasts are still held, but with increasing general protein intake the ecological balance of the gut became much firmer. As this dietary transition occurred a vaccination program was developed, just as the need for it was disappearing.

Before pigbel's exact nature had been worked out we heard of it in places where pork could not be incriminated. I spoke about New Guinea's surgical problems at a hospital in western India in 1968 and found that they saw cases exactly like pigbel. Reports from Bangladesh, Thailand and elsewhere described the same disease, with sudden massive protein intake in people who ordinarily ate very little of it being the common factor.

The GBH physician was a young Englishman, John Richens, who combined exceptional clinical ability with energy that left me breathless. He always carried his camera and amassed a better collection of clinical photographs in a few years than I did in half a lifetime. His pianism was probably the best ever heard in Goroka, and he could have made a career of it if he hadn't studied medicine. GBH had always been blessed with fine paediatricians, as befitted a busy referral hospital, but in the area of adult medicine John Richens was outstanding.

He was an excellent teacher and of great help with the medical students who came to Goroka for six or eight weeks at a time. Looking after them had its problems. One group included two girls, and for safety's sake we accommodated them in a vacant house well inside the compound fence, but on their first night three attempts were made to broach their rooms, so they shifted to the nurses' home. One was so distressed that we had to allow her to return to Port Moresby.

John made supervisory visits to other hospitals and returned with neurosurgical or other problems for me. He brought many cases of pituitary tumour, almost always those that produce growth hormone. In Port Moresby I'd operated on several such patients referred from the highlands, and it now appeared to be largely a highland disease. More than that, most came from Enga Province, in the far west. I returned from one holiday to find two Enga women from the same village and a Southern Highlander with this tumour. This last woman's husband complained that the beautiful girl he married was now ugly, but it seemed to have escaped him that she'd also become totally blind. Sadly, operation did nothing for her eyesight, but at least she went home free of headache.

I forget how I chose which of the Enga women to operate on first, but I remember the close interest the other took in her post-operative progress. After twice watching me changing the daily head dressing she asked when I planned to get on with it and do her operation too. I said I thought she'd like to see that all was well with her friend first. She gave me a big Enga smile and said, 'OK, how about tomorrow?' in its pidgin equivalent.

The highly malignant brain tumours so common in Western countries seemed to be rare, and I saw very few. One of the first was in about 1974, in a Gorokan diagnosed by Alan Shepherd and Frank Wagner, a physician with an interest in radiology. Frank performed a primitive carotid angiogram that nevertheless demonstrated a right frontal lobe tumour. Alan wanted to assist me, and as it was far cheaper for me to go to Goroka than for him, the patient and a relative to come to Port Moresby I spent the weekend there, and on Saturday morning removed what proved to be a fairly slow growing malignancy. All was well for several years until the man strayed too close to his brother's wife, which led to a family fight with bows and arrows. The avenging cuckold scored a bullseye of a kind when he chanced to put an arrow through one of my burr holes. The injury was fatal, and the coronial autopsy revealed recurrent tumour.

A much commoner tumour all over PNG was the meningioma, which isn't malignant but nevertheless has an aggressive tendency to recur if incompletely removed, a feature precisely documented long ago in a landmark paper by my friend Donald Simpson. Their vigorous blood supply and other idiosyncratic features have made meningiomas special challenges since Cushing's day, and like real neurosurgeons usually do I came to enjoy them too. I was fortunate in having a Sikh anaesthetist, Gajinder Oberoi, with skills far above the ordinary, so our patients left the theatre awake.

Sometimes a meningioma so encased the great arteries at the base of the brain that I couldn't achieve complete removal, as recorded in this 1988 family letter.

> On Tuesday I removed a chap's brain tumour – well, almost all of it, and as much as could be removed safely without doing more harm than good. By Saturday morning he was unhappy with his progress, so signed himself out for the day to go and see a local medicine man. How much that cost I do not know, but it will have been much more than the K5 [about $5] for his hospital admission. He came back no better, with a promise from the medicine man that he will deliver his verdict later. On Sunday he was still unimproved, and it may be that he has a bit of a clot collected.

I re-explored him, and sure enough he had a substantial extradural clot, my first such complication in years. Happily he then recovered.

Dr Oberoi, or Roy as I called him, was exactly the one I needed at the top end of the table when I operated on another condition that I collected from all over. This rare tumour, called phaeochromocytoma, usually occurs in the adrenal gland and secretes adrenalin and a related hormone, resulting in wild swings in blood pressure. This can be fatal, before, during or after operation unless counter-active drugs are used expertly, and the operator knows exactly what he is about. A Mayo Clinic surgeon has described removing a phaeo as a fun operation, but I never became that blasé about it. We had some exciting times, including the successful removal of bilateral tumours from a boy whose father's unilateral phaeo I'd removed in Port Moresby more than ten years before. The Lae paediatrician referring the lad had already suspected the diagnosis, which John Richens confirmed by imaging the tumours with our portable ultrasound machine.

A few months later the same doctor sent me another child with bilateral phaeos, from a different tribe, so that there was no possibility of them being related. The odds against seeing two children with such a great rarity in one year must be astronomical, but I was hungry for another. Sure enough, the Lae paediatrician found what he thought was a third case. He wasn't far wrong, because the child had another rare variety of surgically treatable hypertension, as was proven when I removed a shrivelled kidney.

Some conditions common in the West were rarities in Goroka, despite our large referral population. John Richens was there almost three years before he saw a highlander with a myocardial infarct. Apart from arrow wounds in arteries, which were common enough, our people seemed to be almost free of all kinds of vascular disease. Diabetes was rare (although not on the coast), and I saw many more pituitary tumours than cases of diabetes.

Gallstones were rare, always with advanced disease that provides major challenges for young surgeons meeting them once or twice a year, instead of every week as I did in my training days. An inexperienced surgeon in this area can run into trouble and produce serious, sometimes fatal, complications in the kind of case we saw. The simplest approach is to keep out of harm's way by opening the gallbladder, removing the stones and putting in a temporary drain. Not removing the gallbladder sometimes means that gallstones recur in later life, although this isn't as inevitable as many people think. About 1930 my mother-in-law had this limited operation at the hands of her GP and had no more trouble for nearly 40 years. When her pain returned she took to her bed with a hot-water bottle on her old scar, and a few days later this came up like a boil and burst, discharging bilious pus and gallstones. She soon healed and was still symptom-free when she died at 94.

Because the simple drainage operation is regarded as a halfway house, young surgeons sometimes perform it unwillingly, seeing it as an admission of defeat. (A real man takes out the gallbladder!) I aimed to protect my trainees from falling into this error, and developed (so I thought) a new definitive operation, safe and satisfactory in almost anyone's hands. Instead of draining the gallbladder externally I removed the stones and sewed the gallbladder to the immediately adjacent duodenum, with a wide opening in the new party wall. Bile could then run from the liver into the gallbladder and onwards into the gut, hopefully with little risk of recurrent stones. End of problem.

This worked well and spared us (and more importantly, our patients) from difficult and possibly dangerous surgical adventures in what is commonly known as tiger country. After three cases went well I decided that such unorthodox surgery needed the imprimatur of an acknowledged authority, so I wrote to a renowned expert explaining the circumstances in which I worked, why I had done it, and asked for his opinion. He replied saying that he'd never heard of the operation, but readily understood my reasoning. (So he should have, as much of his time was spent dealing with cases referred with the disastrous damage to bile ducts my operation was designed to avoid.) He said that if it worked he saw no reason why I shouldn't continue with it, and asked me to report progress, which I did.

Some time later I opened a surgical journal and read a fine description of a new operation from this man's unit, in which they were doing exactly as I did, although for marginally different reasons. In vain my eyes ran down the list of references for 'Clezy (personal communication)' or some such. Not that it mattered; long afterwards I discovered that Riedel, a German, did 'my operation' a century ago, with the same rationale. I'd invented nothing, but when I described it at a Brisbane meeting the Adelaide surgeon Lehonde Hoare, who had trained a few years ahead of me, said it was the only original idea he'd heard all day. This was generosity born out of old acquaintance, because the ritual three minutes' question period after my paper was memorable only for the numbing silence that guarantees to deflate over-enthusiastic speakers like nothing else does.

My senior trainee was Leonard Kaupa, a highlander with abundant common sense and rapidly maturing ability who had been educated at Geelong Grammar. He often attended to major emergencies without needing help from me, and when I left PNG I rated him as more experienced and more widely competent than I was when I went to Rabaul with my FRCS. So it was common for me to find new cases in my ward that Leonard had been busy dealing with while I was asleep.

Late one night he admitted a friend who had comprehensively torn and broken his right forearm in a car accident. The wounds were ragged and dirty, but Leonard knew what to do as we saw such injuries regularly. The man had a good job, and Goroka's large horsey set regarded him as the best farrier in the country. He was in the private ward, which we habitually visited last when making our rounds. My team and I were discussing a patient in our high dependency unit (the first row in the large public ward, in front of the window into the nurse's station) when a female unknown to us, but apparently a leading equestrienne, strode in. As I paused for breath, and without so much as a 'Good morning,' she asked me for details about the farrier. I said I hadn't yet seen him and that Dr Kaupa had attended to him. She knew he'd been to theatre in the night, so my answer didn't compute. She expostulated, 'But he's your patient, isn't he?'

She had the archetypical imperious and terse proprietary tone we sometimes saw in 'befores', the anglicised pidgin nickname given to foreigners who'd lived in New Guinea before the war and returned afterwards. (Older New Guineans commonly shrugged off their blimpish behaviour with the explanation *emi bipo tasol* – 'he's a before; that's all that need be said'.) By the late 1980s the 'befores' were almost all dead and/or gone, but this lady brought back rancid memories of her type, and for once I lost my cool. 'Look,' I said, 'you don't go into BP's and expect to see Mr Burns or Mr Philp, do you? It's a bit like that here. My name is over his bed and I'll be seeing him in due course, but we have a lot of sick people to see in this ward first.'

Her jaw dropped and she left us without a word, with the New Guinean staff unable to conceal their delight at the put-down that would have branded them as bigheads or sophisticates had it come from any of their mouths. As expected, I found that Leonard's management of his friend's injury was faultless.

Firearms weren't yet widely available, and tribal fighters still used spears, bows and arrows, and axes. These non-explosive injuries meant that warriors (and occasionally, others) suffering them almost always survived if they reached hospital alive. In some months the commonest male adult admission diagnosis was 'arrow wound'. The variety and combination of injuries seemed endless, with our commonest being the arrow in the chest. This produced air leaks and mild internal bleeding but rarely other problems, and was treated by insertion of a chest drain for a couple of days.

I went in one morning to find that Leonard & Co had been busy with half-a-dozen men after a fight between two clans over election results that had seen, according to one side, the wrong candidate elected, undeservedly and perhaps crookedly so. In the front row we had a sorry old man injured more in pride than in person, still in his arse-grass (the bunch of leaves highland men stuff into their belts to cover the buttock cleft). I'd just seen him when a nurse reported that his son was on the phone.

'Tell him he's OK,' I said. 'He'll be ready for home in a day or two.'

'You'd better talk to him,' she said, 'he's calling from New York.' I sprang to and found that the son worked at the PNG mission to the UN. This incident illustrates how great were the changes in New Guinea in a generation.

In my time women and children were rarely injured deliberately in these fights, at least around Goroka. The only female I remember with an arrow injury escaped diagnosis for months. She presented with an abscess behind her left ear, said to have followed an arrow wound. It seemed a minor matter and like so many abscesses its drainage was delegated to the most junior team member, at that time a competent young American. She made an incision, released disappointingly little pus, and that was that.

A few weeks later the patient returned, still draining. This time the junior registrar explored the wound, again with little success. Next time I did it, and failed to explain the ongoing problem. Weeks later she came in yet again, now complaining of something in her right eye, between eyeball and nose. This was obviously an arrow tip, and pulsated. It was finding its own way out successfully and trying to hurry it could only do harm, as its path must have been within a whisker of numerous vital parts of the brain. Another half millimetre or so of arrow tip appeared each day. She interpreted our masterful inactivity as reprehensible dithering and took herself home in disgust, but returned a fortnight later with more than two centimetres protruding into the middle of her field of view. A genuine, if astonishingly indirect, bullseye.

Not unreasonably, she demanded its removal. The wound behind her ear had healed, and apart from the arrow tethering her eyeball slightly, producing double vision, there was no neurological defect. Our eye specialist came to assist if need be, but when I extracted the arrow she bled briskly for a minute or two but had no further problem.

She left us wondering what all the fuss had been about.

The payback principle guaranteed that tribal fighting, and violence generally, had no end. It sometimes came close to home. In 1988 I wrote:

> We are rather nervous on account of a man being axed to death up near the Teachers' College on Tuesday night, with people from [my junior registrar] Kris's village being suspects. The chap had been warned, but after drinking with his friends at the Zokozoi Tavern he was foolish enough to walk home alone in the dark. So there will be a payback sooner or later, and the rule is that the better educated the victim, the better a payback it is. Kris feels that he is likely to be at the top of the list, and has applied for a pistol licence, which I think isn't very sensible. He has moved his family to his wife's uncle's house in North Goroka.

Earlier that year I wrote:

> Iga, our acting matron, has a problem. He is an Okapa, and their national government MP died in Lae on Thursday of complications of untreated high blood pressure. His line has decided that Iga's line worked sorcery on him, and it seems that Iga has been nominated, you might say, as suitable payback material. Fortunately he is married to a woman from the other side of Goroka, so they have gone home to her village. He is an exceptionally good worker as well as a very pleasant chap, so we are more than ordinarily concerned for his safety.

By the mid 1980s travelling on the Highlands Highway was hazardous for both locals and foreigners. In 1986 a Gorokan Christian leader drove a truckload of valuable furniture up from Lae and happened upon a bus hold-up. He sent up a Nehemiah-type prayer and was waved through by the bandits, apparently because they knew him slightly. The bus people didn't fare so well; the driver was relieved of about K200 and passengers were levied K20 each. When an old lady said K5 was all she had, a *raskol* lopped off an ear.

Raskols were sometimes more gentlemanly, but not often. John and Veronica Richens were showing her mother the sights when they were held up close to town. The *raskol* didn't know what to do with a refined English matron, and John had to push things along by asking how much he wanted. He looked them up and down and suggested K20. They handed this over before he had time to change his mind, whereupon he shook hands with them all and waved them on. A few weeks later a busload of nursing students returning from a rural assignment had their money, wristwatches and shoes taken at the same spot, so the Richens family got off lightly.

Personal safety was rarely a major issue for foreigners, but occasionally we had problems. Early one morning we admitted the burly leader of a notorious *raskol* gang long sought by the police who had trapped him at a drinking party. During a wild scuffle he took a bullet in the thigh just above the knee, holing the bone without actually breaking it. The ER nurse was a Salvation Army lad and had been at an evangelistic meeting at which the gangster had professed conversion. This nurse rarely missed an opportunity, so reminded the *raskol* that those who mock God often reap what they sow.

A bellyful of food and drink made early administration of an anaesthetic dangerous, so the staff bandaged his leg and sent him to the ward, where I saw him in the morning. The wound needed exploring under anaesthesia so we added him to the list. It was a straightforward procedure, and he was returned to the ward awake and in good condition. At lunchtime our police chief called, wanting to put the man in gaol. I protested that he had a nasty injury and needed hospital treatment. The officer said emphatically that gaol was the place, because he'd heard that the gang proposed making a rescue attempt, and he didn't want innocent people caught in any crossfire. He'd keep him in the town lock-up (rather than miles away in Goroka's main gaol) for as long as I thought necessary. As this was five minutes' drive away I decided that under the circs we should fall in with this idea. We'd send a nurse up every few hours with injections for pain relief. When asked for a pick-up time I suggested 6 pm.

But this was not to be. He dropped dead at about 5.30 with no warning. A Port Moresby pathologist came up next morning and to our great relief he found a rare condition to explain the sudden death. Already there were rumours in town that a nurse had given a fatal injection. The gang promised to deal with the police, and after taking appropriate revenge in that direction they'd attend to the hospital. We all knew that this was no empty threat, although in the end nothing happened. For weeks the hospital was battened down at sundown, and patients appearing after dark had great difficulty in having the ER door opened. I was offered a transfer but I turned it down, remembering that a New Guinean doctor in a similar situation had refused this option, his reason being that if they really wanted to get him, nowhere in the country was safe. We knew he was right.

I was fortified in my stance a day or two later when reading the passage in the Acts of the Apostles about Paul's apparent danger in Corinth. He had a vision in which he was told not to be afraid, and to stay where he was, because God had many people in that town, and nobody would harm him. Although I read my Bible regularly I don't expect quite such vivid personalised assurances about my safety, my future or more mundane matters on a daily basis, but this morning was different, and the words leapt off the page as God's word for me, so we were greatly encouraged.

All senior specialists had administrative duties, sometimes tedious or irritating but occasionally of interest. The Department once sent a file to Goroka for review shortly after I returned from leave. A planter in an outlying province walked home from a party late on a Friday night and was set upon by hooligans who knocked him briefly unconscious. Someone helped him home, where his astute wife noticed slight but worrying deterioration in consciousness over the next few hours, so she rushed him to the provincial hospital where the duty doctor was a dark-skinned foreigner who, extraordinarily, had spent several years in neurosurgery before coming to PNG. He diagnosed an extradural haematoma requiring urgent removal, which he was competent to do. The wife refused, but agreed to his consulting the regional surgeon by phone. He agreed with the diagnosis and said that, if treatment locally was unacceptable, the chap should be flown to him ASAP. It was now 3 am.

The wife insisted on treatment in Australia despite warnings that her husband could die first. At first light he was put aboard a small twin-engine plane, now so far gone, deeply unconscious and with one pupil dilated, that the doctor had to pass a tube into his windpipe to control his airway. He was operated on immediately he reached hospital in Australia, and spent weeks recovering.

The file came to me because he'd presented his accounts to the Department for payment, on the grounds that his operation couldn't have been performed in New Guinea, and his medical insurance policy had been exhausted by the cost of the chartered plane. The neurosurgeon's fee was $5000. Should the Department pay it?

I said the first doctor could and should have dealt with what he correctly diagnosed as a life-threatening clot, and would have done so without hesitation but for the wife's refusal, and the surgeon he consulted at 3 am was competent to handle the case. The main point to be made was that the family should know they were unbelievably fortunate that he hadn't died long before reaching Australia. As for the surgeon's fee, which was far above the so-called scheduled fee for this particular operation, no doubt it was no more than might sometimes be expected when a plantation owner at the point of death arrives from overseas by chartered aircraft on a Saturday afternoon. Whether or not the Department paid I do not know.

Like many public servants, all of us with a contract requirement that we work ourselves out of our jobs by training our successors, I saw myself as having an open-ended future in PNG. So it came as a very sharp shock indeed when I learnt in 1988 that I was to be offered a twelve months extension only to my contract. This was the government's polite way of telling me my time was up. The news I'd already received that I was to be awarded an OBE may have been a clue that yet another senior public servant was about to be dispensed with, but if it was I missed it.

Our sorrow at the prospect of leaving Goroka, which we loved, was relieved only slightly by the knowledge that it would resolve a barely manageable situation. A new trainee wasn't part of the team, and was unwilling to pull his weight. Worse still, he persistently and proudly refused to follow instructions. The knowledge that the lore of the decolonisation process elsewhere was full of such stories was no comfort.

Many events pointed to it being time to leave. In April I wrote:

> It has been a rather traumatic week. On Tuesday a pilot of a small plane crashed in Simbu [the next province west of Goroka] somewhere about 11 am, and although Leonard was informed around midday he didn't tell me. The first I heard about it was about 3 pm when I was in X-ray with a patient under anaesthesia. The surgical registrar who has been so difficult decided to rush the guy straight to theatre, not properly resuscitated, no blood available, and without telling me what he was doing. By the time I got upstairs he was dead. The junior anaesthetist hadn't called his boss either.

> The chap had a whole lot of serious injuries, and we hoped the autopsy would disclose something untreatable, but it didn't. It's clear that six or eight bags of blood should have been found (which was possible) and pumped into him before anything at all was done. He may have died even then, but the coroner isn't likely to give that much consideration.
>
> The crash investigator tells me he was overloaded 160 kg, which is quite substantial at this altitude, he made a poor approach to the airstrip, and then did the wrong thing when he realised he couldn't land. So it was a disaster from start to finish.
>
> We have of course had our own internal investigation, but the real reason for me not being informed didn't come out. It seems pretty obvious that this was just one more expression of nationalism – the desire to do without the foreigner.

Another 1988 letter included this passage.

> This afternoon my registrar rang me rather cross because he had a patient in theatre with a ruptured appendix, and everybody was there except the anaesthetic service. What to do? I said I'd ring the betting shop, and sure enough the national doctor on duty for anaesthetics was there. Our only functioning ambulance was out on a call so I sent a police vehicle to fetch him, which I imagine was a bit of an indignity. I'll find out tomorrow.

To compound these problems, infrastructure was disintegrating. Villagers who owned the land through which water was piped to Goroka felt that they deserved fatter fees, so pipes were cut repeatedly and we would go for days without running water. One Tuesday

> we persuaded theatre staff to carry water for the morning, but after lunch the senior nurses didn't come back, so several major cases didn't get done. Normally we operate on Wednesday afternoons too, but they jacked up again. I was very cross, and stormed out to ring the *Post-Courier*. After the chap on the line had heard me out I suggested he ring our medical superintendent. The result was a good page 3 story about 'Water crisis at Goroka Hospital' which seems to have stirred up a bit of action. We'll see how long it lasts.

Twenty years later this problem still plagued Goroka.

Water was only one of our troubles. Often we ran out of oxygen, which almost brought the theatres to a standstill, and blood, which we sometimes had to import from Port Moresby. For months the theatre air conditioning functioned on a fierce freeze setting or not at all, which was dangerous for many patients and made working conditions almost unbearable. Was it time to go?

Chapter 14

Home invasion and worse

Law and order was disintegrating long before independence and went into free fall thereafter. If the worst excesses of Africa have not been replicated they seem not far away, with Port Moresby reckoned in 2006 to be the world's least hospitable capital. In a recent letter a Rabaul police officer from my time there described the situation like this:

> Like most of my vintage, I was finished in 1974 when the so-called 'winds of change' blew us out of the country. However PNG has been, to date, the most remarkable period in my life, which was very nearly terminated there when in August 2001 I went back to see the skeletal remains of dear old Rabaul, and Lae, where five *raskols* crossed my path armed with shotguns and bush knives. They held up my borrowed car on one of Lae's main roads at 3 pm on a weekday. My seat belt saved my life in a most unusual way, in that it prevented them dragging me out of the car, in which case they almost certainly would have finished me off and stolen the vehicle, as is their usual fashion.
>
> As they couldn't cope with the seat belt they climbed all over me, knocked me around a little, robbed me of everything of value, even my boots, and fled when another car approached. Barefooted, I got myself to the very police station I'd once commanded (!), finding there a couple of old constables who remembered me favourably. They said they'd 'deal with' my assailants, and took a decoy car to the scene. When the same *raskols* came out again the police 'dealt with' four of them, the fifth had the good luck to escape in the shoot-out.
>
> When you consider that these *raskols* are perpetrating the most horrendous crimes on their own people (gang-raping girls walking to school, or women working in their gardens, cutting off the arms of little children when villagers cannot pay a ransom, murdering their own kind, and other horrible crimes) it's no wonder that the police deal with them.

This was unimaginable in the early 1960s, when we left keys in our cars on the street overnight, and were casual about locking front doors. By the '70s increasing violence of all kinds meant that Port Moresby diplomats, businessmen and others able to afford it took to living in fortresses, with armed guards around the clock, remotely controlled gates, high fences, floodlighting, sirens and dogs.

Most people knew that this protection was more apparent than real. It was rumoured that, for retirement purposes, US embassy staff were credited with double time in PNG, and in 2001 Barbara Bodine, the US ambassador to Yemen (later one of the State Department's woefully miscast proconsuls in Baghdad, between Jay Garner and Paul Bremer) told me that, despite Yemen's booming notoriety, Sana'a was much safer than Port Moresby.

Like old-timers everywhere, long-term PNG residents tended to discount the scary stories that perturbed some newcomers. When we moved to Goroka in 1984 we felt as safe as in College Park, a good Adelaide suburb, but even there John had a narrow escape late at night from a gang wielding bicycle chains a stone's throw from our gate.

Our house near the Goroka hospital was on tall stilts, and we accepted the high Cyclone fence topped with barbed wire as a matter of course. We found it unremarkable that between them the other foreigners in the street had fierce canine guards of almost every legal breed. (Locals called it Dog Street.) Highlanders remained fearful of any but their own dogs, although many coastal criminals had learnt how to deal with them. We resisted the idea of keeping them, on the grounds that they went for brown skin indiscriminately. We wanted PNG friends to feel free to drop in without a guard dog's reception, and were to learn, too late, that a smart animal soon differentiates between friend and foe.

Regular highlands travel went with my position, and friends would stay with Gwen at night, or take her in, whenever I was away, an accepted neighbourly function at that time. As well as visiting hospitals in my own bailiwick I had occasional business in Port Moresby, usually to do with leprosy. I'd written a medical students' manual and each year took part in a week's lecture course.

In 1985 Frank Smith did serial locums and was available to work at GBH for the week I was at the leprosy course. Frank had great experience in chest work, and we always found cases for him. Having been Goroka's surgeon for so long he jumped at the opportunity to return to a place with agreeable memories. We were good friends as well as Christian brothers, so I was glad to have him stay with Gwen while I was away. Off I went on Sunday afternoon's plane to Port Moresby, to be hosted by Ian and Rae Riley. Ian was professor of community medicine, with a long and distinguished research record, and Rae was among the best and most agreeable anaesthetists I've ever had. They were sparkling company, and after many years in PNG they knew it well.

At six on Tuesday morning Ian rattled me awake; Frank was on the phone. I stumbled downstairs to hear, 'You're awake? Well, listen very carefully. We've had the *raskols* in, and we've both been roughed up a bit. Praise God we're all right, but it doesn't matter what you're supposed to be doing today, drop it and get to the airport. Gwen needs you.' He refused to elaborate, and as Ian rushed me out to Jackson's I was more cramped up with fright than ever before or since.

I was in Goroka before 9 am and for once knew nobody in the terminal building who could drive me home. The public phone was u/s (as usual) and the Air Niugini personnel were re-loading the plane, so I grabbed my bag and ran home the kilometre or so. From the top end of our long street I saw police vehicles and clusters of neighbours outside our house. Once inside, I heard the grim story.

Gwen and Frank had talked until about 11 pm and were about to say goodnight and retire when they heard a noise as if someone was meddling with our Suzuki 4WD, so Frank went down the central stairwell and peered outside. Ordinarily security lights came on automatically at dusk, but for once they were out, and he saw nothing. Several *raskols* grabbed him, beat him up, smashed his spectacles, and asked for money. He told them to check his pockets, which clicked with one man, who asked him to write a cheque. Frank didn't think to ask, 'Who to?'

Meanwhile other men ransacked the house, bundled booty into pillowcases and dashed downstairs again, ignoring Gwen in her armchair. Alarmed about Frank, she went down to investigate, and as she stepped into the darkness a man put a knife to her throat, asking, 'Where's the money?' She had K3 only, a trivial amount that he ignored. Then he told her to shut up or else. Two or three were sitting on Frank, so he couldn't help her. The others led her 100 metres down a side street to the double darkness under a stand of trees where five raped her. Somewhere in the middle of all this she cried to God for help. The answer came via a Simbu lad living in a nearby garden house. He grabbed a waddy and rushed to her aid. As her assailants fled nightwatchmen at the nearby Melanesian Institute let fly three arrows, one of which scored and produced a scream.

The Simbu told Gwen he was a Christian and that he'd recognised the gang leader as the Eastern Highlands premier's son. The rescuer's mother appeared and they shepherded her home. Goroka's police chief, who lived opposite us, was away but his wife saw enough to suspect serious mischief so she called the duty officer on a direct line, and he arrived in a full squad car within minutes. One *raskol* was picked up nearby with our portable stereo, and by morning they had arrested all but one rapist, who escaped and was never seen again.

I believe the criminals knew the police chief and I were away, and assumed that Gwen was in the house alone. Regardless, it seemed to be a copycat crime, as Monday's *Post-Courier* (the national daily) had given banner headline treatment to the front-gate ambush and rape of two New Zealanders in Port Moresby.

Considering her ordeal Gwen was in good shape, and friends who had already visited her told me that she comforted them rather than vice versa. As time went by others commented on her serenity and lack of vindictiveness, and some very hard-headed people wondered where her strength came from.

Statements were taken from everyone with anything to contribute, an appropriate medical examination followed, and Gwen was given antibiotics in case any of them had gonorrhoea or syphilis. HIV had not yet appeared in the country. The hospital came to a standstill while New Guinean staff made placards to carry behind an ambulance to the provincial HQ. It was a noisy but orderly demonstration, and the provincial government got the message that the town was sick of violence.

The police rarely caught rapists, and as a case involving the wife of an expatriate public servant was bound to have a high profile, charges were prepared without delay. The public prosecutor, an Australian who was to go on to a judge's bench in Fiji, came and took what he felt was an exceptionally watertight statement from Gwen. This was very different from the usual 'she said, he said' case, and convictions seemed certain.

I phoned the family to say that if they heard (which they did) that yet another Australian woman had been raped in PNG, it was their mother, who was nevertheless amazingly calm. Days later we learnt that our Adelaide house had been broken into at about the same time, which reminded us that in human terms no place is really safe. The idea of leaving PNG therefore didn't enter our heads.

In Goroka we worshipped at the Swiss Mission, properly called the Evangelical Brotherhood Church of Switzerland, where we had close friends. I often played the organ, and was due to preach two Sundays after Gwen's attack. I'd already decided to deal with the life and times of King Uzziah of Judah, a godly and talented man whose reign was marked by exceptional prosperity, but who crashed spectacularly after power went to his head.

The preacher led the service so I was up front with a view of the door when the premier and his minder marched in and took seats in the second row. I didn't know that he'd been a Swiss Mission man years before, but had gradually dropped out as he ascended the power ladder. This was his only church appearance that oldies present remembered, and like them, I knew it had to be related to his son's arrest. I tried to keep my eyes off him as I described Uzziah's rise and fall, and outlined the lessons to be learnt from his history. I'll never know if the premier thought all this was for his benefit. We didn't see him in church again.

Then came the waiting for the first court case, against the premier's son. While it was being prepared a national government heavyweight phoned the prosecutor, desperate to find a way out for his friend, the Eastern Highlands premier. When told that criminal charges once laid couldn't be withdrawn without the best of reasons the politician tried another tack. 'These people are supposed to be Christians, aren't they? Haven't they heard of forgiveness?'

The prosecutor told us this, and named his caller. He had no good reason to do so, and I'll never know if it was a trial balloon to see if we were afraid to go to court. I said we had to respond to this new challenge, and happily he knew his Bible well enough for us to be able to discuss the nature of forgiveness intelligently. We agreed that we were dealing with more than a crime against Gwen, dreadful though that was. It was a violation of womankind in general, and through them a crime against the state. She might choose to forgive on her own behalf, but in a society where rape was epidemic but rarely punished she had no right to forgive on behalf of others. Moreover, people all over PNG knew that the premier's son was the leader of the pack, so aborting proceedings could only be interpreted as vivid and irrefutable confirmation of the widespread belief that there was one law for big men and another for the rest. The case had to go ahead.

So it came to trial. The premier's son, via a good lawyer, pleaded not guilty. He was led into court grinning at his assembled friends and relatives and sat in the dock with his shiny shaven head held high, like a champion prizefighter facing off the fools who thought he'd met his match. Perhaps he believed to the last that his father's position protected him, or that the Simbu's evidence wouldn't stack up. This lad was a convincing witness, and had recognised the premier's son despite the gloom because he'd invited him to join them. The prisoner's big mouth was well known about town, and he lost confidence during the Simbu's evidence.

Gwen was taken through her statement: name, age, occupation, address, and answered clearly, with rare equanimity. As her detailed description of the night's events came out the prisoner crumpled. He didn't change his plea but his body language was unmistakable. His lawyer felt obliged to ask a few questions but knew he could do nothing useful for his client, who got the statutory twelve years with hard labour.

A few weeks later the other three were tried together, which meant another trip to court for us. One man wanted to apologise to Gwen, and wasn't dissuaded when the prosecutor told him that this wouldn't protect him from conviction or sentence. He was brought to us just before the hearing, and seemed genuinely contrite. Gwen told him she forgave him. It is instructive, and says something about the sophists who thought we were splitting hairs in distinguishing between her right to forgive the crime against her, but not against the community, that this unlettered lad had no difficulty in understanding it. Another defendant tried to exculpate himself by insisting that he'd stayed at the house but saw what the others did. The court visited the scene, which anyone with half an eye could see was invisible from our house. All three then pleaded guilty, which spared Gwen giving evidence again. The only item recovered was the stereo.

We settled down again, thinking that our first home invasion would be the last. Not so. Months later we attended a wedding at

Ukarumpa, the Wycliffe Bible Translators headquarters about 90 minutes' drive away, and spent the night with our friends Mike and Suzie Felz. Mike was the Ukarumpa doctor, and besides our medical dealings we had similar approaches to the Christian life.

Next afternoon we found that *raskols* had stood on a petrol drum and smashed a hole in the fibro-cement wall of our living room. The replacement cutlery appealed, as did the stereo. They lipsticked offensive messages on the walls but must have been disturbed, and ran off, dropping the stereo in long grass well away from the house, intending to recover it later. Another New Guinean found it and savoured his good fortune until I met his boss leaving the hospital as I headed home for lunch. He gave me the standard 'G'day. How are ya?' so I told him. He knew that a stereo had been found, so it came back again

We were out for dinner a few months later when it all happened again, with nothing recovered, although the police caught the burglars. They pleaded guilty so we weren't required to attend court. Six years was now the mandatory minimum sentence for breaking and entering.

Next we had the offer of a dog from friends who were 'going finish', as pidgin has it. Three times was enough, so we took it, and were delighted with its behaviour. We acquired a second in the same way, and found their childish antics amusing and instructive. They were pathetically jealous of each other and had individual foibles, but quickly learnt to recognise our Papua New Guinean friends, who had no trouble with them. Gwen's family had never kept dogs and I'd taken no interest in them on the farm, so we both had much to learn. We wouldn't have believed how much we enjoyed them, which made it a wrench to give them away when we departed, even though they went to good homes. And they went with testimonials that we'd had no more trouble, apart from the back fence being cut a couple of times.

I was working long hours, night and day, in a situation that was becoming ever less congenial. I'd rejected a 1987 suggestion that I apply for re-appointment to the UPNG surgical chair that was to become vacant yet again. One evening I answered the phone to hear the unmistakable voice of Carl Castellino, the Indian surgeon for whom I had provided a reference so long ago. He was acting medical superintendent of the hospital in Burnie, where a surgeon was retiring. Was I interested?

Despite Goroka's frustrations both Gwen and I were ambivalent about leaving New Guinea. We had many friends, both national and foreign, and we knew that elderly transplants sometimes failed. Many ex-PNG public servants relocated to Darwin, and there had been a suggestion from the RAH Neurosurgical Unit, which provided services for the Northern Territory, that they find me a position there, as no local surgeon had much neurosurgical experience. We didn't pursue this suggestion, partly because the highland climate had softened us and we felt that Darwin's heat would be more than we could bear.

Time passed and the expected Burnie advertisement didn't appear, and I was wondering if it was all a mirage when Carl rang offering a surgeon/med super job at Queenstown, a then shrivelling mining community on Tasmania's west coast. I declined. Late in the day the Department offered me another contract, to do neurosurgery only, but we felt it was time to leave. I was only half a neurosurgeon anyway, at best, so didn't consider this offer further.

It was time to go, but what was a surgeon rising 59 years of age to do? In my student days Adelaide had too many surgeons, and the situation was far worse now. We didn't even consider another Third World position. We believed that God would take us to Burnie, but were on the way out of PNG before news of my appointment there came through.

About three weeks before we left PNG two prisoners attended my outpatient clinic. The hospital saw many detainees, as illness was a rare legitimate excuse for an outing. Unsurprisingly, they enjoyed admission to the comparative luxury of our wards, and were reluctant to leave. If the crime justified a warder coming in too he was usually as loath to go as the prisoners were.

The first of the pair at my clinic wore the usual gaolbird's surly expression, but the other's appearance was comparatively beatific. He began by telling me in excellent English that he wanted to apologise for what he'd done to my wife and me. I didn't recognise him, and the hair went up on the back of my neck.

'How long are you in for?' I asked, swallowing hard.

'Six years.'

He said he'd become a Christian while in gaol, as a result of visits by local members of Prison Fellowship International, the organisation founded by Charles Colson, Nixon's special counsel during the Watergate affair, who became a Christian while in prison. A short conversation convinced me that he'd been genuinely converted. I took his hand and with moist eyes said I accepted his apology. He came in for removal of a torn knee cartilage, and was an exemplary patient.

I thanked God that however unpleasant and frightening it can be for those whose houses are invaded, or worse, He can bring good out of such things. Meeting this prisoner helped ease my sadness at leaving Goroka.

Chapter 15

Travels and travellers

Although living in New Guinea meant some isolation from family and the cultural attractions of our homelands, the positive features outweighed these disadvantages, at least for most of the time. While few public servants felt they were making history, most were aware of being part of an exciting developmental phase in a unique and wonderful country. By comparison, life in our native lands seemed humdrum.

If initial impressions were of primitive peoples, only the culturally insensitive could fail to be amazed by the complexity of the social organisation of the communities we served. We soon learnt that 'stone age' didn't mean 'primitive' or 'uncivilised'.

New Guinea's 700-plus languages make it a linguist's happy hunting ground, and it is the biggest field of the Summer Institute of Linguistics (SIL), known also as Wycliffe Bible Translators. SIL members around the globe have achieved prominence in most aspects of linguistics and have been leading contributors to literacy in major as well as in so-called minor languages.

Few of us had even basic appreciation of the languages around us, which meant that real understanding of the underlying culture was impossible. But if we were blinkered in the anthropological sense, anyone with eyes could scarcely fail to wonder at the almost infinite variety of plant, animal and bird life that may be eclipsed in some respects by the jungles of South America or Madagascar, but is otherwise unrivalled. Some of us took a professional interest in these matters. One doctor has a bird named after him, and others contributed substantially to the knowledge of other species, with opportunities that would scarcely have been possible at home.

Quite apart from the breadth of professional experience our jobs provided, those whose work involved travelling sometimes had tasks that would have been unimaginable had we not come to New Guinea. Millionaires might swan around the Pacific in their yachts; we had it better on government trawlers, and were paid for it. For example, there can be few more pleasurable official duties than cruising the Milne Bay islands in fair weather, or sailing a smooth and silver sea under an incandescent full moon. And if a line over the stern failed to bring in the best of fish for dinner, the ship's cook had food in the freezer and served it up on time. Well, not always; I made one cookless trip because he'd taken leave to be married, and when we came to prepare our first meal we found he'd taken the tin opener with him, but we managed.

Many a time I sailed through the D'Entrecasteaux Archipelago in Milne Bay Province, a delight in fine weather, with palm-clad islands ringed by golden sand visible in all directions. Of the three major members of the group the steep, conical Goodenough Island is the most striking, with its summit hidden if the clouds are below 2500 m, as they usually are – at least over Goodenough – even when the sky is otherwise clear.

The main reason for my quarterly Milne Bay trips was to operate at the Ubuya leprosy colony, staffed by the United Church, on an islet barely separated from Normanby Island. Simi, an ex-patient from Madang, was Ubuya's physiotherapist. Sometimes I found other work there too. The province had many blind old people, and as I'd learnt to do cataracts under local anaesthesia I did them at Ubuya; there was virtually no chance of them being treated otherwise.

We enjoyed trips to Ubuya because travel on the Health Department workboat *Hekaha* was comfortable, and deck chairs in the breeze under an awning amidships provided almost first class travel. No matter that our skipper was sometimes the sailor said to know every reef in Milne Bay because he'd been on them all. He didn't do it with me, but his reputation presumably explained his reluctance to sail at night. Often we finished work in the late afternoon, and I always wanted to move on, which he did very carefully. Usually we made for Salamo, the provincial United Church HQ a few hours away on Fergusson Island. As well as schools and workshops Salamo had a busy clinic that always produced patients.

I forget why we had to make one trip from Ubuya to Salamo in a private workboat, chugging up the Dobu Channel in the dark, except for a smoky kerosene lantern barely alight in the cabin. Even this was too much for the skipper who slid back the roof and stood one-legged on the forward hatch, head and torso in the breeze, with his other foot on the wheel. We were in deep water, but floating debris was a risk demanding great care, so he didn't dare sail blind. As we approached the mission jetty he switched on a blinding headlight, lined up the two white markers essential for safely navigating the last couple of hundred metres, and came alongside like the professional he was, despite his almost complete illiteracy.

Salamo staff always enjoyed entertaining visitors, as did most outstation folk. Once I was lodged with the station manager and noticed a Matterhorn wall poster. I made some comment, at which the schoolboy son of the house piped up proudly, 'My dad climbed that mountain.' The manager confirmed this, and was persuaded to describe his experience. The other doctor with us (Laurence Malcolm, by this time a health planning consultant, visiting from New Zealand) then told us with justifiable pride about his own recent successful ascent, but a third visitor trumped them both by telling us he was a collateral descendant of Edward Whymper, who led the first party to climb it, at his eighth attempt, in 1865. (He omitted to mention that this achievement was marred by one of the most famous mountaineering accidents, in which four men fell to their deaths during the descent.) I was the only male present without a Matterhorn story.

After a night at Salamo we sailed to the Catholic Mission health centre on the other side of the island, where again we always found patients. Once I was asked to see a nun from Port Moresby who had been ill. She was a member of the Trapp family, of *Sound of Music* fame. So one never knew whom one might meet in Milne Bay.

Another time I planned to sail directly from Ubuya to Dogura, the Anglican Mission headquarters on the Papuan mainland. We were weighing anchor right on dusk when a canoe slid into the Ubuya channel bearing a man and his child with a nasty elbow fracture that needed reduction. He'd recently eaten, so an anaesthetic couldn't be given for several hours. I suggested taking them aboard, to sail on to Mapamoiwa on Fergusson Island, not too far out of our way, and use the health centre facilities there. The father agreed, as returning on one of the numerous small craft crisscrossing the bay would be easy.

We came alongside at Mapamoiwa patrol post about 11 pm and went to the health centre to arouse the medical assistant. He dispatched a minion to fire up the station's generator, upon which the lights in every house on the little outpost came on. As on many outstations, the laid-back inhabitants of Mapamoiwa rarely bothered to switch off their lights. Life was simple, and when the generator died at 10 pm it was bedtime. This night many residents must have been startled at having their bedrooms alight so unexpectedly. The MA gave a good anaesthetic, I reduced the fracture, and we were away in time to pull into Dogura only a couple of hours late.

More than a century ago Samarai was the hectic centre of a goldmining industry, with many of the islands scattered eastwards turning up fortunes. After the mines were worked out the Eastern District, as it then was, lost much of its importance and most of Samarai's pubs rotted until they collapsed. There was little provision for maintenance of remaining buildings but the tiny island clung doggedly to its fading charm. Charm on its own butters no parsnips, so transfers to the backwater of Samarai or anywhere else in Milne Bay Province were rarely regarded as promotions.

An early Papuan graduate from the Suva medical school was Jack Onno, who married Asenatha, a sunny and highly competent Fijian nurse. Jack was among the first Papua New Guineans to become a provincial medical officer, and on the 'make haste slowly' principle his maiden posting at this exalted level was to Samarai. I asked Asenatha, who was smartening up the hospital and had the place humming as never before, how they liked it.

'I love Samarai,' she almost warbled, which was understandable, because the islet and the whole province had a distinctly Polynesian ambience, redolent of home in a way that Port Moresby could never be. 'But Jack hates it. He thinks Reuben'll keep him here forever.'

Dr Reuben Taureka was a few years Jack's senior, and likewise had brought home a Fijian wife, who became a successful Port Moresby businesswoman. She and Asenatha weren't buddies, to put it mildly, which the Onnos feared would blight Jack's career. Reuben had been in and out of parliament since the late 1950s, and at this time was minister for health.

'Don't worry,' I said, 'Reuben won't be minister forever.' I was right. Soon Jack was an Assistant Secretary for Health while Reuben floundered in the surf thrown up by the ambitious new wave of politicians, and retired to the village in confusion and disillusion. This incident reminded me that some Papua New Guineans were like the rest of us, slow to learn the futility of squandering emotional energy on problems that cooler heads would leave to be solved by the passage of time.

I enjoyed all this boating, but most of my travel was by air. The view from the seat next to the pilot of a MAF Cessna could be breathtaking, as we negotiated the Bena Gap or some other famous feature of the highlands that at first sight amounted to interminable jagged and trackless mountains smothered by jungle. Closer inspection might reveal occasional wisps of smoke slowly curling skywards from scattered hamlets, each no more than a handful of dwellings, either round huts or longhouses, depending on the locality. Sometimes a clearing indicated past or present cultivation but some hamlets seemed to be far from gardens. Many were at 2500 m ASL or more, with the single-file tracks into these isolated settlements entirely hidden in foliage. I marvelled at the physical effort required of those living in such isolation should they wish to visit the neighbours, let alone the nearest trade store. No wonder the highlander is a Mr Atlas by comparison with his coastal cousin, and his stamina legendary.

I admired the navigation skills required in this sort of country and saw why pilots had to be checked in to new routes very thoroughly. MAF was punctilious about this but in some commercial airlines it could be inadequate or absent, regardless of what Department of Civil Aviation regulations might demand. Once I flew from Port Moresby to Balimo in the Western Province with a pilot who had never seen that end of Papua. This was safe enough because there were no mountains to cause problems, the sky was cloudless, if smeared with smoke, and we flew over the eastern edge of the largest swamp in the world. Balimo was the only sizeable settlement in many thousands of square miles, with a commercial-quality airstrip.

Three of the four passengers were making for the leprosy centre at Mapoda, a tiny clearing in the jungle two hours upriver from Balimo by outboard canoe, always an unpleasant journey in the scorching sun. We knew enough to suppress any momentary satisfaction when we realised that our blithe pilot was making a landing approach to Mapoda, which would spare us an Aramia river trip. We'd have landed safely but I doubt that he could have taken off again, even empty, from the short strip that was adequate for Cessnas but would have been an iffy challenge for this particular aircraft. We saved him and his employers expensive embarrassment by persuading him to keep flying for a few more minutes.

One flight out of Aitape was with a teenage pilot in the Catholic Mission's tiny Cessna, the smallest of the breed. We were fully laden, and as this was a rather underpowered aircraft I couldn't refrain from commenting on the cross-wind gusting fiercely and not buffered significantly by the trees lining the strip. The pilot grinned and said, 'Watch.' He charged down the runway, lifted the plane a metre or so off the ground and bounced it hard. The rebound gave us enough altitude for our inevitable sideways lurch to be safe. I don't know if this was approved practice but it seems unlikely.

When I first went to Rabaul the only aircraft available for charter were DC-3s, which were expensive, so government departments used them sparingly. The police occasionally did so, as I discovered when it was my turn to be the doctor performing an on-site autopsy at a copra plantation managed by two Australian couples on the south coast of New Britain. Apparently one man had committed suicide with a rifle but the Rabaul police had picked up scuttlebutt at the New Guinea Club bar and decided that the death warranted proper investigation. Like many small communities, Rabaul hummed with gossip; many expats worked on the related principles that nothing is ever as simple as it seems, and there is no smoke without fire.

The DC-3 dropped the detectives and their unhappy doctor in the drizzle at Jacquinot Bay and returned to Rabaul while we crossed the bay in an open launch to the plantation that had been soaked by more than 250 mm of rain in the 48 hours since the shooting. We inspected the living room, noting the bloodstains on the stock of the high-powered rifle and on the coconut matting, and the bullet hole in the ceiling immediately overhead. Witnesses' stories were laboriously recorded, and then came the task of digging up the makeshift coffin from a grave full of mud, and of regulation depth, which wasn't as easy as it may sound. After a monumental effort we exposed the bloated corpse late on a hot soggy afternoon and, collectively holding our breath, rapidly confirmed the witnesses' statements. It was obvious that the chap had been standing up, had put the rifle in his mouth, and had all but blown his head off. We couldn't see the remotest reason for suspecting murder.

Another charter wasn't on, so we had three days to kill until the regular DC-3 passenger service from Lae to Rabaul could be diverted to pick us up. Fortunately the plantation had a well-equipped lugger at the wharf, ideally situated inside a protective inlet, and although we ate in the house we camped on the boat. The rain settled and the Kodak-blue water became glassy clear again, warm and inviting. One detective, astonished that I was an Australian but couldn't swim, offered to teach me. The situation was ideal, and with much encouragement from both men I eventually began to feel comfortable in the flat-calm lukewarm water.

After returning to Rabaul I found that Trish McCosker, a Nonga doctor's wife, was a licensed instructor. She set out to make me confident in the water off the black-sand Nonga beach, but although she did her best I didn't have it in me to become a good swimmer. Tropical seawater up the nose and in the ears should have felt better than the chilly douches I remembered from childhood holidays, but I can't say that it did, so I spent 20 years on tropical coasts and almost ignored waters that tourists paid big money to enjoy.

Although I have many memories of sailing in weather that was near perfect by any measure, it wasn't always like that. In 1962 another possible murder took a Rabaul police officer and the duty doctor (me again) to a remote plantation on the east coast of New Ireland. Our workboat was smaller than average and even before we left Simpson Harbour the sea was rough, so I was hideously green by the time we entered St George's Channel. Crosscurrents caught us as we rounded the southern tip of New Ireland, and the boat's movements lost all rhyme and reason. It began to heave in all directions, as did my stomach. Having brought up absolutely everything and then some I lay down to rest, but as all who have been thoroughly seasick know, there was no rest. Gwen had packed an apple in my bag, and remembering my mother's use of grated apple as a folk remedy for vomiting I took a few bites in desperation, without success.

We struggled up the east coast with seas that originated somewhere near Panama doing their best to swamp us, and bumped into the wharf cushions late in the afternoon, too late for anything but a lot of questions. Neither the policeman nor I could face dinner, which surprised and upset the plantation manager, a brusque and lonely bachelor who had put his cook-boy to some trouble.

Next morning there was another hurried disinterment and a prompt decision that murder was out of the question. Then back on the boat and out to sea. Our hopes that the waves would be smaller were dashed as soon as we were outside the reef. We made Rabaul dizzy and desiccated after 72 of the slowest hours spent on the most useless goose-chase I remember. That utterly wasted apple was almost my only food in that time.

As well as making journeys like these, often we could sit still and have memorable folk come to us. After Australia's restrictions on entry to the Territory were relaxed we saw streams of visitors. Some were old hands, like the anthropologist Margaret Mead who made her name in Samoa and did it again on Manus, which she visited many times. Her Samoan work may have been debunked now (to the satisfaction of some, at least) but she was the queen bee then. She had the ostentatiously unkempt, uncombed and uncorsetted style of many unconventional women of her generation, looking like a windblown haystack on legs, helped along by a gnarled walking stick, considerably longer than she was, that she'd picked up in the bush somewhere. This unimpressive wand must have had mystical meaning, and travelled the world in her hand. By the end of her time in PNG she was the classical incontrovertible authority, and couldn't hide her astonishment and anger when a university student from Manus jumped up at question time to challenge, with brash and disrespectful heat and vigour, her interpretation of material that she'd just presented in a public lecture. The lady had never been contradicted like this, but times were changing. But she was a gifted speaker to the end, and I remember her pinch-hitting for an absent celebrity she had come to hear, when she was called from the front row of the medical school lecture theatre to deliver a lucid and entertaining discourse on nutrition, straight off the top of her head.

I was visiting Port Moresby in about 1965 when a friend lecturing in education at the university had me to dinner at his house to meet Ivan Illich. I'd never heard of the wild-eyed, barefoot guru with the flowing hair sitting cross-legged on the polished hardwood floor and holding forth magisterially on recondite educational matters. When we were introduced his eyebrows arced and he became even more excited, if that were possible. 'Ah, yes,' he purred with a malignant mixture of menace and glee, 'a member of the second oldest profession.' I felt duty bound to defend myself but soon hit the wall. I still wonder if my friend set me up, because Illich took me as a cue to serve us bullet points from his wide-ranging critique of Western medicine, published years later. Arguing with him was like trying to pick up mercury from the floor, and soon I was happy to let someone else try it.

George Wald, a Nobel laureate for his work on the chemistry of vision, took time out from Harvard to ponder the meaning of life and the nature of things. He chose New Guinea in which to do it, and somehow met Valerie Taylor. He took an immediate liking to her, decided she was working well below her potential, and said that if she wished to change up from nursing to doctoring he would guarantee her entrance to Harvard Medical School. Flattered as she was by this magnificent offer she saw too many imponderables for such a move to be realistic, but his encouragement reignited her intermittent ambition to study medicine at UPNG. She'd been among the minority of foreign residents bold enough to take PNG citizenship during the six-week window after independence, so could attend university at very little cost, and did so. Her nursing experience gave her a head start, and she became an excellent doctor.

David Hamilton, long-time surgeon in Rabaul, says he knew Valerie as a nurse in Madang in the 1960s, a medical student and intern in Port Moresby, a popular and successful Rabaul GP in the '80s, and finally as the medical superintendent of Quilpie Hospital, 1000 kilometres west of Brisbane in the 1990s, when he visited the far west as locum flying surgeon. She flourished in each situation.

In 1986 Sankar Sinha phoned to say that one of America's most distinguished surgical scientists, Dr James C. Thompson, professor of surgery at the University of Texas Medical Branch at Galveston, was visiting PNG as a tourist. The Port Moresby surgeons had enjoyed entertaining the Thompsons, and Sankar asked me to do something for them in Goroka. It was the weekend of the Highlands Show, a unique spectacle alternating between Goroka and Mount Hagen in which anything up to 75,000 warriors gathered from all over in their headdresses and tribal regalia, with drums, shields, spears, bows and arrows and axes. Caparisoned in more bird of paradise plumes than we could have believed existed in all the jungles of New Guinea, and with faces painted white, red, yellow, ochre, blue and black with brilliant natural pigments, they sang, boomed, drummed, danced and stomped in the dust of the showgrounds for hours on end. Camera-toting tourists from all over the world clicked and clicked and clicked. Stone age they might be, but if an outsider needed convincing that the highlanders were richly cultured, seeing this show was enough, or should have been.

With so many visitors in town every hire car in Goroka was booked weeks before, so after their visit to the showgrounds we lent the Thompsons our Suzuki to explore a little of the Highlands Highway before I showed Jim around the hospital. I demonstrated two cases of ruptured spleen, proven by ultrasound, being treated conservatively, which interested him. He was no less impressed by the diminutive night watchman at the front door, a Kukukuku warrior with a quiver full of arrows and a bow almost half as long again as he was. The little man escorted us home in the dark to prove that he was more than just a pretty face.

On his return to Galveston Jim wrote us a gracious letter of thanks, inviting us to call on him should we ever be in the US. The opportunity might have come in 1993, but our schedule was too tight, with a surgical meeting in Hong Kong followed immediately by the International Leprosy Congress in Orlando, Florida. This was the meeting at which WHO repeated its brash claim that leprosy would cease to be a public health problem by the turn of the century, by which they meant that its incidence would fall below one in 10,000. Paul Brand made a brilliant speech at the opening session, in which he gently reminded us that within living memory the same prediction had been made about tuberculosis with the same confidence, and look where we were now. Even if history didn't repeat itself there would still be vast numbers of ex-patients with ongoing deformities requiring skilful individualised management. He argued calmly but passionately for the rights of the individual that were all too often crushed beneath the juggernaut of public health policy. His lifelong concern for the needs of individuals came through as his professional credo, and the applause was deafening. Few who heard him will forget that speech.

After Orlando we had friends to visit in Augusta, Phoenix, Calgary, Winnipeg and Dublin as well as in several cities in the UK and Switzerland. There was no time whatever to allow us to backtrack to Galveston.

Our Augusta friends were the Felz family who had lived at Ukarumpa, the SIL headquarters down the road from Goroka. Mike and his boys were baseball fanatics and a little in awe of this old man who had pitched in the first game played under lights in Australia.

They niggled me until I agreed to give a demonstration, but seemed unable to make allowance for the 40 years' interval since I'd last stood on a pitcher's mound, and couldn't hide their disdain and disappointment when they saw me in action on their makeshift diamond.

The morning Gwen and I left Augusta the family dropped us at the airport before driving on to Atlanta to see the Braves play. Knowing that I'd never seen a big league match they'd begged us to join them, but our onwards bookings made it impossible. 'Next year?' Mike suggested. 'OK,' I replied, a little too easily, but as time went by the idea grew, and seemed justifiable if I combined it with a visit to Jim Thompson. Then I could go on to a UK meeting that I wanted to attend anyway. So I called in Jim's offer, which he promised to make good with embarrassing enthusiasm and generosity. He invited me to talk to his students, and would arrange visits to each of Galveston's special units and meetings with their directors, one of the best known of whom was Dr David Herndon at the Shriners Burns Institute. This personalised opportunity to see something of the workings of one of the most highly regarded surgical departments in North America was too good to miss, and I set about organising my year's program accordingly. Everything fell into place perfectly. The Braves were playing a home game on a certain Saturday in mid-September, and the preceding few days suited Jim Thompson exactly.

I dug out my best New Guinea slides, prepared my lecture, and made my bookings. Then came news of the baseball strike. Gwen planned to stay at home anyway, after being exhausted by the previous year's frenetic around-the-world trip, and suggested that I cancel out. I waved Jim's detailed program at her and said I couldn't bring myself to ask him to postpone all this until the next year. Anyway, there was still time for the baseball players to buckle. As the record shows, they stayed out, but I went to Galveston anyway, where I learnt about legendary Southern hospitality as well as many surgical matters.

Galveston's specialty is seafood. The welcoming dinner at the Thompson residence was but the beginning of the most memorable week's eating of my life. By day I was treated equally well in the hospital where I met a breed of outstanding clinical and technical surgeons with complementary skills in the basic sciences that would have allowed them to pursue careers as academic researchers and never lift a scalpel again, had they so desired. The all-round capacity of some of these men and women was breathtaking. For example, the head of colorectal surgery was not just a superb surgeon; he worked on the genetics of colorectal cancer at the molecular level.

My enthusiasm for the minilap cholecystectomy (described in a later chapter) was at its height at this time, and when I met the chief of hepatobiliary surgery, whose unit received referrals from all over southern USA, I told him about it. That morning he had discharged a patient after repairing bile ducts damaged during laparoscopic cholecystectomy elsewhere, so he saw my point. My feelings on the subject were reinforced in Augusta days later when I watched a surgical resident operating laparoscopically under supervision. He battled on and on, and I shivered as he kept poking his cautery in a northwesterly direction in fruitless efforts to control minor but annoying bleeding. I was leaning against the back wall talking quietly with the operating room supervisor, a burly sergeant-major type, when she sighed theatrically and opined, well above a whisper, 'Darktar, what sarm of these people fagairt is that one hour in here carsts as march as a night in the harspital.' Not for me, I told myself yet again.

Jim Thompson had the typical American professor's office, wallpapered with framed membership certificates, awards and photographs of meetings with other surgical stars. He also had what might pass for a framed text for a researcher or anyone else: 'Babe Ruth struck out 1132 times.'

After Galveston I spent the weekend with Mike and Suzie Felz in Augusta. They were most apologetic about the baseball strike, and told me things would be better next year, but I'm yet to see the Braves play.

In 1995 our friends Barry and Robin Hicks, workers with the Sudan Interior Mission (SIM) in Ethiopia many years earlier, were at Soddo, the grotty capital of the densely populated Wolaita province in the south. Barry was surgeon, and the only expatriate, at the government hospital, a stark square two-storey building built long ago by SIM but taken over by the government during the time of the Derg, the communist regime that overthrew Haile Selassie. The hospital served a wide area, and the shortage of medical supplies was only one of Barry's frustrations. Between the lines the Hicks letters suggested that Barry needed to talk out his difficulties with another surgeon, so I offered to spend a month with them.

He met me at the airport in his Land Rover and set off for Soddo with minimum delay. After leaving the rich grasslands surrounding Addis Ababa the narrow crumbling tarmac of the highway to Kenya crossed the Ethiopian slice of the Great Rift Valley, at first densely settled farmland, then thorn-bush country. The dusty road ran south as far as the bustling market town of Shashamane, whose chief claim to fame is that it's the headquarters of Ethiopia's Rastafarian community. AGIP petrol stations and the oily Italian-style fried fish and salad at the Zwai restaurant were reminders of the colonial past. After negotiating Shashamane's frenzy of every-direction pedestrians, bicycles, pony-carts, donkeys and lorries we turned west onto an unsealed road and climbed into the mountainous Wolaita province, with village huts now thatched, and round rather than square. Eight hours out of Addis we pulled into the Hicks' yard, weary and dusty.

Soddo was a typical spreading African town of ramshackle shops and houses, separated by deeply furrowed muddy streets. The rich soil and high rainfall in this region produced enough food in good years, but there was no cushion if the rains failed.

Most of the young doctors at the hospital were impressively indolent, despite being bright enough. The nurse-anaesthetist and the obstetrician downed tools at 5 pm, with neither available for emergencies at night or weekends. Ward nurses were, in general, irresponsible and unreliable, as I saw for myself. New Guinea was never like this, I said.

In Derg times Cubans worked at Soddo but couldn't have been up to the usual high standard of Havana-trained doctors, because perceptive locals called their hospital 'The Slaughterhouse'. After Barry began demonstrating good results his surgical workload ballooned, but in coping with it he was obstructed at every level, largely because most of his Ethiopian colleagues abhorred foreigners. Theatre staff might or might not appear for duty, so planning a day's operating was next to impossible. Nevertheless he managed to do an amazing amount of work, giving his own anaesthetics when necessary. He employed a bright schoolboy and taught him how to mind the anaesthetic machine, which worked well.

Goitres, prostates, hernias, intestinal obstruction, burns and caesarean sections made up most of his work. With extensive thoracic and vascular experience, Barry handled a wide range of cases. Nowadays few general surgeons are competent to replace the oesophagus, as I saw him do for an Eritrean who had mistaken hydrochloric acid for soft drink months before. The resulting stricture didn't respond to dilatation, and we operated on a very thin man, which usually makes things easier. Barry excised the wooden remnant of the oesophagus and replaced it with stomach pulled up into the neck. The only post-operative investigation was a chest X-ray taken because of a fever. We didn't find its cause, and it subsided without treatment. The man was much fatter when he came for review a year later.

In poor countries women deliver at home, which causes many problems all over the Third World, and at Soddo we saw ruptured uteri and vesico-vaginal fistulae (VVFs). Women who labour at home for anything up to a week, and survive, sometimes develop a direct connection between bladder and vagina from prolonged pressure of the baby's head on the party wall between these structures. The result is constant uncontrolled leakage of urine, with the woman becoming an outcast, a smelly burden to herself and her family. Thousands suffer this disaster every year, and most have no alternative but to endure it.

Reg and Catherine Hamlin made Addis Ababa the fistula capital of the world, and all our cases went to the Fistula Hospital. One weekend at Soddo we happened upon a tiny woman in hard and obstructed labour in hospital, with the duty doctor quite unconcerned that she'd had a VVF repaired after her last terrible pregnancy. We took her straight to theatre and delivered her by caesarean section, hoping to avoid a recurrent fistula.

Enthusiasts are struggling against great odds to improve basic maternity services in many countries, but if a doctor, a citizen of the land with the highest VVF profile in the world, apparently neither knows nor cares that vaginal delivery after fistula repair is a recipe for disaster, what hope have mothers living in less enlightened countries?

A hospital worker asked Barry to talk to his father about a vasectomy because he already had thirteen children, and little to feed them on. This delicate matter seemed to be dealt with most easily over a meal, so we were invited to a neat village house for lunch. This consisted largely of injera, to me an unappetising local flat bread with the appearance and consistency of grey tripe, doused with curried vegetables. The meal was rounded off with coffee that I'd been warned about: very strong, very salty, and with lashings of rancid butter on top. As in so many cultures, to refuse was to offend.

The only way to handle this challenge was to hold my breath and attempt complicated mental arithmetic while downing it in one go. The old lady with the kettle saw this and deduced that I liked it, so backtracked and poured me another, right to the brim. In Ethiopia, and in many other countries, you'll be served again and again until you leave something in the cup or on the plate. One lesson was enough, and I'm unlikely to make such an error again.

Chapter 16

Around the world on two rolls of film

When we went to Rabaul in 1961 we were incubating no fanciful plans for the future. We were little more than innocents abroad, and simply saw ourselves as taking the next step on the road we believed God had planned. This is no boast – ambition minus imagination is an oxymoron, and neither of us would claim great imagination. Our temperaments, upbringing and faith in what the Bible says about the peace of God gave us confidence that He knew what was ahead. This meant that we lacked some of the common in-built triggers that otherwise might have challenged our day-at-a-time contentment.

An unexpected advantage of government service was that I could go on leave relaxed and detached, without paying someone to look after things, hopefully as well as I did. In addition, the PHD was sympathetic to officers attending overseas meetings, especially when they paid their own way, as I usually did. When I learnt of surgeons in Asia and Africa who were expert in diseases I was treating, but about which I'd learnt next to nothing during my training, I decided to see them onsite and in action. When leprosy became a special interest I attended the quinquennial international leprosy congresses.

My first professionally important journey was nothing to speak of in the touristy sense, medical or otherwise, but was special for the best of reasons. My initial TPNG contract was for 21 months work followed by three months leave, with fares paid to my home state. Our first leave was due in late 1962, when the RACS was to hold a final fellowship examination in Melbourne. On becoming an English fellow I'd declared that this was the last qualification I would ever seek, but a farsighted surgical visitor to Rabaul set out to convince me that it was sensible to obtain the Australasian qualification too. He argued that this would be useful, if not essential, should I wish to continue working when I returned home. I saw myself in New Guinea for the rest of my working life, and more letters behind my name seemed unimportant, but my visitor was persuasive so eventually I agreed that it might be prudent to join the local College. I'd give it one shot, but no more.

After working in surgical isolation in Rabaul I needed refreshment if I was to have any hope of passing a stiff exam, so I tested the casual offer one of Peter Martin's surgical visitors had made to John Fisher and me. John Loewenthal was professor of surgery at the University of Sydney, and his vascular interest brought him to Chelmsford in 1959. When Peter proudly introduced his Australian crew Prof. Loewenthal issued us a warm 'If ever there's anything I can do …'

He was as good as his word, so *en route* to Melbourne I spent three weeks at the Royal Prince Alfred Hospital where he and his staff did their best to get me up to speed. One junior was Tom Reeve, recently returned from the US with his FACS. He too was due to front up in Melbourne, a requirement that seemed to chafe a little. Tom was to become a world authority on goitre surgery, and a notable president of our College.

Another reluctant examinee was Ken Jamieson, an outstanding neurosurgeon who headed the frantically busy Brisbane unit. He held a Master of Surgery degree, but management insisted that he sit the FRACS. When I brought him a Rabaul nurse with a brain tumour he seemed to regard his forthcoming trip to Melbourne as a great nuisance. Sadly, Ken was to die quite young, dropping dead while mowing his lawn before his daughter's wedding.

I was far from the only FRCS sitting that Australasian Part 2, and recognised several other candidates as well as the two Adelaide examiners on whose list I was. This had to be an administrative bungle, and whether I'd drawn a long or a short straw I didn't know, but I feared the worst. My dismay went up a few notches when my long case was an old man with multiple arterial problems, common enough in Chelmsford but far removed from Rabaul's surgical bill of fare. Somehow I satisfied the examiners, and could now say in complete confidence that this was the last qualification I would ever seek.

We spent the fortnight before Christmas at Cooee, partly because I was to give the address at the Naracoorte High School speech night. I tried to transmit something of the excitement of living and working in New Guinea. The school's proud motto was *Carpe diem*, so I challenged students to do exactly that, and test the proposition that the grass in the next paddock sometimes looks greener for sound reasons.

The school council chairman, a self-made worthy, mouthed a 'thank you' before exerting his right of reply. In essence, he said that while it might be all very well for graduands to consider working in exotic places, even in Adelaide, Naracoorte would always provide satisfying careers for the best students, so please stay here; we need you. (Take that, Clezy.)

In 1966 the Western Pacific Orthopaedic Association held meetings in Hong Kong and Singapore, so I took the opportunity to visit the home of anterior fusion for spinal TB. Harry Fang, an articulate pioneer of this operation, gave cutting-edge presentations on this and other procedures being refined in Hong Kong. A popular lecturer and a classy operator, he performed an almost bloodless anterior fusion on a child. It was a fresh case, and I saw that this was the time to operate, rather than after a year or more of drug treatment as I had sometimes done. Later I was to abandon anterior fusion except in certain specific situations.

I saw Grace Warren in Singapore, on her regular visit to operate at a government leprosy hospital. Although the modern operation for footdrop was pioneered there, few Singapore surgeons touched leprosy patients, and for years Grace did most of it. Some of her methods had been discarded in Karigiri but her work was highly regarded, and she was a morale booster for both staff and inmates.

In 1968 the 9th International Leprosy Congress was in London, and I brought my leave forward to include visits to India and Africa, with Gwen meeting me in London. The cheapest route began with a Port Moresby–Hong Kong flight. I sat between an old lady bubbling with childish excitement on her first flight ever, and a Melbourne trade teacher seconded to the ILO, bound for a briefing in Geneva before his assignment in India. Despite much travel he was terrified of take-off and landing, and as we began rolling he went dumb in mid-sentence, grabbed the armrests, clenched his teeth and screwed his eyes up tight. I've never seen anyone stream sweat and over-breathe like it. When the seatbelt sign went off he relaxed and apologised as profusely as he'd perspired, swearing that his white-knuckling was absolutely uncontrollable. Asked why he did so much flying when he was so terrified by it, he said it paid very well indeed. We had a repeat performance during the descent into Kai Tak.

I visited Hong Kong for two reasons. First, I wanted to see Grace

Warren on her home turf, the Mission to Lepers leprosarium Hay Ling Chau, on an island in the harbour. Second, I wished to visit Dr S.F. Lam, an orthopaedic surgeon who had been a gracious host to Ian Reid, a Port Moresby surgeon. Ian sent packs of the famed Goroka coffee, which I delivered when I tracked Dr Lam down at the Queen Elizabeth Hospital, Kowloon.

SF was busy with private patients so left me with his juniors, who were pleased to show me how much work they did. Their ward full of trauma was enough to keep a well-staffed department busy. They treated tibial fractures by traditional methods, except that at about four weeks they applied a below-knee walking cast (the Sarmiento plaster).

When SF took me for lunch he made a few remarks that introduced me to the Byzantine complexities of medical politics in Hong Kong, which persist to this day. Surgeons are aware of these things and others would be bored by their description. Suffice it to say that it is almost beyond belief that grown men, up to and including world-class professors, can out-do the greatest prima donnas of all time as do the surgical demigods of Hong Kong, where jealousy, bitterness and one-upmanship flourish as nowhere else on earth.

Our lunch ended when SF had to rush off to his children's school. Such was the overcrowding in Hong Kong schools that a child who attended morning classes this year had them in the afternoon next year. I thought New Guinea could do with this system.

Next day I rode out to Hay Ling Chau in the mission launch. As Grace showed me her cases it became obvious that leprosy was more aggressive in Hong Kong than in New Guinea, with skin lesions angrier and more numerous. And rather than provide special footwear she tailored feet with an ulcer history to fit ordinary plimsolls (tennis shoes). Paul Brand was opposed to foot surgery unless it was absolutely necessary, but Chinese wouldn't wear shoes that were visibly different.

Allan Waudby of the Mission to Lepers took me to the airport, where I met Jean Gardiner, an English physio returning from Taipei after visiting Grace's team there. Years later Jean helped me in Indonesia, and again in PNG. We met for the last time in Jerusalem in 1985, when we found ourselves in the same pew at St George's Church. She was preparing patients for Grace's next visit.

I flew to Calcutta with Lufthansa, faintly amused that our pilot was Captain Doctor somebody. At Dum Dum airport the trademark Lufthansa efficiency vanished, with one battered bus making three trips for 70 passengers. Even these were more than expected, and we overwhelmed the immigration section. Most were waved straight past the health office, but then struck a bottleneck while liquor permits were issued to all and sundry. As we drove into the city my forgotten first impressions of India from 1964 came back – the all-pervading smell of cow, the headlights of approaching vehicles flashing on and off right up until the last moment, the ramshackle sweet stalls and other tiny shops dimly lit by kerosene lanterns or naked light bulbs, the screeching transistor radios and the throbbing, threadbare, bony hordes of India's poor.

Next morning I flew to Madras and caught the slow train to Katpadi, the station for Karigiri and Vellore.

> More and more of India is coming back. The streaky, peeling, blistering, fading paint on everything, crows everywhere, the filthiest children on the face of the earth, the ticket scalpers, wanting to guarantee me a seat for five rupees. And the spitting! At least Hong Kong has notices everywhere, trying to discourage it, not that it helps.

I found Karigiri greatly changed in four years, with more wards and other new buildings to allow expansion of research in many areas of pathology, up to and including culture of the leprosy bacillus in mouse footpads, which the Karigiri team had recently achieved, for the first time in India. Surgeon Saku and physician Benty Karat each had large and almost sumptuous offices, his in particular exuding an up-market aura, a jarring departure in a previously strictly utilitarian institution.

The weather was oppressively hot and dry, so a long ward round with Benty was exhausting, despite being of great interest. He showed me several things I'd never seen, some not described in the literature. He had cases of leprous inflammation of muscle tissue, which he'd found was not uncommon, and showed me erythema nodosum on the back of the tongue. He'd observed that about ten per cent of lepromatous leprosy cases had the upper cornea exposed, which he ascribed to leprous involvement of Muller's muscle, a tiny structure that helps elevate the upper lid.

My diary reads:

> The staff is now enormous, and I've never seen such detailed (and complicated) case notes. How long this sort of thing can be justified I don't know. If you can do multiple stool fats, C-reactive protein studies and the like, but have to send to Delhi to get a patient's brother to give him a pint of blood, it seems a curiously unbalanced set-up.

Saku Karat strongly disapproved of itinerant surgery, basing her opinion on poor late results she saw when reviewing cases Bill Lennox had operated on at Vadathorasalur, a couple of hours south of Vellore. This was hard to accept because I knew Bill made sure that the physiotherapy was up to standard; there had to be other explanations for his alleged unsatisfactory outcomes. At Saku's follow-up clinic I found Karigiri cases with imperfect results, which I put down to inadequate supervision of trainee surgeons that I observed for myself. Part of the problem was that Saku was discarding some of Paul's methods, re-inventing the wheel and performing procedures that I knew had been proved to be unreliable. I was dismayed that his pioneer work was being dispensed with so readily, and felt that the Karigiri surgical program was doomed.

But I could only applaud the Karats' great expansion of clinics throughout the Guddyatham *taluk*, where paramedical workers supervised the drug treatment of thousands of cases. We saw 140 review patients the day I went out with the team. Once again I was astonished at the detailed notes, and saw a man with the simplest and most stable type of leprosy who had a 26-page chart, mostly blank. There has been a great research output from the Guddyatham work, and it maintained its reputation as a model control program for many years.

Another visitor, an eminent Copenhagen dermatologist, Professor Lomholt, was keen to visit the Danish hospital in South Arcot, and as I was to visit Ernest Fritschi, now in charge at Vadathorasalur, close to the Danish mission, we went together. As always, the Fritschis were delighted to entertain visitors and Ernest almost exhausted us, showing us a great variety of cases. Because of the heat he operated at night, and we had a couple of sessions from 6 pm to midnight or so. We each operated with the other assisting, and found that we'd each developed subtle modifications of technique since Ernest had been my teacher four years before. As usual, our own way of doing things seemed best.

Ernest was distraught because Karigiri's expansion since the Karats' return was soaking up a disproportionate share of mission money, to the detriment of its other hospitals. I knew the Karats were dissatisfied with what they regarded as an almost derisory level of funding, and also that the Karigiri budget had long been a chronic source of tension between the numerous Mission to Lepers institutions in India. All had unmet needs, and inevitably the annual budgetary attempts to square the circle failed. Benty Karat was one of the brightest people in clinical leprosy, with exceptional laboratory skills as well. As far as the global leprosy effort was concerned it was a great pity that he and Saku voted with their feet and returned to England.

When we returned from Vadathorasalur the Karats were helping to select 120 winners from 3800 applicants for first year places at the Christian Medical College in Vellore. Karigiri was therefore at a standstill, so I visited Dr H. Srinivasan, an innovative orthopaedic surgeon working in professional isolation at the original government leprosarium for Madras state on the outskirts of Chingleput, a city south-east of Vellore. He had few visitors and enjoyed showing me his cases, on some of which he had performed his own modification of Brand procedures. His senior physio was a man whose hands Paul had operated on ten years previously, with perfect results even after that time.

The Srinivasans lived simply and Mrs S apologised that they were strict vegetarians. I didn't mind; most vegetarians are good cooks. She was no exception, and served us a tasty meal. She worked as a doctor and he was rated as a Senior Scientific Officer, but he couldn't afford to go to the London meeting, although several other staff members did, at government expense.

I spent my last night in Vellore with Australians friends Frank and Val Garlick. Frank headed a CMCH surgical unit but saw little justification for being there, and spent half his time trying to keep his staff occupied. For his 23 public and eight private beds he had two other qualified surgeons, a registrar, four second-year trainees and five interns. No wonder he felt superfluous. Later he became a mentor to Christian medical students in India, before going off for a long stint in Nepal. He was the first recipient of the RACS International Medal.

Earlier I mentioned a visit to western India, to the Wanless Hospital, Miraj, but not the circumstances. The nearby Richardson Memorial Leprosy Hospital was another TLM place, managed by

Trixie McKay, the Australian matron at Karigiri early in our time there. She was desperate for someone to operate on about a dozen cases, and as suitable physiotherapy was available I agreed to do them. In addition, I demonstrated the latest method of reconstruction of the nasal deformity peculiar to leprosy, with the Wanless ENT surgeon as assistant, after which we reversed roles.

I told Wanless staff about surgical problems in New Guinea, and attended a gala farewell party for Jim Donaldson, their American orthopaedist, who was also a fine general surgeon. His son Stephen, now a noted fantasy novelist, was still a child.

Next stop Bombay, to revisit Noshir Antia. I was surprised to find him about to abandon his large US-funded research program in burns and leprosy to go to London to work with Sir Peter Medawar on transplantation immunology. He had little previous laboratory experience and seemed quite vague about what he would be doing. For the foremost plastic surgeon in India to give up clinical work in his 40s and plunge into high-powered laboratory research needed explanation. I suspected, perhaps unkindly, that he was looking for an out from India, and this was an honourable way to do it.

Noshir said he believed units shouldn't be built around personalities, and as he'd headed the Tata Department of Plastic Surgery for five years it was time to move on. This seemed facile and unconvincing. He said with great confidence that all the work done in the last 100 years (including Brand's) was nothing compared to the footpad work. (The culture of leprosy bacilli in footpads of mice, achieved in 1960 by Charles Shepard in Atlanta, Georgia, for the first time allowed laboratory testing of antibiotics and many other seminal investigations in leprosy.)

When I left Bombay I still had a worthwhile number of rupees, and couldn't miss the notice at the airport saying that taking Indian currency out of the country was illegal. A single bank stall was open but the teller refused to change them because I couldn't produce the chit from where I'd bought them. I assured him I'd come by them in India, but he was unmoved. Regulations were regulations. There were no shops, no beggars, no way of disposing of the troublesome currency. I fronted up to the departure desk to find I was required to sign a bold-type declaration that I wasn't taking rupees out of the country. I explained my predicament to the clerk, who emitted a tired recitation in Bombay Welsh that it was forbidden to take Indian currency out of India.

'Look here,' I said, waving my grubby banknotes, 'I can't go down the street and spend them; it's too far. This bank won't take them and I'm not tearing them up. What am I to do?'

He leant forward and said, his head going like a metronome, 'Sar, I am telling, it is forbidden to take Indian currency out of the country. Have … you … any … Indian … currency?' At long last the penny dropped, or was it the rupee? I looked him in the eye and said, 'No, sir.'

'Thankyou, sar,' he said as he ticked some box, stamped my card and waved me through.

I flew into Addis Ababa on 28 July. I wrote:

> Africa at last, so different, exciting, and full of extraordinary things … Addis is a contradictory mixture of ultramodern buildings (including the splendid Africa Hall, with its glorious stained-glass window) and slums, with no sewerage, and armed men everywhere … Lovely university buildings, even a music faculty, would you believe it, but only 40 Ethiopian doctors so far. More embassies than anywhere else except Washington DC. The emperor has 8000 bodyguards. Gum-trees everywhere.

David Ward, the physio heading the Karigiri department in our time, met me. He'd been seconded to ALERT (the All-Africa Leprosy Research and Training Centre) by the Mission to Lepers. The institution was housed in an old asylum-type leprosy hospital, and although the main buildings were irretrievably grim the staff housing was excellent, having been built by a well-heeled Swedish charity. I envied the Wards their lovely Scandinavian-finish home.

Like some other institutions with input from multiple bodies, ALERT was somewhat directionless, a situation exacerbated by the management style of its elderly medical director, an otherwise worthy man who grated on his staff. The Ministry of Health had lost its enthusiasm and didn't seem to care if ALERT survived or not. According to David it had been on the point of folding until Paul Brand's recent arrival on a double mission: to steady the ship, and to spend six months training their new surgeon Luther Fisher, a young American orthopaedist.

Stanley Browne, a senior British leprologist, and Paul had been drivers in setting up the place, and felt duty-bound to make sure it was salvaged. Stanley had been a Baptist missionary in the Congo for almost 30 years, and being well aware of the philosophical and practical differences between French and English approaches to the disease, wanted to see 'our' sort of leprosy work properly established in Africa. Specialised training of doctors was important but the main need was for paramedical workers, who could best be trained under African conditions. Addis Ababa aimed to be a centre of leadership in many respects, so apart from its high incidence of leprosy it seemed to offer other advantages.

ALERT was a great idea that wasn't working out in practice, despite having hand-picked, high-quality staff with significant research experience, and a large patient load. David was quite depressed, pining for India.

> He says he doesn't find anything he can like in the Ethiopian people. They're violent, always fighting, corrupt in the extreme, and promiscuous beyond belief. WHO found an 80% VD rate in town and set up a lot of clinics, but when they stopped funding them the government closed them. There was such an outcry from uni students that clinics had to be re-opened, just for them.
>
> Ethiopians are lighter than many other Africans, and see themselves as a race apart. They regard the rest as black men and are so scathing that many students from other countries have packed up and gone home.
>
> July 29. This evening the available male staff (David, Paul, Felton Ross [leprosy physician with huge experience] and Red Fisher) came over to talk about surgical developments in New Guinea. I made the point that surgery has been the draw-card to bring general medical people into leprosy work, and also to make patients more interested in their disease.
>
> PB says the words 'Surgery is a bridge between leprosy and general medicine' ought be written in letters of gold, and was disappointed that the time is not ripe for me to plug this home to various people in Addis who are yet to be persuaded. It may be that they will bring me back from Nairobi in about a fortnight if a meeting can be arranged. Paul wants me to see Bechelli [head of leprosy at WHO headquarters]

in Geneva, who also needs convincing that surgery in leprosy is worthwhile.

Then on to Entebbe, the airport for Kampala, Uganda, where orthopaedic surgeon Ron Huckstep met me in his big Citroen, the model looking like a whale. He had trouble with its radiator, which kept boiling. The only way to handle this was to switch the engine off whenever possible, so we freewheeled downhill at 80 mph with not so much as a seatbelt between us, windows open, and Ron shouting against the wind, 'I hope you're insured.' This on the highway with the worst accident rate per mile in the whole world.

Ron began his medical training as a teenager in a Japanese concentration camp after his capture in Shanghai, where his father was in business. He was fortunate enough to be imprisoned with doctors who taught him anatomy and other subjects. At war's end he fronted up to Cambridge University and asked for admission, which was denied because he hadn't matriculated. Not easily put off, he described his background, and after hearing his story the authorities were so thoroughly gobsmacked that they felt unable to refuse him admission. So he became the first non-matriculant ever admitted to the Cambridge medical course, *ad eundum gradum* from the University of Hard Knocks, or some such.

His resourcefulness didn't end there. Shortly after graduation he was holidaying in Kenya, in Mau Mau times, when a typhoid epidemic broke out in a prison camp, and somehow he was asked to take charge. He agreed, with one proviso: he needed full laboratory and secretarial support. Amazingly, this was forthcoming, and not only did he treat and document 1300 cases, he wrote a MD thesis and a standard monograph on typhoid fever. When I met him he had chapters on this disease in three major textbooks.

Typhoid wasn't yet a problem in New Guinea; my main reason for visiting him was to see his polio work, which had brought him thoroughly deserved renown. At a time when most people in the developing world saw splints as impossibly expensive he was making them cheaply and fitting them to children by the thousand, many of them first requiring tendon-lengthening operations that he devised or standardised.

He begins the day at 5.30, eats almost no breakfast or lunch, currently swims 400 yards a day and is working up to 600. Calls himself a sun-worshipper. He has three offices, two full-time secretaries and a large staff of orthopaedic assistants he has trained himself, plus nurses and voluntary workers of many kinds.

He has established a factory making crutches and calipers, the former out of split wood and 6 inches of broom handle, and the latter from quarter-inch reinforcing rods with clogs on the bottom and a little leather here and there. They cost about a pound sterling. Their caliper bank is huge, and his record is fitting 194 in one day.

His unit's enormous output resulted in part from his innate ability to enthuse others to a point marginally short of worship. I saw what seemed to be scores of staff and volunteers whose sole apparent aim in life was to please Ron Huckstep. He seemed to be extremely disorganised, but his achievements, then and since, belie this totally. As well as the polio work he had a large talipes (clubfoot) clinic that ran like clockwork, and had developed a superb paraplegic unit like no other in the developing world, with self-help being the watchword.

Much Ugandan paraplegia was due to road trauma, which filled the hospital wards. The previous week the wife of the professor of paediatrics had died in a car accident and he had been seriously injured. Violence of every kind was rife, with Uganda said to have the highest murder rate in Africa. Crime was such a problem that the death penalty was being introduced for some categories of theft. It was impossible to insure a car not fitted with a burglar alarm and steering lock.

Despite such disincentives, Kampala was the happy home of a large number of outstanding medical expatriates, with Huckstep amongst the better known. Denis Burkitt was away, but I met other notable people, including a Scotsman, Joe Shepherd, who years later became professor of surgery at the University of Tasmania, where he identified and studied a huge lineage with a rare endocrine disorder that brought him enduring fame in the annals of endocrinology, and until he died in 2002 a trip to Hobart was a must for endocrine surgeons visiting Australia.

All this was far in the future when Joe took me on a ward round with his Kampala students. Although he still did general surgery he majored in paediatrics, with a particular interest in cleft lip and palate, and Hirschsprung's disease, a congenital bowel disorder causing severe and sometimes life-threatening constipation. He published theoretical work on it, and may well have made major contributions to its treatment had he stayed in paediatric surgery.

Joe introduced me to Lindsay Grigg, an Australian cardiac surgeon trained in London under Bill Cleland, another Australian. Lindsay was new to Uganda after three years in Hong Kong, where he said he'd suffered continuous harassment at the hands of G.B. Ong, a great surgeon but also the great-grandfather of all autocrats. He described his Hong Kong time with a curious mixture of humour and bitterness.

Next I visited Imre Loefler, an extroverted German giant, ex-Hungary, who joined the wartime army at fourteen. He worked for years in an upcountry Catholic mission hospital before moving to Kampala, where he was now a senior surgeon of great energy and ability. His ward was half full of fractured femurs, but he also had cutaneous diphtheria (which I've never seen again), a recovering extradural haematoma case that had been comatose without pupillary signs, and numerous urethral strictures, with their cause not apparent at that time.

John Taylor, a surgical registrar, took me home for lunch, and while he worried about an Israeli at the hospital (for whom a neurosurgeon had come from Jerusalem by chartered jet, to do negative burr-holes) his wife took me to the Africa Day do at the university.

> There was a quite good Swahili opera about friendship, and then dancing by students from Kenya, Tanzania and India. Finally the Heartbeat of Africa musicians and dancers came on. The orchestra was dressed in what looked like white nightdresses and brown tapa cloth scarves, and belted out a great rhythm. The dancing was hot stuff too, except that most of the girls were pretty skinny, with the strangest assortment of bust-lines more or less covered by funny little bras made out of yellow net. This lot went to Expo 67 in London (where they were required to wear Maidenform bras), but to my mind they weren't a patch on a Hagen *sing sing*.

I'd hoped to visit Murchison Falls, a popular tourist site, but the planes were booked out, so without seeing anything of the wilds of Uganda I set off for Nairobi to visit Michael Wood. The drive out to Entebbe in an East African Airlines minibus was even more hair-raising than the trip in with Ron Huckstep. We queued while four people each handled our tickets. Baggage seemed to be a problem, and for the first time ever they put my briefcase on the scales and informed me seriously that I was seven kilograms over, so I asked the clerk his name and wrote it down. He then looked inside the briefcase and decided that all was OK. Laurence Malcolm taught me this trick, which he said would overcome almost any difficulties with air travel.

Long after returning to New Guinea I learnt that Michael Wood's letter replying to my enquiry about visiting him had gone down in an air crash, so I arrived in Nairobi unannounced. After finding my way to a cheap Indian hotel I tried contacting him and found that he wasn't even in the country. He was a plastic surgeon and ran the African Medical and Research Foundation, based in Nairobi, which I assumed would mean that he lived there, but I was wrong. He had a farm in northern Tanzania, where he was a citizen, and escaped to the privacy of his property in his own plane whenever possible. His wife was a member of the Buxton family, famous in the missionary annals of Africa.

It was a Friday long weekend, so after making useless phone calls I wandered around by myself, and particularly enjoyed the Nairobi National Park a mere five miles outside the city. Fenced on three sides, it spread out over 30,000 acres and boasted lion, hippo, rhino, zebra, giraffe, antelope of several kinds, jackals and many other animals, all quite used to tourists. Maybe there were elephants too, but I didn't see them.

> Monday evening MW picked me up in his brand new bright red Porsche. We screamed down a wet road at a frightening pace, to dinner with a Mrs Noad, a dainty Englishwoman who looks after him a bit when he is in town. She has an interesting mud house with round rooms, but got up very nicely, and elegantly furnished. The silver was the best and most profuse I have ever seen. This lady runs a school for children of diplomats and the like. She has some connection with Jomo Kenyatta, correcting his written English and so on.

The African Medical and Research Foundation was Wood's baby, for which he was to be knighted. Its main activity was its flying doctor service, different from Australia's in that most people needing surgery were brought to Nairobi, except for eye patients, which they managed in peripheral hospitals. This was possible because the female eye specialist had a pilot's licence. With a series of energetic young American plastic surgeons on hand they did reconstructive work in several Nairobi hospitals, mostly for burns and hyena bites when I was with them. They ran a daily radio help-line for peripheral, mostly mission, hospitals that seemed a very useful consultant service. Years later I met a retired worker from one such outstation, and she described Wood's outfit as their lifeline.

As well as clinical work there was research into Burkitt's lymphoma in association with Dr Henle, a leading Pittsburgh immunologist. I flew with their team to Shirati, on the shore of Lake Victoria in Tanzania, to collect serum from apparently healed Burkitt patients and their relatives. American Mennonites ran a fine hospital at Shirati, with pelvic sepsis and uterine fibroids two of their biggest problems. They delivered 900 babies a year, but even so infertility (secondary to pelvic sepsis) was a common complaint. Their leprosy department was complete with a Vellore-trained physio who made good footwear and a few artificial legs. Bob Cochrane, who first fired Paul Brand's interest in leprosy, had visited recently, and I signed the visitors' book a few lines below him.

Back in Nairobi that evening I'd just sat down to dinner when in walked a high-coloured, beaming Harry Rees, an elderly obstetrician from Port Moresby. I hadn't known that he intended visiting Africa, let alone that we'd be there at the same time. The preternatural pink was sunburn, the result of his successful ascent of Mount Kenya. He had some sort of heart trouble and his doctor had banned reckless activity. Harry worked in African mission hospitals for many years before coming to PNG, with never enough spare time for mountaineering. Now was his great opportunity, and as Nairobi boasted good cardiologists he saw no reason why he shouldn't attempt Mt Kenya. He was on his way home to tell his doctor all about it, and expected a good chewing out.

For me, Rhodesia was next. This came about because I'd corresponded with two well-known stamp collectors there for several years. Most knowledgeable people would agree that the postage stamps of Rhodesia provide one of Africa's richest fields of philatelic interest. Darrell Dale, a retired Bulawayo banker, had a wonderful collection that made him one of the most eminent of many philatelists in Rhodesia. Even now, years after his death, one occasionally sees items at auction with the notation 'ex-Dale' attesting their distinguished provenance.

My other correspondent was John Strong, a Bulawayo surgeon and not too far behind-the-scenes politician, a regular *éminence grise*. He too had a fabulous collection containing exceptional rarities, but had accumulated it in a great hurry, reputedly as a form of portable wealth, and most of the real philatelists regarded him as a gauche and presumptuous Johnny-come-lately. When I told him I planned to visit Africa he suggested that I attend the first Rhodesian International Medical Congress in Bulawayo. He and Darrell would accommodate me for a few days each and show me their treasures. With their country in the international spotlight this offer seemed too good to refuse.

Ian Smith's white minority Rhodesia Front government had made a unilateral declaration of independence on 11 November 1965 rather than give up their version of apartheid, benign by South African standards perhaps, but apartheid nonetheless. Sanctions were imposed, not entirely successfully, the porous border with Portuguese East being one well-known leak. Even so, much of the surprising economic resilience of the rebel regime was due to rapid and diverse development of import substitution industries, with successful production of advanced pharmaceuticals, for example. Comparable achievements right across the board meant that the government felt able to thumb its nose at the rest of the world, and it delighted in doing so.

But the publicity machine worked overtime, and this excellent medical meeting was one more example of it. The call of the wild drew an astonishing array of talent and the Rhodesians went out of their way to entertain and amuse. One plenary session was on organ transplantation, at first sight a rather highfalutin' subject for a meeting in the middle of Africa in 1968, but after Christiaan Barnard's recent heart transplants in Cape Town transplantation in general was suddenly a hot topic.

On what might be called Transplant Day, Richard Lillehei, an American pioneer of pancreatic transplantation for diabetes, gave a fascinating account of his unique experience. Roy Calne, a world authority on kidney grafting in his early 30s, and now Europe's trailblazer in liver transplantation, gave a similarly polished and riveting account of promising liver work being done in his department at Cambridge.

Then Barnard came on. Tall, brisk, Hollywood-handsome, with one boyish tuft standing away from his otherwise neatly parted black hair, he presented his material very well. He made a lovely crack about the change in the atrial incision in his second case. 'This is now called the Cooley technique.' [Cooley was a protégé of Michael DeBakey, and stories of the relationship between these two legendary egomaniacal heart surgeons are classic accounts of flint on flint.] He got a great ovation from the packed hall, and then Charles Rob moderated a brilliant display of wit and wisdom from these chaps. Lillehei nearly brought the house down when he said: 'There's one thing about surgeons – we may be wrong, but we're never in doubt.' He drew even louder laughter when he made reference to a society of vascular surgeons whose motto was alleged to be 'Out of blocked arteries much money flows'.

But for once, and only once in my experience, the Bulawayo banquet upstaged the rest of the meeting. Most congress dinners are memorable for being dull in the extreme, and poor value for money, with the first course often the first problem: 'Is this meant to be hot soup, or cold soup?' I've dined at many such expensive boards, and the gala event at the Grand Hotel in Bulawayo was by far the most outstanding, the proverbial quantum leap ahead of any other. The food was superb, but that was but the beginning.

The MC was Stan Kaplan, a Bulawayo physician. In welcoming the overseas guests he told of his trip to Edinburgh to sit their Royal College of Physicians finals, at which an examiner tried to be clever. 'So you're from Africa? Dr Livingstone, I presume?' Dr Kaplan flashed back, 'No, sir. Stanley.'

Prime Minister Smith was guest speaker, and John Strong managed to have us seated just below the top table. Christiaan Barnard was opposite me with Mary Strong on his left, obliquely opposite John. To my left was a Bulawayo anaesthetist (another stamp collector) who confided late in the evening that Barnard was so difficult in theatre that anaesthetists detested working for him. (He had many detractors; I heard another topdrawer South African speak snootily of 'the Barnard epiphenomenon'.) To my right sat Dr Louise Westwater, a public health official who worked in Port Moresby many years later.

> Barnard was very tired after his trip to Australia and Bangkok, and also because he was dancing at the Stork Club until all hours this morning. He wore a superbly cut dinner jacket and a white polo neck shirt, apparently the latest style. No bow tie necessary. This drew a remark from Sydney Gellis [American paediatrician and writer] to the effect that with all the ties given out this week, it was a shame nobody thought to give him one.
>
> Barnard told a marvellous story about a spectator who identified him at a bullfight in Lisbon. When he crawled out from under the avalanche of photographers that had immediately descended on him from nowhere, one of them remembered what Mother had taught him and said, 'Thank you, Dr DeBakey.' This came out when I asked him if DeBakey was going his own way [in respect of heart transplantation] and he said he was.
>
> He and John talked about Persian carpets. The Shah gave him a beauty, and he has a couple of others he seems very proud of. I asked him if Darcy Sutherland [outstanding Australian heart surgeon, from Adelaide] would be doing the first heart transplant in Australia, and he said he didn't think so. [Correct.] He also talked about where he would go if he had to leave RSA. He says Italy, as he likes the people so much.

> The toast problem was overcome by having 'The loyal toast' and then 'The land we live in.' (Loyal though they wished to be to her person, white Rhodesians felt unable to toast Elizabeth as Queen of England.) Ian Smith made a speech that began with plenty of firm Rhodesian stuff. Then he told jokes, three about testicles, each worse than the last, followed by a fourth about Kenneth Kaunda's, mixing racism and gross obscenity. Much of the house was convulsed with laughter, but many guests were appalled by his lack of taste. When he asked the lady beside him how she thought he was going, she said, 'Sir, I think you'd better stop.' So he wound up pretty quickly.
>
> I thought Sir Derrick Dunlop (retired professor of medicine, Edinburgh) would have a stroke, and many others at the top table and elsewhere were visibly dismayed at Smith's performance. Poor Mary Strong, well-bred convent-educated girl that she was, idolised him, and looked as if somebody had thrashed her. John was most incensed. He left the table and spoke to Dunlop, trying to smooth it over, and then

went away to decide what had to be done. He spoke sharply to Smith's private secretary, which no doubt got back to him, because at the end of the program he made an impromptu and all too obvious stab at a face-saving speech, this time from the cabaret dais, on his way out. After some more of the same Rhodesia Front verbiage he'd dished out earlier in the evening he made appreciative remarks about the fine flow of English from Sir Derrick, who'd replied to the toast to the guests.

At 1 am the final surprise came when newsboys brought in the *Bulawayo Chronicle* with a dummy front page about the congress and the banquet. They had photographed several tables at about 8.30, including ours, this to please John, I guess. I suppose I will never again have my picture taken at the dinner table and see it in the newspaper before the meal is over.

We then went home and commiserated. I told John I thought it would be a nine days' wonder, if that, but he felt that Smith's crudity had given the office of prime minister a body blow, which was something Rhodesia's image could ill afford. And it was ammunition for the opposition, who'd said repeatedly that Smith was a boor, unfit to run the country. Assurances from Illingworth [author of a British paediatric textbook] that the PM's jokes were only what were to be expected at a medical dinner didn't help. A week ago John was dreaming of cabinet rank; now he says he is finished with politics. [Not likely; after the next election he was Senator Strong.] He hardly slept, nor did I – there wasn't much time for it between 3 am and the appearance of a uniformed servant at my door at 6.20 with tea and biscuits on a silver tray, as he does every morning. At least he didn't ask yet again if he could run my bath.

In between meetings I found that my philatelic friends possessed surprisingly large quantities of the rare trial printings of the new Rhodesian stamps produced by Mardons, a Salisbury printing company, who experimented extensively with both paper and gum before settling on specifications for the first definitive issue. John and Darrell were prepared to sell or exchange some of their precious duplicates, and this was the foundation for my specialised collection of this interesting period in Mardons' evolving experience in stamp production.

I also learnt that John had been a medical officer on the *Penola*,

John Rymill's Antarctic exploration vessel. He was interested to learn that I was born a mere 30 miles from the Rymill property near Penola.

Nobody visiting this part of the world should miss the Victoria Falls, and few of us did. I joined a post-congress tour of Wankie Game Park, memorable for great herds of elephant as well as other animals that I'd seen outside Nairobi. After Wankie we went to the stately but somewhat run-down Victoria Falls Hotel, and were up early for a launch trip on the Zambezi, where we came upon a large school of hippos gambolling in the shallows.

> After lunch we had a trip to a model Matebele village, where they gave us a description (which I didn't follow) of the three-wife system they have here. Then we went to the falls, a truly magnificent sight, much better at ground level than from the air. (I took a 15-minute flip at lunchtime, which gave a fine panoramic but foreshortened view.) Twice as long, and twice as high as Niagara, with the depths of the gorge out of sight. The roar isn't quite deafening, and the half-mile or so walk (raincoats provided!) along the lip of the opposite side of the gorge, in and out of clouds of spray, is unforgettable. No wonder the locals told Livingstone the falls' name was 'The smoke that roars'. Seventy-five million gallons a minute is almost beyond comprehension. Right now it is below full flood, which occurs in May and June, when the cloud of spray is so thick that it conceals the waterfall.
>
> Then we were taken to see David Livingstone's statue, a larger-than-life bronze dwarfed by a gnarled baobab tree that must have stood here long before Livingstone. The sculptor has caught the intense, searching gaze of the explorer–missionary most realistically. I wonder how long this memorial will survive the changes happening to this country?

On returning to the hotel I flopped into a cane chair on the tiled patio overlooking the bridge and the never-ending cloud from the falls thundering away in the distance. I noticed Sir Derrick Dunlop sitting alone, so I joined him, saying that I remembered the lecture on heart failure that he gave in Adelaide almost 20 years previously. I knew he had left the chair some years before, and suggested that he must have retired young, which he had. He said he'd seen too many men hang around their departments long after they should have gone, expecting to be treated as oracles. He had decided to retire before he became pontifical. I said that in Australia we had a great and elderly medical scientist with an opinion on every subject under the sun, who was always ready to give voice on any of them, in and out of season.

'And who might that be?' he asked.

'Sir Macfarlane Burnet.'

'You couldn't give a better example of what I mean,' he chortled. 'The last time I saw Mac Burnet he spent a solid hour telling me how medical students should be taught. When he went to the Walter and Eliza [one of the world's great medical research centres, the Walter and Eliza Hall Institute in Melbourne] he made sure he had nothing whatever to do with medical students. I've taught them all my life, but he felt able to lecture me on how to do it. Yes, an oracle alright.'

We then got talking about a certain distinguished conference speaker, and DD said that on the Wankie tour he'd shown himself incredibly ignorant about everything but his own line of work. He asked childishly ingenuous questions about animals, and when told that African elephants were dangerous, and would kill you, he asked, 'Would they eat you?' Sir Derrick assured me that the great man was perfectly serious.

He and I then dined together (wonderful steak, followed by peach flambé again) and the talk turned to New Guinea and why I had gone there. He wanted to know if I was still a Christian, and said that although he regarded Christ as the greatest man who ever lived, he couldn't believe. We had some talk about prayer and guidance, and it was quite clear that he knows all about these things in theory – as any educated man of his day did.

He made withering comments about various government leaders he has met here (the health minister is fifth-rate) but has been fascinated by the congress, and agrees that the session on transplantation could properly be described as historic. He is under the spell of Barnard, but remarked that fame of this type is heady wine for a young man.

After a final relaxed day with my Bulawayo hosts I flew to Johannesburg for the night and then on to Lagos with Panam.

We put down at Kinshasa, supposedly for 35 minutes, but it was an hour and a half before we took off again. This is a hot, dry, flat, smoky place, and we were shepherded into a stuffy upstairs room with armed guards at the door. RSA passport holders weren't allowed off the plane.

Just after we landed an Air Congo plane came in, and the ground staff boxed our luggage with theirs, which explained the long delay. When finally we were aboard I sat with an American, and had to move over for a Congolese to sit between us. The incensed Yank muttered that he hoped the chap had bathed in the last 6 weeks. Being a French speaker the Congolese seemed not to follow this, although the tone of voice must have said it all. The stewardess said we could sit somewhere else if we liked, and apologised for putting a black man alongside us. (Foreign relations, Panam version, 1968.)

I visited Nigeria to see John Lawson, a gregarious English professor of obstetrics and gynaecology at Ibadan, and the senior author of a long-lasting textbook written from a tropical perspective. Amongst other things, he was known for his large experience of vesico-vaginal fistulae and had developed technical refinements of the operation to repair them. John spoke at the 1967 symposium of the Papua and New Guinea Medical Society, reporting on his research on malaria in pregnancy, and gave a general invitation to any of us visiting Africa to call on him in Ibadan.

I arrived in the middle of the butchery that was the Biafran War, essentially a southern Nigerian struggle between the majority laid-back Yoruba and the minority Ibo. The Ibo had a strong work ethic and occupied what most Yoruba regarded as a dangerously disproportionate share of key posts in both public and private sectors, and they were now paying for it. A million Ibo died, but as in most civil wars, the whole country paid for it and is still doing so, generations later.

Surprisingly, our plane was allowed into Lagos after the curfew. The city was in total darkness, the government having found that throwing the main switches was the only way to enforce a blackout. By the time we'd been frisked and our luggage searched it was 7 pm. (They were very thorough, and discovered my hernia.) The curfew was strict, and rather than attempt to find a more salubrious place for the night I was advised to put up at the airport hotel, a seedy establishment where I ate a doubtful dinner. Then there was nothing to do but go to bed by the light of what remained of a candle, lit with matches that they sold me for sixpence, which I thought was a bit steep.

There was more frisking and luggage searching next morning before we boarded the Ibadan flight. John Lawson's secretary met me, and as John was up to his ears in the clinic he handed me over to Victor Ngu, the first Nigerian professor of surgery, and a former trainee of Peter Martin's at the Hammersmith, an experience he remembered favourably. He showed me around the surgical wards, crammed with the military casualties that clogged the hospital. I saw an amazing number of gunshot wounds to the head with little damage, and such things as through-and-through injuries of the neck, many with hopeless brachial plexus injuries. There were no Ibo among them.

The war was fought far from the capital but it affected everyone. Next morning I met J.O. Oluwasanmi, who'd been an intern in Chelmsford in my time. He was Ibadan's only plastic surgeon, and showed me many maxillo-facial injuries from the war that occupied most of his time. Then he took me to Professor Odeku, a US-trained neurosurgeon of great renown and prodigious energy who, amongst other things, was dean of the medical school. I'd already learnt that the East African was laid-back by comparison with the West African, of whom Dr Odeku was perhaps an extreme example. He was the only neurosurgeon between Salisbury and Dakar.

Next I visited the orthopaedic department, swamped by war casualties, a situation that may have been partly responsible for their conservative attitude to spinal TB, on which they rarely operated. When I asked about their management of polio deformities they said this was all very difficult, with splints costing hundreds of pounds. I began to describe what I'd seen in Uganda, which brought the languid response, 'Huckstep? Yes, we've heard of him.' Next subject.

This was a vivid demonstration of the fact that the spread of a new idea may be impossible without fire in the belly. Sadly, there was none of the right sort in the orthopaedic people I met in Ibadan. Years later Ron made a world tour promoting his methods, sponsored by the Commonwealth Fund, but as far as I know the only place it really caught on was in Honiara in the Solomon Islands. The protectorate's enterprising Irish surgeon, Tony Cross, became an enthusiast and quickly attracted the nucleus of workers that had made the Uganda work possible. They did excellent Huckstep-type work for years, until a hormone-powered disaster came out of left field and all but destroyed the team. The next blow was Tony's retirement, with the program almost dying when he departed. Nigeria could have used him.

John Lawson's wife was in England, as many Ibadan wives were, so on Sunday he took me to Ilesha Hospital, a Wesley Guild institution 75 miles out. We picked up a hitchhiking soldier and a uniformed policeman, which he liked to do for protection in an increasingly lawless society. We drove through thick bush, even denser than that around Madang, and I noticed that Nigerians didn't prune their cocoa as was usual in New Guinea, so that their plantations looked ugly and straggly.

'You'll meet David Frost's sister today,' John said with what sounded like pride. He almost ran us off the road when I asked who David Frost was. The sister was the wife of Andrew Pearson, an ex-China Inland Mission doctor and now medical superintendent of Ilesha. The Pearsons enjoyed entertaining the Lawsons, and during afternoon tea they and John chewed over the war from the expatriate perspective.

Many years later a doctor from Nigeria visited PNG to promote continuing medical education for GPs. I happened to be in Port Moresby staying with Iain and Riita-Liisa Aitken when the visitor and his wife came to tea. I said I'd been to Nigeria long ago, visiting John Lawson. Did they perhaps know him?

'Oh yes, we know John well,' beamed the lady. I went on to say that one Sunday he had taken me out to a mission hospital where I met David Frost's sister. I was halfway into this sentence when the lady's buckteeth seemed suddenly familiar. 'It was you, wasn't it?' It was.

Years later I was seated next to a Chinese doctor at a dinner in Tasmania and learnt that she'd worked in an African mission hospital, which turned out to be Ilesha. She told me about her pre-service interview with the Pearsons, who were on leave in London. They invited her to meet them at an address that the Monopoly board told her was in a posh area, and as she approached the grand residence it seemed an increasingly unlikely meeting place for missionaries. It was Frost's house, which he lent to his sister and her husband whenever they went home.

When leaving Nigeria I struck the same problem that marked my departure from India. With a local five-pound note (worth over seven sterling) in my pocket I gazed at the notice, in letters a foot high, threatening dire penalties for travellers caught taking Nigerian currency out. There was no airport bank, and shops were far away. There were enough soldiers about to repel an invasion, as well as hordes of other uniformed officials, eyes everywhere, so I was disinclined to do anything rash. Without doubt, the Bombay shadow play wasn't an option.

Close by I spied a group of memsahibs, clearly a gaggle of prosperous company wives merrily farewelling one of their friends who was off to England on leave. I approached them and explained my problem. I still maintained a cheque account in London, so I asked if anyone would take my Nigerian money and pay into my account whatever she regarded as the sterling equivalent. They were familiar with this dodge and several would have happily done the needful. I handed over my fiver and my banking details, and left the country pleased with my resourcefulness.

But nothing happened. Bank statement after bank statement showed no credits not otherwise explicable. When travellers' tales came up at dinner parties I told the story of the five-pound note that disappeared into the purse of a refined Englishwoman at the Lagos airport, and raised a laugh every time. Then, nine years later, six pounds odd was paid into my London account, with my copy of the pay-in slip giving a lady's name and address. This had to be my long-lost fiver, so I composed a light-hearted thank-you note saying that for years I'd been telling a tale about the charming lady with the honest face who'd so sweetly agreed to pinch-hit as a moneychanger in Lagos. I was still trying to work out whether she'd now ruined my story, or improved it. She felt no compulsion to reply, so I'll never know if she could cope with my sense of humour.

One reason for my African journey was to visit French leprosy work in Mali, but I still had no visa. I was to overnight in Abidjan in the Ivory Coast, and had been assured in Lagos that this would give me enough time to get it. Abidjan was a paradoxical mixture of the ecstatically ultramodern cheek by jowl with age-old traditional mud and daub, spread out on a steamy delta, with water in every direction. The airline put me up at the dowdy Hotel du Parc, a fading and almost empty French relic cumbering the ground in a good location. Glitzy shops were across the road, but I wondered how anyone could afford to patronise them. There were few tourists, so some Abidjan residents had to have money. After a little searching I found a smart but, by local standards, not too expensive restaurant, and ate well.

Still reeling from French coffee, I made my way into the street and was accosted by a sad young African who pulled a curling paperback *L'anglais vivant* from his pocket and asked me to help him with his translation. It was awful stuff, French crudely transliterated into English, and he won't get far with it – such things as 'Turn into the passive: The boy listened to the noise.' I had to say I couldn't help him.

Next morning I found the Malian Embassy and managed to energise the pair of clerks lolling under a sluggish fan, smoking vile cigarettes, into issuing a visa in about two hours. This was a task that promised to stretch them, judging from the way they blinked. While it was being done I wandered down a wide boulevard and happened upon a City Hall reception for the president of Ghana. Sweat-shiny Ivorian drummers throbbed loudly on the lawn, watched by hordes of local elite attired in light linen and dark glasses. The Ghanaian and other dignitaries applauded politely and rushed off to their next appointment. Police sirens wailed as the cavalcade of black Mercedes and their outriders sped off, with the VIPs last, in a 600-series.

At the airport I met Peace Corps people from Sierra Leone who were at the Hotel d'Ivoire last night, where they were treated contemptuously. The girl was the only one with any French, and out of curiosity asked the African on the desk how old the hotel was. He snapped that he hated curiosity and hated Americans. This was as ridiculous as could be, the Hotel d'Ivoire being in the US-owned Intercontinental chain.

I flew to Bamako in a creaking Ilyushin 4-engined turboprop owned by Air Mali's bankers. Dr Pierre Giraudeaux met me and guided me through customs without a hitch, which I gathered was some achievement. We drove several kilometres out of town in his crinkled baby Renault to the Institut Marchoux, a sprawling complex of cavernous two-storey buildings that had housed the regional tropical medicine centre when the French expected to rule their slice of Africa forever. Now its principal activity was leprosy research and treatment. Living on site were 350 patients, some under active treatment in wards, but most in cottages for the outcast, homeless and hopeless. Amongst them I saw my first Tuareg, a young woman with the trademark blue facial tattoo.

Pierre had even less English than I did French. His favourite phrase was 'Quite terrible'. His wife was in France recovering from a road accident, and he was no cook, so we existed largely on greasy green salad and watery red *vin ordinaire*. We got on well, and he showed me many interesting patients and the elaborate documentation dealing with their experiments with long-acting sulphonamides for leprosy. The French had something akin to xenophobic distrust of dapsone, the drug used almost universally elsewhere, and which had been introduced into clinical practice by a team led by Bob Cochrane that had included Doug Russell, long before he came to New Guinea.

Another French idiosyncrasy was their belief that many paralysed leprous nerves could be revived, partly or completely, by dissecting scar tissue away from them. I wanted to see patients with plantar ulcers that the Marchoux team claimed to cure by decompressing the major nerve supplying sole skin. Paul Brand and everyone else I knew found this incredible, and I hoped to see cases and their records, as well as actual operations. I found their post-operative cases unconvincing, largely because their sensory maps and muscle-strength records weren't detailed enough for proper before-and-after assessment to be possible. I saw demonstration operations, which in cases of plantar ulcer involved very extensive decompression of nerve and artery that I've never seen elsewhere. Such procedures were likely to keep patients off their feet for long enough to allow some ulcers to heal, at least temporarily, whether or not nerve function improved. Despite these so-called curative operations, each morning a long line of patients waited for dressings at the ulcer clinic. Many had made themselves simple sandals out of discarded car tyres, but there appeared to be no emphasis on the importance of footwear, and it didn't seem to matter to the staff whether sandals were worn or not.

Pierre suggested that I pay my respects to the minister for health, and drove me to a stately building on a rise on the edge of Bamako, which was as flat as a billiard table otherwise. This elegant edifice had been the admin headquarters in colonial times, and now housed key members of the government. The minister for health was away so I met the prime minister instead. He was a quiet young pharmacist sitting at an almost bare desk in an enormous and equally bare and musty room with five-metre ceilings. What must have been the original heavy Second Empire curtains were drawn, so that after coming in from the blinding sun it took us a while to see the PM in the gloom.

With a dusty half-dead potted palm and a rusty, clattering electric fan for company, his secretary plugged away on her noisy old typewriter at a metal desk in the wide corridor outside.

The PM wore a shabby brown-check safari suit with cigarette burns on one lapel darned none too successfully. He spoke little English, so such conversation as there was took place between him and Pierre. I left with the impression that seeing a visitor from the other side of the world had made his day. He didn't last long – a military coup dealt with him a few months later.

Pierre said Mali was dirt-poor, essentially a low-grade slab of Sahara. From the air the best of it looked to be one-thorn-bush-to-the-acre country, but it must have had strategic significance to the French, who opened the Dakar–Bamako railroad in 1905. The unprepossessing Bamako CBD amounted to no more than a clump of dilapidated colonial buildings, smart enough in their day perhaps, but secondhand-looking now, after enduring a century of sandblasting by winds howling across the desert that stretched away to infinity in all directions. Cheap market stalls surrounded the CBD, but with little of the colour that I'd seen elsewhere. Close by, with a fine view of the Niger (the sluggish and precarious lifeline of the country), a tall hotel was going up very slowly, hopefully in time for the Pan–African Games.

A little further out were a surprisingly large number of embassies, representing countries that rushed in with assistance when Mali gained independence. The USA had aimed to replace France as the dominant power, but lost interest when it became clear that communist countries were much preferred. Russia, China, North Korea and North Vietnam were there in strength, doing their bit to introduce what would one day be called appropriate technology. We visited the Mali Ceramique factory, donated by North Korea, where I bought a couple of Tombouctou bowls, rather crude work but nevertheless genuine souvenirs of the fabled city that I'd have visited had there been the time.

From the beginning Mali tried to punch above its weight, perhaps fired by subliminal communal consciousness of the glory days of its distant past when its kings were rich and influential. When Russian tanks rolled into Prague the only African applause was from Bamako, and when white-governed Rhodesia rebelled, and the Organisation of African Unity decided that member countries should break diplomatic ties with England, only Mali did so. They soon discovered, although I wondered how and why, that having no British consular services in Bamako was most inconvenient.

The permit essential for photography was unobtainable in the time available, so I left Mali with no visual record of my visit. I was glad to go because London was next stop, where Gwen met me for the leprosy meeting. This was the one great occasion when most of the household names in the leprosy world were seen in one place at one time, like a rare planetary conjunction. I found that this world sustained an extraordinary number of tall poppies with a brittleness of personality quite out of keeping with their eminence.

This was my first experience of a multilingual conference, with proceedings in English, French, Spanish and Portuguese. Perhaps I shouldn't have been astonished that translators sometimes stumbled, especially at question time or when an inconsiderate lecturer departed from the script that he'd passed in well before his presentation. A Brazilian delegate jumped up to berate a huffy English pathologist who was so far ahead of the Portuguese translator that she gave up. This provoked a shrill and undignified three-cornered barney, from which there could be only one winner, the pathologist, with the tearful translator in her glassed-in cubby a bad last.

This congress was notable for two reasons. It was the first at which much preliminary work was presented on clinical experience with the new drugs that were to revolutionise the treatment of leprosy. And it was the first at which most major papers were by laboratory-based scientists rather than by those who were primarily leprosy doctors. These trends could only continue, and 40 years after London the International Leprosy Association still struggled to come to terms with the new realities; on the one hand there was (and is) the geometrically progressive profusion of increasingly recondite pure science, on the other the burgeoning numerical and practical prominence of paramedical fieldworkers. To this latter group any talk of the relevance of nonsense DNA in the leprosy genome and all similar esotery is double-distilled nonsense, and always will be. A single conference cannot satisfy the needs of such disparate groups of participants.

The surgical sessions were an important feature, but with my Karigiri training only four years behind me I heard little that was new. But it was of lasting pleasure to meet people I knew by name only, as well as old friends. We sat with some at the banquet, most memorably with Paul and Margaret Brand. This meal was at the Savoy Hotel in a vast room apparently designed with the Hall of Mirrors in mind. I first met croquette potatoes at the Savoy, and it was the first time I saw the after-dinner speaker announced by a character from a Punch and Judy show bellowing, 'Oyez! Oyez! My lords, ladies and gentlemen …'

Then on to Geneva. Inscrutable diplomat that he was, Dr Bechelli received me graciously at WHO headquarters and patiently heard my enthusiastic sales pitch for reconstructive surgery in leprosy. Sanguine enough to see that it was all rather like water off a duck's back, I took my leave without illusions. My chief memory of the WHO building is the siesta room for top brass, next door to their top-floor restaurant. An Australian with access to this sumptuous, softly lit sanctum showed me the long line of luxurious black leather couches, and assured me that they were well used. 'The index of activity isn't very high around here,' he said.

It was Toronto next stop, where Gwen's cousin Allan, who had married us, was the representative in Canada of the Bolivian Indian Mission. The Burrows took us to Niagara, a spectacle that compared badly with the Victoria Falls.

We had good friends in New York, Thom and Vonnie Marubbio. He'd been a doctor at the Lutheran hospital at Wapenamanda in the Western Highlands, and we struck up a friendship on my first visit there. He was on study leave at St Luke's Hospital and had a staff flat where they put us up for a few days. As well as doing the usual New York things we went to a piano recital in the Metropolitan Museum of Art auditorium. The pianist was Lili Kraus, a Hungarian, one of the first overseas artists to visit Australia after World War II. I heard her in Adelaide in 1946, and remembered her playing a Schubert sonata in which there is a long sparkling scalar passage. On reaching it she threw back her head to the sword-swallowing position and gazed at the ceiling for what seemed minutes on end while her hands flew up and down the keyboard with breathtaking accuracy. 'Look, Mum, no hands' isn't quite right, but is near enough. Now, more than 20 years later, she played the same sonata, and at the very same bar up went her head, exactly as I'd seen in Adelaide. Some concert artists boast that every recital is a new interpretation. Not this lady.

After New York we flew to New Orleans, to be met by a driver from Carville, the only leprosy hospital on the North American mainland, where Paul Brand worked between teaching tours and consultancies around the world. The resident surgeon, a big man physically, had Gwen and me to afternoon tea, and didn't hide his chagrin that the Public Health Service had seen fit to employ Paul. ('He's nart even a citizen, f'Gard's sake.') He saw to it that Paul did no operating, and was restricted to the biomechanical research that had long fascinated him, which he seemed to find fulfilling enough. He was only 55, and it is hard to believe that he was content to relinquish operative surgery, but he showed no sign of dissatisfaction with his lot at Carville.

We were now on the homeward run. Another friend from New Guinea, Dan Kleinig from the Wapenamanda hospital, visited the Marubbios a week before us, on his way home after passing the English fellowship. After several failed shots at the FRACS his desire for a postgraduate qualification had driven him to give it one last throw in London. A congratulatory letter was in order, so I wrote an aerogram, somewhere between New Orleans and LA.

After checking in for the trans-Pacific flight I noticed a pillar-box, which reminded me of the aerogram in my pocket. As I dropped it through the slot someone grabbed my elbow. I turned and saw Dan Kleinig. After we exchanged the extra-warm greetings well known to all who've run into friends unexpectedly, far from home, I burbled, 'I've just posted you a letter, to Wapenamanda.' The Kleinigs were on a different flight, and the odds against our meeting the instant I was posting Dan's letter must be enormous. This is but one of many extraordinary coincidences that have been a feature of our lives, and I've often suggested that such preposterously unlikely events are evidence of God's sense of humour. He is making fun of statistical theory, a human invention. (The Byethorn story in Chapter 2 is another example.)

Yet another occurred in 1973, the year of the Bergen leprosy meeting. When I was on Aoba in the New Hebrides, operating on leprosy patients, the doctor at the Australian Churches of Christ hospital at Nduindui at the other end of the island invited me down for a weekend, and collected me in his little American-built motorboat of WW2 vintage. Halfway along the north coast its notoriously unreliable motor sputtered and stopped. My host tried everything he knew to restart it without success. We were unpleasantly low in choppy water with ten centimetres of freeboard, fully laden with vegetables as well as four souls. With wind and waves driving us towards a shore consisting of fiendishly sharp rocks without an inch of beach for miles (they weren't called the New Hebrides for nothing) we jettisoned the veggies. The sun was sinking fast and chatter ceased as we tried to work out what to do. I think we all prayed. I certainly did. To our great relief a Chinese-owned trader, coasting the island to buy copra, hove into sight. Seeing that we were in trouble they put on speed and took us aboard, and our recalcitrant launch in tow, just in time.

In an earlier chapter I described my working visit to Indonesia on my way home from Bergen. One Sunday morning in Medan an Australian railway engineer on official business came to church and introduced himself afterwards. The Leprosy Mission nurses invited him for lunch, partly as a foil for me, and partly out of the goodness of their hearts. One girl was a member of the Churches of Christ, as was our guest. Somehow it came out that he too had been to Nduidui, and knew the motorboat that had given me my biggest fright in a very long time. He made light of it, and said it once broke its moorings in a storm and was given up for lost. Weeks later it turned up on a distant island. In the many years since that Indonesian trip I've never met anyone else who has been to Aoba, let alone to Nduindui.

Chapter 17

Burnie, Tasmania

When we left PNG a surgical position was available in Burnie because there was, and still is, a widespread belief in Australian medical and some other circles that rural practice is for those lacking the ambition, drive and/or ability to succeed in the city. This is a simplistic and totally erroneous and distorted view, as was demonstrated long ago by Professor Max Kamien, of the University of Western Australia. His survey in that state showed that the doctors most likely to find satisfaction working in country areas were those who'd been born there. He said medical schools should target country students in an effort to solve the problem of finding doctors happy to work away from metropolitan areas. Most of the medical workforce has been brought up in the city, which accounts for their anti-rural bias, and may explain why there was only one other Australian-born specialist on the hospital staff when I went to Burnie.

The transition to Tasmania from the New Guinea highlands and half a lifetime of Third World surgery was much less painful and complicated than it might have been. At that time taking a vehicle to Tasmania during the summer holidays usually meant booking a ferry passage months ahead, which of course we hadn't done. Trevor foresaw our problem and rang the ticket office as soon as he had our approximate date. Miraculously, and due to a cancellation, there was a single space remaining on the very night he and Nancy were booked back after their annual Adelaide holiday, but no more for weeks. So we crossed Bass Strait with our elderly Volvo at exactly the right time.

The Northwest Regional Hospital held a long lease on a furnished flat for the use of new specialist staff while they settled in. A locum surgeon vacated it as we arrived, so we were able to drive off the ferry at Devonport, half an hour from Burnie, and directly to our temporary new home, where we unpacked and stocked the kitchen before nightfall.

A supercilious mainland journalist once described Burnie as a grotty little mill town, which like much fine copy was quite misleading. It is a major port on the north-west coast, handling exports of timber, paper, minerals, dairy products and vegetables in particular. The two big employers were the Australian Pulp and Paper Mills, and Tioxide, the latter processing the titanium dioxide that forms the white base for oil paint. The climate is mild, due to the water-bath effect of Bass Strait, and snowflakes are seen in the air every seven years or so, but don't make it to the ground. There is plenty of winter snow a few kilometres inland, and even in summer there may be sudden snowfalls on the peaks, and violent weather that has been the death of many unwary bushwalkers.

Burnie is hilly, with the only land suitable for an airport about 20 kilometres away at Wynyard. The immediate hinterland is largely taken up with dairying, and beyond that lies the Tasmanian bush that attracts tourists from all over. Many overseas travel companies tout Tasmania as the most wonderful island anywhere, after Moorea.

The two general surgeons, Carl Castellino and Alan Scott, welcomed me enthusiastically. Alan was Scottish but had been in Australia for many years. He handled the vascular surgery in Burnie, of which there was plenty. The deadly combination of heavy smoking and too much cream meant that many locals suffered blocked arteries, and he was kept very busy. About eighteen months after I arrived he moved to Launceston where another vascular surgeon shared the workload. Alan and I shared a ward for that time, and became good friends. We had different ways of doing many things but could argue our positions without damaging the friendship, which persists as firmly as ever. He was to be the sole personal visitor we entertained in our six years in Yemen, and I will remember him forever for that kindness, amongst many others.

In Burnie he and I made a combined ward round on Friday mornings, teaching undergraduates and the young doctors working for us. For me these sessions became the highlight of the week, and I continued them until I finished in Burnie. The pattern of my own training days was not for me; lengthy discussions with students around the bed are too stressful for many patients. Simple cases are safe enough, but when it comes to talking about unpleasant features of a disease I have always held that bedside teaching is inappropriate and can be unduly frightening. Sometimes a student will give an incorrect answer to a question that alarms the patient more than does the truth. So for me a teaching round has two parts: a business session in the wards, and then detailed discussion over coffee, in comfort.

These sessions produced surprises and the occasional *faux pas*. One morning we were discussing unusual presentations of appendicitis, and I told the students about my son's experience a fortnight before his wedding, in which he had the typical appendix bellyache, fever and loss of appetite, but his main complaint was a sharp burning pain in the pit of his stomach every time he emptied his bladder, especially with the last few drops. I asked them to explain this unusual symptom. The University of Tasmania derived significant income from overseas students, many in the medical faculty. One lad, an elegant product of the posh school that calls itself the Eton of Africa, put his hand up immediately. I welcomed his promptness because it was rare for him to be ahead of the others.

'Yes, Joe,' I said, 'why did John have that pain?'

'Gonorrhoea,' he replied with great confidence. When calm returned I told him gently that he was wrong, and explained that if the appendix is stuck to the bladder, as in his case, the process of passing urine drags on it, causing pain.

My public hospital contract was for a notional sixteen hours a week, plus on-call and callback. This provided as much income as I'd earned in PNG and allowed plenty of time for private work, but there were no suitable rooms available when I arrived. Never an entrepreneur, I felt that things were bound to be slow initially and I was unwilling to take on major expense, so when the North West Private Hospital offered the use of a visitors' consulting suite on an hourly basis we accepted without hesitation. At first Gwen did all the paperwork, except for typing replies to referring doctors, which I did at home.

The other Burnie surgeons didn't conduct public clinics, but saw all their patients in their private rooms. With an inbuilt bias towards the public system derived from my time in New Guinea I decided that I would hold an outpatient clinic in the hospital, but soon found it unsatisfactory and inefficient, with half the patients turning out to have private insurance anyway. Any minor procedure I wanted to do on the spot, such as dealing with an ingrown toenail under local anaesthesia, seemed a great imposition on the nursing staff. After months of struggling with the system I decided that Carl and Alan were right to see all their patients in their rooms for the best of reasons, so I did the same.

My office was very quiet for many months, and almost the only private patients I ever saw locally were disgruntled people who for one reason or another were dissatisfied with the other surgeons, but never with any solid basis that I could discover. I collected the occasional fresh customer when I was on call for emergencies, but otherwise I saw few private patients until Alan departed for Launceston.

Somebody suggested that I'd do well to consult out of town, which proved to be true, and the Smithton Medical Practice was the first to welcome me. Gwen and I visited Smithton, the centre of a rich dairying district about 80 kilometres west of Burnie, every third Tuesday afternoon, and never tired of the scenic drive along the coast. Soon we added Ulverstone, nearby to our east, and later still Devonport, so that we were out of town every Tuesday afternoon. The elderly, in particular, were pleased to get a surgical opinion locally, and these peripheral clinics became very busy.

In the first few months we spent many hours looking for a suitable house until the agents must have reckoned we were impossible to please. The problem was that every attractive property we saw was far bigger than we required, and beyond what we judged to be our means. Fortunately the hospital wasn't pressing us to leave the short-term accommodation, which was wonderfully situated with the windows facing the north-west. As winter came on Gwen found she didn't need a cardigan indoors in the daytime.

That spring a 'For Sale' sign went up on the vacant block next door. The idea of building hadn't occurred to us but we were suddenly attracted to it, even though the block fell away from the road quite steeply, and was narrower than we thought ideal. Weather-wise its orientation was perfect, and the price was right, so we bought it. Our well-designed flat gave us ideas about layout, and Milton Smith, a talented Ulverstone draftsman, converted them to practicality. The erection of a distinctly non-standard dwelling on a steep block took rather longer and was much more costly than we had bargained for, and the builders said that it was their most difficult house ever. We moved into a delightful modern two-storey all-electric house that continued to satisfy us but, as always, we would make a few alterations if we were doing it again.

We worshipped at the Baptist Church, partly because the interim pastor had been a missionary in the PNG highlands and also because we knew they were looking for an organist. We would have been almost as comfortable at the Uniting Church, where Gwen was to make many friends.

After trailing around the world with me for so many years without complaint, all too often with children but without me, Gwen was looking forward to putting roots down. When we married she had a brother in Bolivia and a sister in Borneo, both missionaries, so the idea of living abroad didn't faze her, but the need to send our first three girls to Australia for their secondary schooling was more painful for her than I realised at the time. She always found packing, even to go on annual leave, more of a trial than a pleasure, and undoubtedly a less peripatetic life would have suited her better. Being married to a surgeon can bring its own problems, but she was unfailingly loving, helpful and supportive, right to the end of my career and beyond. One hears of combative wives and family fights, but I know about them in theory only, because Gwen has always been such a model of graciousness. When I first set eyes on her I knew she was special, but I couldn't have dreamed what a Godsend she was to be. When I was awarded the RACS International Medal at a College dinner I told the guests it was really half hers, so vital was her support. So when we left PNG she thoroughly deserved a place to call home at long last.

Soon after our arrival she noticed how friendly the supermarket girls were, and felt a sense of community in Burnie that big cities often lack. By Australian standards it ranked as a city, with more than 25,000 inhabitants then, but it has shrivelled in the last few years, after the closure of Tioxide and finally of the paper mill.

Despite the warmth of my welcome, settling in at the hospital had a problem or two. After being the surgeon of last resort, as a rule, for so many years it came as a shock to find the nursing staff sometimes looking sideways at this chap from the wilds of New Guinea, with some behaving as if I was Alan's registrar. The first time I treated a ruptured spleen non-operatively proved to be quite a challenge. It soon became obvious to me that the patient was not bleeding to death, and I was relieved when it became clear to the many doubters also that all was well.

I had three operating sessions a week but very few patients, so Alan asked me to chip away at his waiting list, consisting mostly of people with varicose veins, primary and recurrent hernias, and gallstones. These complaints were uncommon in PNG but I'd had plenty of practice with them in England, so I did my best to clear up Alan's backlog while waiting for my ship to come in.

We'd been in Burnie a few months when the phone rang at midnight; this was rare, and was usually a wrong number. A local GP offered the ritual but unconvincing apology for disturbing me at such an hour ('Not at all, Paul') and then said he was at the Voyager Hotel with Tammy Wynette, and wanted me to see her.

'With who?' I asked blearily, my grammar a bit limp at that hour. After wondering aloud where I'd been all my life he said the lady had given a concert in Burnie that night and had collapsed afterwards with severe abdominal pain. Similar trouble in Queensland a few weeks before had been investigated and put down to residual gallstones after previous surgery. He wanted me to see her before he gave her the shot she was demanding, and said that if I identified myself to her bodyguard outside the hotel I would be admitted.

Sure enough, a big bruiser was waiting for me, and led me to the lady's suite, the best in the house. The dishevelled GP and the expensively casual boyfriend were sipping scotch, paying scant attention to the faded bottle blonde dressed (undressed, more like it) in an expensive-looking negligee, groaning on the king-size bed. Between them they told me the history included seventeen operations, mostly at the hands of a plastic surgical team with a global brief, as far as I could see, but one scar had to be the work of a biliary surgeon. The lady flinched before I touched her, and I soon satisfied myself that this was no surgical emergency, although I thought her pain was genuine. She apologised for not remembering the name of the injection she knew she needed, but mumbled about Peth-something several times.

'You'd better give her some Pethidine,' I told the GP, who had his syringe at the ready. 'A hundred should be enough.'

'Ah, yes,' she sighed, and relaxed before the needle hit her. I offered reassurance that all would be well and rose to go home, but she insisted that I wait a few minutes in case the injection needed topping up. As I don't drink scotch they found me some soft stuff while we waited for the Pethidine to take effect, which it did. I was leaving when the boyfriend asked, 'What's the damage, doc?' This matter had slipped my mind; after all, I had entered private practice very recently.

'I don't know,' I said. 'Paul, what's the fee for calling a surgeon out in the middle of the night?'

The men almost choked on their drinks and then Paul sputtered, 'How about a hundred?' so the boyfriend pulled out a wad of notes about the size of the bedroll people carry onto night trains in India and carefully peeled off my hundred.

Robyn and Michael were holidaying with us at the time, and at breakfast Michael said he thought he'd heard me go out in the night, so I told them the story. He guffawed at my naiveté. 'What? A *hundred*? She's a multimillionaire. She must have more platinum discs than anyone else in the whole world, and you charged her peanuts.' He then told me all I needed to know about Tammy Wynette, and then some. And, of course, who is singing next time I turn on the radio?

I hadn't been in Burnie long when I realised that the traditional incision we made to remove the gallbladder was too long. Laparoscopic cholecystectomy was being introduced elsewhere, but there were numerous reports of catastrophic injuries to bile ducts and other vital structures, so like some others of my vintage I decided that I was too old to learn this new technique. As an alternative, surgeons in Scotland described a small incision that they found satisfactory, and recommended preoperative ultrasound examination to localise the gallbladder exactly so that the incision could be made right over it. This seemed rather impractical and unnecessary, as variations in the gallbladder's position are minor and of negligible importance.

A thin old lady wanting repair of a hernia the size of a golf ball high in her midriff at the same time as her gallbladder operation helped me stumble on a better approach. I made a five centimetre transverse incision over the hernia from the midline towards the right, and found that the most critical part of the biliary system's anatomy was clearly visible in the middle of the wound. The position of the gallbladder itself was unimportant, as it could be mobilised quite easily through this short incision.

So I gave up my previous incision, which amounted to something like the middle two-fourths of a conventional so-called Kocher. I now used a short transverse incision just to the right of the midline, which allowed adequate exposure and a much less painful recovery than did Kocher's incision. I performed this so-called minilap-cholecystectomy for the rest of my time, and found that more than half my patients, whether in the public or the private hospital, were able to go home the day after operation. After operating on hundreds of people of all sizes, extending the wound to whatever length was necessary to allow a safe view of the gallbladder and bile ducts, I found that the commonest incision length was between five and six centimetres.

As more reports appeared of bile duct injuries at laparoscopic cholecystectomy (LC) some people felt that I became obsessional about the virtues of the minilap-cholecystectomy (MC). A paper I gave about it at a College meeting drew little public support, although several surgeons admitted over coffee that they did something similar. Laparoscopic equipment and techniques have improved, and bile duct injury is now less common, but the incidence stubbornly remains rather higher at LC than with open operation. Truly comparable figures are difficult to obtain, but I thought it significant that our trainees had all seen bile duct injuries, whereas I didn't until I was at least 50 years old.

My enthusiasm was encouraged further by a paper in the *Lancet* from Professor Alan Johnson's unit in Sheffield, reporting the first truly controlled trial of MC versus LC, which failed to confirm superiority of the latter procedure. The same issue included editorial comment from my old friend Noshir Antia, now a passionate campaigner for simple and effective methods in every area of medical practice. He castigated the Indian surgical establishment for its unthinking adoption of procedures such as LC when the vast majority of the population couldn't bear the costs involved in the provision of increasingly expensive equipment for laparoscopic surgery.

I'd known Alan's father Dr Douglas Johnson in London when he was the secretary of the Christian Medical Fellowship, following his long and wise leadership of the Inter-Varsity Fellowship, a conservative organisation with Oxbridge beginnings. For many years around mid-century DJ was a major influence on evangelical Christendom in universities right across Britain, and thus on evangelicalism at home and abroad. His spiritual legacy is huge. Alan had his father's faith and gracious manner, and I very much enjoyed a visit to Sheffield in 1996 to see his unit in action. Their technique for MC was almost identical to mine.

I was well aware that my attempts to promote a simpler operation branded me as a troglodyte when almost everybody else was doing laparoscopic cholecystectomy, but when the Asian Surgical Association advertised a 1997 meeting on 'Cost-effective Surgery for Asia' I thought that at last I'd found the forum I needed, and flew to Hong Kong full of enthusiasm. A glance at the program showed that fully two per cent of speakers could be said to be paying attention to the stated theme of the conference. It was a large meeting with parallel sessions, and the one that included my paper drew less than 30 people. The only question I remember was from a Dutch academic who asked if my patients could go home the same day. I'd already told the meeting that more than half went home after one night in hospital. If the Dutchman supposed that this was a disadvantage by comparison with outpatient surgery in the usual Asian context he clearly had no idea of realities in this part of the world, and there was certainly no time to teach him. This meeting, more than anything else, convinced me that I was wasting my breath promoting MC.

Despite my initial dearth of private patients in Burnie I was persuaded to become chairman of the Medical Staff Committee at the private hospital for much the same reason that I had become dean in Port Moresby. I was a newcomer with no obvious axe to grind, which some others were perceived, rightly or wrongly, to have. I was to hold this position for about eight years. No doubt this brought extra consideration from the manager, who found us progressively more spacious consulting rooms as our business expanded.

In 1994 a new public hospital was built a stone's throw from the private one, and then a building linking them, to house private consulting suites and imaging and pathology departments to serve both hospitals. Apart from our Tuesday afternoon trips out of town my day's work was now all under one roof. In the office we employed a full-time secretary plus another part-time girl, and for my three consulting sessions in Burnie Gwen came in to help handle the paperwork. This gave her a genuine stake in the company and an understanding of the business. Patients liked her, and this must have helped.

Life in Tasmania became even more enjoyable when Meredith joined a Launceston general practice in 1992. After graduation from the UPNG and her compulsory two-year internship she had commenced training in obstetrics and gynaecology at PMGH. She passed the first part of the MRCOG diploma, as it then was, and was about to go to England to finish her training when she met Ian Ross, an architectural draftsman from Brisbane, who was working at a Port Moresby vocational school run by the Salvation Army. They married in January 1980 and left PNG for Brisbane.

As an overseas graduate wishing to practise in Australia Meredith had to pass the examination for foreign doctors, then known as the AMEC, and was the first Australian-born doctor to do so. The clinical part of the examination was easy enough but she found the English test very difficult; no wonder Indonesian, Vietnamese and other foreign candidates had such trouble. And not only they: years later another Australian-born UPNG graduate, back from England with the MRCOG, failed the obstetrics section of the AMEC on the stated grounds that his answers were those of a specialist, not those to be expected from a final year medical student.

More recently the xenophobic aura surrounding Australian treatment of foreign medical graduates has been fading, but we still hear occasional complaints of unfairness, particularly from specialists wishing to work here. Australian training in all specialties is of a high standard by any measure, and our various Colleges are justifiably proud of their products, but the closed shop argument heard from both local and overseas graduates is becoming ever more difficult to refute. After examining the situation for years, in 2002 the Australian Competition and Consumer Commission expressed the view, with refined and diplomatic circumlocution, that the Royal Australasian College of Surgeons might be improperly limiting access to surgical training.

Meredith's desire to complete her specialist training in Australia came to nothing, as in the early 1980s there were more than enough Brisbane graduates to fill the available training posts there, which effectively excluded outsiders. She and Ian were disinclined to try interstate, so she settled for the Diploma in Obstetrics, which allowed her to practise GP obstetrics but required her to pass on complicated cases to specialists. After spending years supervising her juniors performing caesarean sections this must have been a comedown, but she accepted it happily enough. With a husband and three children to look after, until her elder son Andrew joined the workforce elsewhere, part-time general practice in Launceston suited her well. The Rosses are active in the Salvation Army there, and have various other community interests.

Our third daughter Kate graduated from the Adelaide University Medical School and went on to train in infectious diseases. She worked full-time in HIV/AIDS in Sydney for some years before becoming a staff specialist in general infectious diseases, and ultimately departmental head, at the Prince of Wales Hospital. She and Patrick Versace, an ophthalmologist specialising in refractive surgery, have two boys.

This is the place to mention the rest of the family. Shirley matriculated from Port Moresby and lived with the Trevor Clezys in Launceston while training as an infant teacher. She married Robert Culhane, a carpenter and joiner with Bible college training. Later they became Bachelors of Theology in Melbourne. Rob went on to do an MA while they were Presbyterian home missionaries in Flemington before moving to a Churches of Christ congregation in Balwyn. He went back to building for several years, but was ordained as an Anglican minister in 2007. They have three children.

John studied electronic engineering in Adelaide, became a software engineer, and married Tiffany Ferguson with whom he has six sons and three daughters. They spent several years abroad, most recently in Germany where their older three became genuinely bilingual. Their first son was born in Tel Aviv and their fifth in Ulm. Their home church is an independent congregation in Adelaide.

With our children, and theirs, so scattered it mattered little where we lived. Tasmania is unquestionably isolated from the rest of Australia and the world, but we managed to see our family more often than many parents do. And while Burnie could never provide the same variety of surgical work that New Guinea did it was still more attractive in this respect than many other cities in rural Australia could have been.

For example, about two years after our arrival Burnie's senior physician, Mike Templer, a no-nonsense ex-British Army consultant, had me see a lady with a brain tumour and a tiny lung shadow of uncertain nature, presumably related. He asked me to biopsy one of them, and after seeing the patient I said it would be better and easier for her, and for me, if I removed the brain tumour rather than biopsy the lung lesion, with the probable additional advantage of relieving the headache, at least temporarily. Probably both tumours were secondary deposits from elsewhere, and in my view the Hobart neurosurgeons were too busy to take on obviously incurable patients.

I soon found that the notion of an elective craniotomy being performed in Burnie was novel, almost hilariously so, but one theatre nurse reluctantly admitted neurosurgical experience, and eventually an anaesthetist agreed to play ball. I opened the lady's head and found a large deposit of melanoma in her right frontal lobe, and although I removed it I knew she was incurable. She went off to the Intensive Care Unit and made an uninterrupted recovery from the surgery. As the nurses were fearful about managing the case I kept as close an eye on her as had been my routine in Goroka. I was miffed when on the second post-operative day the ICU registrar, a trainee physician, felt that slight drowsiness warranted a CT scan, and ordered it. It was no more than a mild case of 'second day slump', and neither the alarm nor the expense was necessary.

A few weeks later John Liddell, Hobart's senior neurosurgeon, phoned saying that he felt I should know that a complaint had been passed up the nursing hierarchy because I'd performed an elective craniotomy in the absence of neurosurgically specialised ICU nursing staff. I explained the situation and he sounded satisfied. He said that as far as he knew nothing had been put on paper, to which I replied that should it come to that my response would be that I had been doing craniotomies for 30 years without much noticing the absence of specialist nursing staff. Happily I heard no more.

The surgery of the oesophagus is another area not normally regarded as within the general surgeon's bailiwick, but once again New Guinea experience proved useful. My first case happened by accident, when our ENT surgeon removed a thin old war veteran's cancerous larynx. The cancer had recurred after radiotherapy, more extensively than preoperative investigations suggested, and invaded his upper gullet. My colleague was perfectly capable of doing the excision but lacked experience of the best method of replacing missing gullet.

As a rule the simplest way of handling this situation is to open the abdomen and mobilise the stomach so that it hangs on its southern blood supply, and then core out the oesophagus by manual dissection from above and below without otherwise opening the chest. This is usually a straightforward procedure, with little bleeding. When the surgeon's hand is behind the heart it jumps a bit, but this rarely does harm. One then hauls on the top end of the oesophagus and, hey presto, the stomach appears in the neck, where it will reach as high as the back of the tongue if need be. All went well, and the veteran went home happy.

The Australia-wide orthopaedic manpower shortage made it difficult for the Burnie hospital to maintain these specialists on staff, and in the early 1990s we went for months at a time without them, although we usually had a doctor with considerable orthopaedic experience who functioned as a registrar. Having treated fractures for all my time in PNG it seemed ridiculous to send simple cases to Launceston, 150 kilometres away, and between us the registrar and I managed most fractures. I never became truly familiar and comfortable with modern orthopaedic hardware, much more complicated than the nails, plates and screws I'd used in PNG, but the registrar and the theatre staff were fully conversant with our equipment, and between us we made a team. When open operation was indicated it often happened that I exposed the fracture and then did little more than watch the others for the rest of it. The few referrals we made were complicated cases, or occasionally because patients demanded specialist treatment, as was their right.

Tasmania has the purest air on earth, and therefore many locals had severe solar skin damage, which meant that skin cancer was a perpetual surgical problem. Many cases were suitable for excision in the office, and as time went by I extended the range of what I did there, either in Burnie or at my outlying clinics. When vasectomy became popular men seemed more relaxed in the office setting than in the hospital's Day Surgery Suite, and I performed hundreds there. I also operated on many cases of carpal tunnel compression in the office under local anaesthetic, using a semi-closed method Peter Martin taught me in Chelmsford, which I have never seen used by anyone else.

One of the pleasures of Burnie was that as well as teaching medical students we had interns and general surgical trainees, usually of a high standard, on rotation from Hobart or Melbourne. Juniors with enquiring minds helped maintain an alert and energetic atmosphere, and our trainees seemed to enjoy Burnie. Carl did most of the colorectal work, and I had experience in some areas, such as parotid surgery and hand surgery, in which he wasn't much interested, so between us we provided a fairly broad experience for our juniors, most of whom left convinced that the positives of country practice far outweighed the negatives. Sadly, this enthusiasm rarely survived the subsequent blandishments of metropolitan life, but eventually one of our ex-registrars, David Finkelde, phoned from Melbourne where he was spending a post-fellowship year in breast and endocrine surgery, telling me he'd like to set up in Burnie. As I was past retiring age and the College has a very proper policy that old surgeons shouldn't hold onto posts when young ones are ready, willing and able to take over, I could only welcome him.

He came, and did well. As I expected, there was insufficient work to keep three full-time general surgeons busy, so I looked towards retirement, and closed the business in late 1998.

Both Gwen and I were young at heart, and giving it all away seemed premature. I'd already enquired about surgical vacancies in mission hospitals, which I knew were always crying out for staff. We offered for a year, expecting to be posted to some oppressively hot place that might well be too much for us. Jibla Baptist Hospital in Yemen needed a locum surgeon for a year, from a date that suited us exactly. At over 2000 m ASL, Jibla sat in the floor of a valley, with a climate that was second to none. And so began a new, rich and exciting chapter in our lives, most of which we wouldn't have missed for anything. It introduced us to some great saints, a wonderful country, and gave us front seats at a deadly clash between Christianity and fundamentalist Islam.

Chapter 18

Jibla Baptist Hospital, Yemen

The response of almost everyone was 'Where?' We could at least place the country in the south-west of the Arabian Peninsula, and knew that there had been two Yemens until fairly recently. (That's one of the benefits of stamp collecting.) We told those interested that if they pictured Arabia as a giant axe-head slashing south-east into the Indian Ocean, Yemen was at the bottom of the sharp edge. The country was about eight times the size of Tasmania and mostly desert, but had a population roughly the size of Australia's.

We'd heard of the exploits of the south Arabian travellers Freya Stark and Wilfred Thesiger, but otherwise our knowledge of the region was sketchy, and we had no idea of the unique features that make Yemen a wonderland for tourists (when there are any) and the object of a love affair for most foreigners who live there. We wouldn't have believed how passionately we would come to identify with the land and its people in about six years.

Two or three weeks after we announced our intention of going there almost everybody knew where Yemen was, with our newspapers giving major treatment to the kidnapping that led to the death of the tourist from Sydney. Some friends and acquaintances questioned our sanity, or at least our wisdom, in going to such a wild place. But Jibla staff were unperturbed by this or any other kidnapping, and nobody there suggested that we think again. We'd prayed that God would lead us in the right direction, and saw no reason to back out.

Management sent us an excellent information pack. JBH had been founded about 35 years before by a dynamic American doctor, Jim Young, who had been working in Gaza but wanted to move deeper into the Arab world. He couldn't have chosen a country more isolated than North Yemen, where a line of *imam*s from one family had ruled for 1000 years and had deliberately kept foreign influence to a minimum. The *imam* had a few Italian doctors in his service, and welcomed the prospect of a second opinion being available. Accompanying the Youngs were Ethne Stainer, an Australian nurse raised in the remote Fead Islands in New Guinea, and Maria Hidalgo, a lady from Barcelona. All three were blessed with boundless energy, enthusiasm, initiative and faith. Gaza had made them fluent in Arabic, and they adapted to the Yemeni dialect with ease.

They were given a ward on the top floor of the old Taiz hospital, but when other doctors' patients began flooding upstairs in embarrassing numbers Dr Young saw good reasons why he and his team would do better to work on their own. He aimed to establish a hospital far enough from other facilities to be seen as independent, but near enough to a major city to minimise communication problems with the outside world. After a careful search and much prayer he accepted the offer of a 99-year lease on what we've been told was a disused Jewish burial ground at Jibla, an historic town set in a deep and winding valley a few kilometres south of Ibb, the capital of the Ibb governorate, otherwise known as the Green Province.

JBH eventually had 75 beds, and because Dr Young had great surgical ability he attracted patients from all over. He retired in the 1980s, and was followed by other career staff for several years. More recently, retired surgeons had filled for three months at a time until Dr Judy Williams, a board-certified American, arrived in early 1999. Being IMB career staff she had to begin with a year's formal Arabic study, so we went to Jibla expecting to stay for that year.

Yemen is well off the beaten track. Gulf Air, Emirates and Royal Jordanian all flew out of Melbourne to the hubs of their respective networks, with much delayed connecting flights to Sana'a. We chose Gulf Air, which meant almost 24 hours in Bahrain before a very early flight that arrived at the drab and dreary Moscow-minimalist Sana'a International Airport at 4.30 am.

Staff from Jibla met us, whizzed us along the airport highway to the city centre and down a warren of narrow bustling streets to the mission guesthouse, where we cleaned up before the four-hour drive down a spectacular mountain road. We were too weary to pay attention to the famed architectural wonders of Sana'a or to the features of the highway, but we were alert enough to notice our driver's wariness of other vehicles that could be following us, and sensed his relief when a highway patrol car escorted us between two towns in a troublesome area. Jibla vehicles were well known to the soldiers manning the eight or nine checkpoints, and there was little delay anywhere.

A simple Western-style house was ready for us on the bottom terrace of the beautifully laid-out hospital compound that stretched for six or seven levels up one steep side of the *wadi*, with Jibla town opposite us. Like most Yemeni upland towns, Jibla is built on ground too steep for agriculture, with each house having several storeys. Because chipping its foundations out of solid rock is the most difficult part of building a house, Yemenis usually settle for a small footprint and add two to five or more floors of high quality stonework. Windows tend to be in pairs, and almost invariably each has a further half-moon window at the top, picked out in multicoloured glass. The effect at night is almost magical, when all lights seem to be on, despite the high price of electricity. Jibla stretches up the side of the *wadi* for 100 metres or more and when lit up could almost be mistaken for the Sydney CBD. So with gum trees all over the compound and recognisable weeds – oxalis and morning glory – in the garden, we felt quite at home.

Arwa, queen of all Yemen, had her palace here 1000 years ago, and its crumbling remains are still visible. A lady of great resourcefulness, she had an aqueduct built to bring water from a spring half a day's walk further up the mountain. It still runs but isn't truly functional. Her mosque, one of many in the town, attracts pilgrims from all over the world. Ordinary tourists were rarely seen in Jibla in the late 1990s, partly because of negative travel advisories, and also because well-founded stories about stone-throwing boys tended to discourage the few who braved this part of the country.

We spent a few days recovering from our jetlag and then took the in-house two-week survival Arabic course designed for short-term workers, taught by Ismail Ghorbani, a pharmacy assistant with fair English. Neither Gwen nor I are natural linguists, but it's almost impossible anyway for people of our age to learn Arabic, generally acknowledged to be one of the most difficult major languages. For native English speakers it has some very foreign sounds that increase its difficulty, and my developing familial deafness made matters worse. (That was my excuse, anyway.) Ismail did his best to give us the rudiments, and enthused me to struggle on, largely with the aid of an Arabic Bible that has the short vowels marked, as do children's textbooks. Despite much effort I remained far from fluent, but could manage a ward round on my own provided that nothing more than my limited selection of stock phrases was required. The daunting differences between the Jibla *patois*, ordinary spoken Arabic and the formal written language may help explain why I picked up almost none of the chatter that went on in the operating room. But for the few Yemeni staff with fair to good English I'd have found communication difficult. They complimented me on my efforts, but didn't disagree convincingly when I said that if I worked in Yemen for another century I might speak their language properly.

When we began there were many Americans, and a few others, on the staff with formal language training. Most Indian and Filipino contract staff spoke Arabic well enough for ordinary purposes, but few could read or write it. I made an effort to do both. Arabic script comes naturally to a left-hander, and I often wished I was young enough for a serious attempt at the language to be realistic.

Language was our only real problem. Despite the great cultural differences between New Guinea and Yemen, our previous experience must have helped make settling in easy. We were used to being members of a small expatriate community. And Jibla was scarcely a hardship post. The dirt-floored shops at the bottom of the hill had an adequate range of ordinary groceries and fruit and veg, and most other items we could possibly desire were available in Ibb.

Mission policy was all foreign staff be Christians, and we soon found a warmth, and a spiritual depth, on the compound that are sometimes less prominent features of mission hospitals than they should be. We enjoyed JBH so much that I wished we'd heard of its need for a surgeon long ago. We were to make lifelong friends amongst the American, Dutch, Swiss, Indian, Filipino and Mexican staff. That first year only three of ten doctors were American (one of whom wasn't IMB staff) but many nurses and ancillary personnel were Southern Baptists with long experience of the Middle East.

There was far more work than one surgeon could reasonably be expected to do, and I was amazed that Jim Young had been able to cope with it. One needs a break occasionally if minor disagreements with fellow-workers are to be evanescent rather than festering, and if errors resulting from snap decisions are to be kept to a minimum. Gwen and I both so loved Jibla and everything about it that we had no hesitation in agreeing to return when that was put to us. We found that three months at home after a year away allowed us to see almost as much of our family as if we were in Burnie, except for Meredith and her lot in Launceston, whom we saw frequently.

Security was tight. A fenced compound meant that our houses were considered safe, and pedestrian access to the hospital itself was via a single gate. A squad of soldiers was based just inside this gate and relieved men of their weapons. A second guarded barrier separated the outpatient from the inpatient buildings, and only those with a valid reason were allowed inside.

The Jibla working day was a new experience. The clinic opened at six and was supposed to finish by 2 pm, except for emergencies. Foreign staff met in the chapel at 6.30 each morning, with most of us in rotation being responsible for leading a brief service. I was in the ward by about seven, and aimed to finish my rounds in time to be home for breakfast and the BBC radio news. Monday to Thursday I was in the operating suite from 8.30 until well into the afternoon, lunching somewhere between 1.30 and four, and then returned for whatever operations remained to be done.

We had an excellent anaesthetic service, provided at various times by an American male nurse, an Indian GP–anaesthetist, an Australian part way through his specialist training, a couple of Indian and several Yemeni nurse–anaesthetists. The most experienced of the Yemenis was Abdul Kareem Mubeni, who began his career as a cleaner. Ethne soon promoted him to the operating room where he later became a scrub nurse and eventually an anaesthetist. Despite his lack of formal qualifications he was highly competent. Ethne taught him Australian English, and he bridged the language gap for me many times.

We worked a split weekend, with Friday a day off as a concession to Yemeni staff and Sunday for the foreigners. My surgical outpatient clinic was on Saturday and ran from 8.30 until I'd seen all comers, which might be 3 pm. In between cases on operating days I saw more outpatients from distant villages in the recovery room, so that in the course of a week I might see close to 100 outpatients. I refused to operate on Saturdays after finishing my clinic, except for emergencies. Often people from far away were slightly peeved at having to stay in one of Jibla's 'one sheet' or 'no sheet' hotels until Monday morning.

Monday had a way of filling itself up in this way, so I made few other deliberate bookings for that day.

Orderly planning of operating lists was all but impossible. Often I came to agreement with patients about dates for operation and then had them fail to arrive. There were many reasons for such unpredictability: difficulty in raising the estimated fees for non-emergency admissions, travel problems, a forgotten wedding or some other celebration that took priority over an operation, or patients might simply misread the date on the admission form.

To complicate matters still further, new patients arrived daily from great distances, fasting and with money in hand, expecting same-day operation, most commonly for tubal ligations, hernias or piles. They regarded any delay as indicating laziness or poor management on our part. Often I saw men with hernias of up to ten years duration who were upset because I wouldn't operate on them immediately. Women, in particular, seemed to think that the only way to get prompt attention was to moan, groan and otherwise act as if they were *in extremis*, in striking contrast to PNG villagers' behaviour, where almost unbelievable stoicism was the rule. Soon I learnt that the more dramatic the presentation the less likely I would be to find a problem needing urgent attention. Women often came in doubled up and waving three ultrasound reports describing gallstones (from three different GPs, who all seemed to have ultrasound machines in their offices), complaining of agonising pain and inability to eat for weeks, but with no convincing abnormality to find on abdominal examination.

As one never knew what a day would bring I soon saw that rather than postpone straightforward day cases it was easier to get on and deal with them. With three operating rooms and a fast turn-around (better than he'd ever seen anywhere, according to a visiting Melbourne anaesthetist) it was possible to add several such patients to any day's list.

We saw groin hernias almost daily, not only because they are unusually prevalent, as in much of Africa, but also because Yemenis regard any lump with great suspicion. I tried to persuade old men with hernias at minimal risk of strangulation that they didn't need operation, but the almost invariable response was that the hernia was painful, and therefore justified repair.

We managed almost all hernias as outpatients, using the technique I call modified Shouldice, with excellent results. We saw many recurrences, first operated on elsewhere, mostly in a certain city two hours north of us, but sometimes in Saudi Arabia, where about a million Yemenis worked until the First Gulf War, when most were expelled. Exploration of Saudi-operated cases showed that despite the generally high medical standards in the kingdom there are operators there with little idea of hernia surgery.

Nowadays most hernia repairs include the insertion of expensive plastic mesh of some kind, but using it was almost prohibitive in Yemen, where it tripled our fee. I therefore obtained nylon mosquito netting, cut it into small squares and sterilised it. I learnt of this alternative at a 1998 meeting of the Association of Rural Surgeons of India, whose members had used it for many years. I found it easier to handle than the stiffer material provided in Burnie. Costing about a cent a case, it proved entirely satisfactory.

Mesh relies on vigorous scar tissue formation for its permanent beneficial effect. Excessive scarring, entrapping nerves, may explain several troubling reports of chronic groin pain in these patients, so I used it only when I judged the patient's own tissues inadequate to prevent recurrence.

Piles were another daily problem, and of particular importance because Yemenis believe them to cause impotence. Old men with multiple wives complained bitterly of piles when nothing worth treating could be found, but even so, many warranted operation. Usually the 'eleven o'clock' pile was by far the largest, something quite exceptional in my experience elsewhere.

Many children and some adults came for tonsillectomy, which our GPs were doing very freely when we first arrived. I saw some that warranted operation, but usually I declined because I doubted that recurrent tonsillitis was their problem. All over the country people seemed to believe that if tonsils were enlarged they were diseased. Parents were astonished at a refusal, and rarely comprehended when I told them, as I often did, 'This is a hospital, not a shop.' If they argued the point my compromise was to endorse a reappointment slip saying that I'd see the patient at any time with an attack of acute tonsillitis. Only two returned to me, but no doubt some found other doctors more accommodating.

A Sana'a businessman said he needed antibiotics for a sore throat every fortnight, and asked me to remove his tonsils. As usual, he was fasting and expected operation that day. He had no enlarged lymph nodes in the neck, and I saw no tonsils, and no throat abnormality of any kind. I told him so and elicited the information that he'd had a tonsillectomy three years previously, so what he expected me to do this time I didn't know. He departed with his belief shaken, if not shattered, that an operation will fix just about anything.

That first year when I was a solo surgeon with no junior staff the last thing I needed to be doing was social tonsillectomy. Often I operated until six, or even later, and before going to bed I made a round of my major cases. Every surgical patient seemed to want to talk, which took extra time. All this meant that I worked harder in the year I turned 70 than I'd ever done before. It would have been impossible had I been called out of bed often. The usual nocturnal emergency was a caesarean section, which most of our GPs were well able to perform.

While most patients came from the densely populated Ibb governorate, we continued to attract custom from all over Yemen even though there are now many government and private hospitals. Our fees, while steep enough for the average citizen of one of the poorest nations on earth, were far below those charged in regular private hospitals, and didn't prevent us treating many poor people. Even so, I often wondered where they found the money. Our administrator's poor fund helped provide free treatment for the many Jibla poor, but otherwise elective surgery had to be paid for up front.

At first I saw the fee schedule as complicated, but it worked well. Each operation was itemised, and then there was the daily bed fee, and standard charges for all the drugs, IV fluids, catheters and other disposables. Most patients left hospital with a refund.

The four local specialties were gunshot wounds, burns, kidney stones and congenital abnormalities. Gunshot wounds (GSW) were common because until recently every self-respecting male carried his firearm, as provided for in the constitution. Even machine-guns are permitted for personal protection. A law allowing town officials to proclaim 'no gun' areas wasn't acted on for years, but by 2004 Sana'a and some other cities had done so. There are said to be more firearms per head in Yemen than anywhere else, and until the Jibla shootings it was unusual for us to be without GSW inpatients. Most were said to be accidental even when it was obviously impossible for this to be the truth. I heard many ingenious stories and felt that many a feud was settled, or prolonged, by something described as an accident, or as self-inflicted. Fortunately the hospital security squad, led by a Yemeni army captain, handled the medico-legal aspects, and we were never required to give evidence in court.

I saw four or five people hit by falling bullets, which must be expected to happen, given the local custom of firing live rounds into the air as part of wedding and other celebrations, apparently in the belief that bullets just keep going upwards. Gwen came close to having personal experience of this injury. Boys on the hill sometimes threw stones onto the roofs of nearby houses, and ours occasionally qualified. One Thursday afternoon – the favourite day for weddings – she heard a loud thwack on the roof, but without the subsequent clatter that stones make. She thought no more about it until she changed our sheets and found a little collection of plywood chips on her side of the bed at about chest height. Immediately above it was a neat hole in the ceiling, and closer inspection of the bedding revealed a slit that went almost right through the heavy ticking mattress.

So we were very thankful that she hadn't been having her afternoon nap, which could have meant a Kalashnikov bullet in the chest. When telling our family and friends of this incident we reminded them that when they prayed for our safety they were casting their nets rather wider than usual.

Burns were common because bottled gas was cheap, with poor Yemenis often able to afford it. There are many possible leakage sites between the bottle and the jet of a locally made stove, and all too often flash fires in kitchens brought us badly burnt mothers and children, and occasionally grandma as well. Most female attire was highly flammable and we saw burns severe by any standards, of a type that would be managed in major burns units in the developed world, but around Jibla the buck stopped with us.

Because there was too much other work for the solo surgeon – and some locums lacked burns experience anyway – our GPs had managed most burns for years. Each morning the GP on roster to the operating room did the dressings, sometimes with no one person in effective overall charge. Skin grafts were done too late, with contractures developing, so when I'd been on staff long enough to feel able to speak up I asked for burns to be admitted as surgical problems. Most Yemenis saw skin grafting as a last resort, and breaking this entrenched belief was difficult, but when Judy came we at least had her taking full responsibility for burn care, and she provided by far the best service in our part of Yemen.

Stones in the urinary tract were common for the usual reasons – poor general nutrition and very chalky water in short supply, so people drank little. I operated on several every week, usually for a single big stone in one kidney. In the West these would be treated by lithotripsy (smashing with ultrasound) that was available in the capital but was far more expensive than a few nights at JBH.

My approach to the kidney was the old-fashioned lumbotomy that many urologists have never seen. With the patient face down I made a vertical incision about eight to ten centimetres from the mid-line, just outside the edge of the longitudinal muscles. This is the quickest and easiest route to the kidney. Often a stone can be removed without lifting the kidney from its bed. In 20 per cent of cases we removed a rib to allow safe exposure of the kidney. Patients living on the highway departed after three or four nights, but if home was down rough unpaved roads, real 4WD country, an extra night in was usual.

More old men came for open prostatectomy each year. As any urology ward nurse knows, unexpected post-operative bleeding can be annoying, and ever since Rabaul I'd looked for the best way to prevent it with certainty, all the more important in places where blood may be in short supply. My favourite catheter was unavailable, and sometimes I resorted to packing a long gauze roll into the prostatic cavity. This was completely reliable, but the downside was that removing the pack after about 48 hours meant another minor operation.

When I was on leave a Canadian surgeon, Ken Foster, used a trick he'd learnt from a Pakistani urologist, in which a heavy nylon purse-string stitch is passed around the bladder neck behind the catheter, with the ends brought out just above the pubis and tied over a swab. The suture is removed at about 48 hours, too soon for any risk of permanent narrowing of the bladder outlet. This was so simple and successful that I used it routinely.

Congenital abnormalities of many kinds were very common, no doubt because this has always been a highly inbred society, in striking contrast to the situation in New Guinea, where inflexible kinship laws ensure that people marry out. In Yemen arranged marriages are the rule, with a quarter of the girls marrying a first cousin on their father's side, and almost as many some other blood relative. This must explain the high incidence of such things as imperforate anus, our commonest problem, but many other abnormalities too, such as spina bifida, hydrocephalus, cleft lip and palate, omphalocoele, clubfoot, hypospadias, epispadias and others. We treated all but the hydrocephalus and spina bifida cases, which we sent to a Sana'a neurosurgical unit.

Although I was old enough to be Judy's father, and a product of a very different system with different ways of doing many things, we worked together well. She was an excellent clinician and a well-trained, skilful surgeon. Occasionally we helped each other with major cases where we expected trouble. I remember assisting her with a lobectomy for a hydatid of the lung in a teenage girl where complications made the much simpler enucleation (shelling it out) inappropriate. It was a perfect operation, and she lost no more than a couple of spoonfuls of blood from start to finish. Judy's thyroidectomies likewise were bloodless. On top of this expertise she had organisational and management skills that Bill Koehn agreed were exceptional.

As in many other mountainous areas, goitre is very common, and many women came asking for removal of their neck lumps. Some we sent away to take iodised salt, but we saw many thyroids large enough to justify operation. Many Yemenis had marginal calcium stores and developed symptomatic hypocalcaemia if stressed by another illness. Judy felt that the fundamental problem, in women at least, was vitamin D deficiency secondary to the almost total protection from the sun provided by female apparel, and explained the 'hungry bone' phenomenon, particularly severe after operations for toxic goitre. We were experienced thyroidectomists and took great care to preserve the parathyroid glands and their blood supply, but even so we had an annoying incidence of transient post-operative hypocalcaemia, sometimes within 24 hours of operation. Even junior nurse aides were able to diagnose it. There was a research project here, but we could scarcely expect patients to pay for repeated serum calcium tests, so usually managed without them.

Judy had learnt modern methods of treating imperforate anus, so I was more than happy to leave those cases to her. I did the cleft lips and palates, except for palatal clefts that seemed too difficult, which we tried to refer to the Dutch Interplast team that visited the country twice a year. Later we had charity visits from an Indian plastic surgeon in private practice in Sana'a.

One morning I operated on three sisters with cleft lips. The extraordinary thing about this family, from a truly remote village, was that the eldest girl had the most severe cleft and the youngest the mildest. An older brother with bilateral complete clefts had died in infancy, and a normal younger sister was at home. Cleft lip is commonly familial, but the odds against a decreasing severity through a family of five must be astronomical. Their father had a simple explanation – he and his wife were getting better at making babies.

They certainly make them, with the average woman having seven living children. Girls usually marry between fifteen and nineteen (some as young as nine), with many years of fertility ahead. Despite the poverty large families are expected, and 20 or more pregnancies are not uncommon. Days before writing this I operated on a girl of 28 who'd had eleven pregnancies. Incessant breeding takes its toll, and Yemen is said to have the highest maternal mortality in the world, 850 per 100,000 live births. When tubal ligation became popular, despite widespread fundamentalist disapproval, women with only six or seven children asked for it, and we did up to 200 a month at the end of 2002. Three or four men a month asked for vasectomy. This simpler (but more time-consuming) operation remained unpopular because many men nursed dreams of taking another wife and having children by her.

Yemen is an extremely conservative society where most women cover completely in black when out of the house, except in Sana'a and Aden, where one sometimes sees a face. If the veil is lifted it reveals no more than a couple of centimetres around the eyes. In hospital a sick woman usually exposes her face, and when she begins to cover up again she is clearly on the mend, whatever she may say. In the West the reappearance of mirror and make-up is a similar sure sign of recovery. Our female nursing aides wore white face covering and long black gowns, except for those in the operating room who wore blue. One was admitted to the ward with abdominal pain and uncovered like the rest. When asked to see her I didn't recognise her because I'd never seen her face, and I never saw it again.

Casual conversation between the sexes scarcely occurs outside the family circle, and even in the hospital situation one was careful to avoid more than fleeting eye contact with female Yemeni staff, as this is regarded as a sexual act. This made prolonged discussion about a patient, or anything else, a slightly awkward experience. Nursing work is one of the few approved female occupations in our part of Yemen and girls enjoyed it, partly because it legitimised the inevitable minor contact they had with men on the staff, but the faintest suggestion of familiarity could be highly offensive. A young Australian anaesthetist, well liked by everybody, took a phone message for an aide who was assisting at an operation and tried to attract her attention by tapping her on the shoulder. If looks could have killed …

Seven male Yemeni nurses had certificates; the rest were aides trained on the job. Some had worked at Jibla for many years and were highly competent, but I saw little of the initiative that we expected of our staff in New Guinea. Female theatre nurses in the West become used to the exposure of male genitalia during the course of some operations, but our girls wouldn't assist under such circumstances, except when the patient was a small boy. And in the wards no female Yemeni could nurse men, and vice versa.

We saw some marriages of equals, but in general Yemeni women seemed to be second-class citizens, totally under the control of their menfolk. Whether this is truly Islamic or an unrelated Arab cultural trait is a matter of perennial debate. Those who protest that Islam gives women dignity and equality have to contend with the fact that the fountainhead of Islam, the Kingdom of Saudi Arabia, whose ruler is Keeper of the Holy Places (the cities of Mecca and Medina) has been notorious for suppression of women's rights, with its neighbour, Yemen, not far behind. Occasional and sometimes quite remarkable exceptions only go to prove the rule.

Islam allows a man four wives at a time, provided that they are treated equally, but few Yemeni men can support that many. Two wives aren't rare but more is distinctly uncommon. Divorce is not uncommon, with the children almost always going to the father, whose property they are. Regardless of the rights and wrongs of the case it is usual for the wife to take nothing from the marriage that she didn't bring into it. And contrary to the custom in some other Muslim countries, divorced women in Yemen frequently remarry. No woman could give permission for operation but any male family member able to put his thumbprint to paper could do it for her. Women who drove a car were quite rare, and none could travel outside the country without the permission of their menfolk.

More girls' schools means that female literacy is rising, and many girls now attend university, although some villagers still see the risks of such unsupervised adventures as too great. Recently a young woman from a conservative village persuaded her parents to allow her to enrol in medicine at Sana'a University, thus becoming the first female tertiary student from her area. When they didn't hear from her and enquired at the medical faculty they were told she'd disappeared. The authorities said she must have been a bad girl, and suggested that she'd run away with a man.

The parents didn't accept this explanation, and found another family, originally from Iraq, with a similar experience. Together they pursued the matter and found that in the course of a few years sixteen female medical students had disappeared. Except for these two, every family chose to believe that their daughters had shamed them, and did nothing, apart from working out what to tell the neighbours. Eventually it came out that all sixteen had been murdered. Recognisable body parts were found in the anatomy department.

As in many other countries, justice can be rough. A friend of ours who visited the local prison found a woman and her baby incarcerated because her husband, the driver in a fatal accident, had absconded. The authorities pulled them in as a reliable means of bringing him home.

Despite the traditional separation of the sexes nature takes a hand often enough for many women to be imprisoned for extramarital pregnancy. After delivery the standard punishment is 100 lashes, by instalment if need be. The man involved rarely feels the lash, paternity being less self-evident than maternity. We knew of a girl imprisoned after alleging impregnation by her father, who escaped by simple denial of the rape she insisted had occurred.

Death sentences for murder can be escaped if the bereaved family accepts blood money. I had a murderer in for a major operation and found him unusually anxious to return to prison instead of enjoying the much greater comfort of JBH. When I expressed surprise he said he had to pay for the two guards per shift watching him, and every day in hospital was money he couldn't afford as he was still raising the blood money.

Yemenis enjoyed hospital unless they were acutely conscious of the daily bed charge. They would lie flat for as long as possible after operation, and I was never able to do a morning round and see my patients up and taking an interest things. Women made the most of their time in hospital, as it might well be the only holiday they ever had.

In our first year Gwen and I had a long weekend in Sana'a while Judy came down to mind the shop. This time we were awake and enjoyed the four-hour journey, which begins with a steep descent of about 200 metres into the broad valley north of Ibb. The highway next climbs another 1000 metres over the Sumara Pass, snaking around the mountains, sometimes with three or four loops of tail visible. There seem to be more blind corners than straight stretches of road, but this doesn't deter Yemenis, who gaily take risks that appall even moderately careful foreign motorists. Most drive as if unaware that vehicles crashing through the occasional guardrails may face an unbroken drop of hundreds of metres. That is, unless they catch on one of the 20 or 30 or more narrow terraces that allow food crops to be grown on what would be considered impossibly steep ground in most parts of the world. Dry-stone walls thousands of years old are all over the highlands to minimise run-off in the wet season, and to maximise the cultivable area.

Looking down, one sees rocky outcrops providing precarious sites for villages, with more almost vertical drops to settlements far below. Some are served by hazardous vehicle tracks, but others can be reached on foot only. Carrying in the stone for the houses, often built of material obtained from a great distance, must have required enormous stamina.

The highway passes through several busy market villages and two substantial towns, Yarim and Dhamar, the latter about halfway between Ibb and Sana'a, and from which our doctors saw many patients each day. Dhamar is a major commercial centre in a valley ten to fifteen kilometres broad, with thousands of hectares irrigated for grain and vegetables. Here the road is fairly straight, but impatient drivers pass as recklessly as they do on the mountain sections.

Branching valleys intersect the plain, and on strategic high points the crumbling remains of Turkish forts are reminders that the rulers of the Ottoman Empire thought they had control. It was an illusion that they ever did, which may explain the total absence of anything resembling the post-colonial cringe so easily discernable in many other countries, even 50 years after independence. A Yemeni looks you in the eye and expects to be treated as an equal.

At the northern end of the Dhamar plain the road makes a long steep traverse over another pass onto a higher plateau dominated by Sana'a, itself encircled by jagged bare mountains. Old Sana'a is a UNESCO World Heritage site on account of its unique architectural style. Houses of five to seven storeys built of stone and red brick line its narrow winding streets, and are decorated with the standard Yemeni highland windows, each with its half-moon top, and with window surrounds, doorframes and balconies whitewashed. Each storey is marked off externally with an intricate frieze of endless variety. The overall effect is of gingerbread houses. This style extends outside the wall into modern Sana'a, with houses in the best areas successfully melding it with modern Arab designs. Those in the cheaper suburbs have the same basic Sana'a pattern, but with much less decoration.

We tramped ourselves footsore on that first visit, up and down the cobbled alleys of Old Sana'a, the air heavy with the scents, some subtle, some pungent, of many kinds of merchandise. One alley was all dry goods, the next all groceries, spices, metalwork, curios and antiques, *jambiyas* (the curved dagger worn in a gold-embroidered belt by the well-dressed Yemeni male), second-hand car parts, cloth, jewellery and so on; shops of each trade lumped together as in so much of the East. As well as all these cramped little stalls hundreds of small traders sat on the ground with their wares, anything from cheap watches, shirts and plastic sandals to myrrh and frankincense, hair and other dyes (especially henna, a Yemeni favourite). We saw walking spruikers with men's suit jackets (but not trousers, because these couldn't be tried on in public), matches, washers for gas bottles, second-hand flour bags, perfume and much more. They jostled with pushcarts full of oranges or other garden produce. It seemed that half of Sana'a was out shopping, and in whatever direction we walked it was like swimming against an incoming tide.

It was therefore something of a relief to pass through the great arched red-brick south gate, Bab al Yemen, and cross the stampeding traffic of Zubairi Street. From the safety of the pavement on the other side of Zubairi we viewed a panorama exactly as it appears on the back of the 1000 riyal banknote, the medieval walled wonderland of high-rise houses and minarets that is Old Sana'a. We revisited the old city repeatedly, spellbound by the sights and sounds of this great *suq*, utterly different from Crawford Market or its equivalents, or the umpteen Chinatowns around the world.

Although Sana'a is ancient, certainly as old as Damascus, at various times several other cities were capitals of kingdoms occupying areas roughly corresponding to modern Yemen. Marib, a dry, sandy governorate east of Sana'a, and inhabited nowadays by notoriously recalcitrant tribesmen, has monuments and partly uncovered rich remains of what some say was the Queen of Sheba's empire. And 50 kilometres north of Jibla, at Dhofar, a shabby village on a sharp, bald hill is all that marks the decline and fall of the Himyarite kingdom, whose capital Dhofar was almost 2000 years ago. No fancy architecture here now; unimaginative and unskilled builders gathered whatever stones lay around and slapped them together to produce single-storey, haphazardly multi-hued houses. Here and there an otherwise rough and rubbishy wall incorporates a priceless relic from Himyarite times – a bull's head, carved flowers, an inscription in a long-lost language, or some other stony reminder that a wealthy society once occupied what is now hopelessly impoverished semi-desert. Grubby, dusty peasant lads, brashly calling themselves guides, descend on the rare visitor and are able to point out, but not to explain, the trove used so casually as building material. They know it must all mean something, because German archaeologists working here on and off for years have constructed a little museum in the village to display some of their precious discoveries. Much must still lie under the ground. The National Museum in Sana'a contains a great collection of relics of this and other prehistoric south Arabian kingdoms.

Like capital cities everywhere, Sana'a is expanding rapidly, and has a population of well over a million. The water table is sinking fast, with a solution to this serious problem nowhere in sight. Infrastructure lags far behind housing development, and such amenities as sewerage and garbage collection are poor quality, which doesn't encourage tidiness. It has been said that Yemen's national flower is the pink plastic bag (PPB) that lies around in its thousands in many parts of Sana'a as well as all over the country. A particularly dense growth of PPBs usually means that a *qat suq* is nearby. *Qat* is the leaf that most male Yemenis stuff into one cheek by the handful and chew for hours every afternoon. Many women have the habit too. *Qat* comes from the topmost fronds of shrubs grown on thousands of hectares of prime land, and long ago displacing coffee and other less lucrative crops. Ideally it is bought fresh, and comes in various grades. It is clearly addictive and faintly soporific, but its visible effects are otherwise quite mild. It seems to relieve hunger, judging by the number of men who can afford it, but not food, for themselves and their families. The president has sworn off it in an effort to undermine the habit, but such a deeply ingrained cultural trait as the *qat* session appears all but ineradicable.

Even quite modest houses have a special *mafraj* (men's room) that serves little purpose apart from providing a place for them to lounge on cushions around the walls and quietly chew all the afternoon, with long silences occasionally broken for gossip, business or reminiscences. Sometimes there will be a *narghil*, or hookah, to provide variation in the entertainment for a few senior members of the group. Yemenis living in the US said the best *qat* is found in New York, imported illegally from the Ethiopian highlands at great expense, so once the habit has a hold it must be difficult to break.

Apart from that weekend away, and a fortnight's Spanish holiday in September, I rarely left the compound in 1999. Sometimes I shopped with Gwen at the foot of our hill, and occasionally we visited other foreigners in Ibb or elsewhere, all living in rental properties, usually on the ground floor, with their landlords upstairs. And a couple of times a year a local big man, Sheikh Abdul Aziz al Hubayshi, invited Bill Koehn and whoever he wished to bring with him to lunch. This old sheikh had a strong social conscience and did much good work in the community, financing an orphanage amongst other things. He lived on a peak in old Ibb, in a six-storey house approached via steep cobbled streets at the apex of the valley running north from the city. Once he owned land as far as he could see, and despite his simple appearance he was still very wealthy.

We met him in his *mafraj*, where he sat with his toothless mouth full of *qat*. Bill took a cushion at his side and chatted in Arabic, as the sheikh spoke no English, although it's hard to believe he didn't understand it. Various other male Yemeni guests appeared and greeted him respectfully, stooping low to pass him. Eventually a waiter summoned us to the dining room, another long thin room with its carpet covered with plastic to protect it from the dozens of plates and bowls of food.

We were served a mixture of traditional Yemeni and foreign foods. I went for brown rice and roast chicken, and dodged salad, yoghurt and various hot Yemeni dishes. Squatting on the floor and eating with the right hand only is quite an art, and I only managed by sitting on a thick cushion.

After the meal we washed our hands in scented water and moved to another *mafraj* on the top floor for glasses of Yemeni tea, very sweet, black and deliciously spiced with cardamom. This room was unusual in having picture windows, allowing views for miles down the valley. The chandelier and the high, decorated ceiling made it a delightful room, despite the plastic protecting the carpet. Walls displayed framed photographs of the sheikh in company with various Arab dignitaries, some dating from his stint as ambassador to Egypt in Nasser's time. After two glasses of tea we were off, passing the afternoon visitors on their way in with their PPBs full of *qat*. No Yemeni female was visible, unless a small girl cautiously poked her head around a doorjamb. All this was unimaginable when we made that 1998 offer to work somewhere overseas.

When we learnt that JBH was at an elevation of 2000 metres we knew heat wouldn't be a problem, but until we saw it we couldn't believe what a wonderful climate Jibla enjoyed. When we arrived in February 1999 all Yemen was as dry as outback Australia in midsummer, but otherwise the highland weather was ideal, with cool nights and clear crisp mornings. Showers fell sporadically as midyear approached, when it rained almost every afternoon. Again, the mornings were crisp and clear, with clouds appearing towards midday. There was none of the uncertain drizzle so common at home; we had sharp storms with thundering drum-rolls that echoed around the valley for 20 minutes or more. In PNG we'd experienced thunderbolts that made the ground shake, but the continuous rumble so common at Jibla was something new.

With 1500 millimetres or more of rain annually, most of it in four or five months, we understood why even the Romans knew that Ibb was green. For much of the year our house, and the whole compound, was surrounded by lush lawn and garden that made Jibla a little Eden. The climate in Burnie is one of the best in Australia, but Jibla was even better. Gwen's niggling asthma disappeared after a few days there, and even the occasional dust storm didn't stir it up.

From the dates and bananas of the Red Sea littoral to the mouth-watering grapes of the highlands the markets were packed with a luxurious variety of fruit and vegetables, all with the homegrown flavour that plastic-looking produce sold in supermarkets always lacks. And the hospital was an exceptionally friendly place, so that living at Jibla was no hardship. Our compound was a favourite R & R site for Christians working in other parts of Yemen, and from elsewhere in the region. Someone once described the Jibla compound as a colony of heaven. Only those who have been there can fully understand why we loved it.

Chapter 19

Over and out

Time was when almost everyone on earth could recall where they were when Jack Kennedy was shot. Pride of place now passes to 11 September 2001, a more significant watershed in history, on a par with the bombing of Nagasaki and Hiroshima, insofar as it introduced a new, almost unthinkable form of warfare. Guerilla fighting wasn't new, but its locus was the jungle. Now the World Trade Center and the Pentagon, supremely and ostentatiously invincible symbols of unparalleled economic and military power, were shown to be pathetically vulnerable to moderately imaginative suicide bombers.

We were enjoying a fortnight in England visiting old friends, and on 9/11 were with Bert and Nina Wilken at their lovely North Lincolnshire home. Gwen and Nina were out shopping for items unobtainable in Yemen while I luxuriated in the autumn sun, reading the morning papers, when the phone rang. It was the Wilkens' daughter, asking if I had the TV on. I didn't, but from her urgent tone I knew I was missing something. I switched on as that plane hit the second tower, outdoing anything that Orson Welles could have dreamt up. It was rebroadcast *ad nauseam*, and the possible implications for foreigners living in the Middle East quickly became apparent.

Next day's papers covered these events from every angle. The story that struck me most was about the young entrepreneurs, rolling in their millions, whose deaths some journo thought more noteworthy than those of thousands of ordinary folk. A more crass example and more telling illustration of contemporary values is barely imaginable.

Embassies sent warning emails, and we heard that some valued colleagues were leaving Jibla. We knew that the Koehns had stayed on, against peremptory consular advice, during the First Gulf War and Yemen's 1993–1994 civil war. Bill maintained that only a mandatory evacuation notice would shift him. Noncompliance is said to result in passport withdrawal and a stiff fine, a threat that brings US citizens to heel. During the civil war many staff members of various nationalities had followed embassy advice, but to a man (to a woman, actually) felt so guilty about abandoning their colleagues for the beaches of Cyprus that they vowed never to do it again. So this time the old hands stayed put, but several new-chums didn't.

We were booked out of Manchester on 18 September, and saw no reason not to return to Jibla. We found it a different place, with a seriously depleted staff, so that for months it was difficult to maintain a 24/7 service. Not much was said, but soon I sensed a niggling undercurrent of sadness, disappointment, even anger, that close and trusted colleagues had left so hurriedly. We'd been short-staffed for most of the year anyway, and were now unpleasantly busy, which doubtless made us less tolerant. When a fellow-worker said to Gwen, with a rare dash of vinegar, 'Isn't it odd that it's the most confident and talkative Christians that've gone?' I saw that the problem had to be faced head-on.

I was on the preaching roster at the end of the month, and set out to scratch the scabs. I began by confessing to being guilty of passing judgement on departed colleagues. Slow, embarrassed nods confirmed my suspicion that I wasn't alone. I said that, commencing with the flight into Egypt, even Jesus had avoided danger on several recorded occasions, because his time had not yet come, according to John's gospel. And the apostle Paul often moved on because it was too dangerous to stay put, but nobody had ever dared label him a deserter.

I said that in the present instance we couldn't expect God to give the same guidance to everyone because, despite superficial appearances, our circumstances differed. For example, some had contracts so close to expiry that a few weeks scarcely mattered, so why were we openly (or secretly) aggrieved that they'd left so precipitately? Others had frantic children phoning day after day, imploring them to leave Yemen, which must have been difficult to handle. (Our family trusted us to use on-the-spot information rather than rely solely on advisories from over-cautious embassies.) I think my sermon helped defuse an awkward situation, and I heard nothing more that could be construed as criticism of our departed co-workers.

Bill's imperturbability reassured us, and I detected no anxiety in those who remained. Safety measures, already firmly in place, were beefed up. For weeks we had a gun truck sitting outside the hospital, and our security squad looked even more alert than usual. Travellers had to take a soldier with them, even for the few kilometres to Ibb. Journeys beyond Ibb required advance notice to Security, who expected us to be off the roads before dark.

In the event, Yemen was quieter than most countries in the region. The government allowed one large public protest in Sana'a, after which it was business as usual. The *mullah*s were ordered, not entirely successfully, to refrain from inflammatory speechifying. Eventually some foreigners returned to JBH, but potential new staffers without previous Middle East experience cancelled out, so we had to struggle on with inadequate human resources, trying to function as a proper hospital. Patients continued flocking in, undeterred by fiery sermons from the mosques.

In May 2002 our situation was complicated by the fall of a long-feared axe. JBH was one of the last overseas institutions of any kind that the Southern Baptists maintained. Funding from, and administrative support in, the US would cease from 1 June, and attempts would be made to find new owners. For years the IMB had talked of closing Jibla, but a few board members objected firmly enough to prevent it. They reasoned that Yemen was in a different category from other places, where schools and hospitals had been handed over to national churches. Those pressing for closure argued that because there was no visible church in Yemen despite more than 30 years' work, the hospital was plainly ineffective, and therefore wasn't worth maintaining. In October 2002 an IMB spokesman went on record describing the Jibla work disparagingly as pre-evangelism.

Service restrictions were already in place. In late 2000 Richmond met Jibla management in London and said, 'Downsize or be shut down,' with no room whatever for negotiation. The delivery room closed, despite Yemen's scandalous maternal mortality rate, and various other services were curtailed. All this angered the locals. We shrank from 75 to 44 beds, which we used more efficiently, and outpatient surgery expanded. We were now essentially a surgical, gynaecological and paediatric hospital, and remained uncomfortably busy.

Before I learnt of the London ultimatum I protested about the delivery room's closure to a visiting IMB heavy. 'That decision was made locally,' he said smoothly. I was stunned. Later I discovered that he'd told me a half-truth; the IMB had offered two alternatives only: major service reduction or closure. I had to agree that the most efficient way to downsize was to cease providing maternity services. Nevertheless this seemed, and still does, an almost unbelievably callous action by leaders of the richest protestant church in North America. At about this time I said that if I were a Southern Baptist I'd be finding another denomination.

The May 2002 announcement had one sweetener: the IMB would continue supporting any of its staff electing to stay on under a new administration. Friends of Jibla in the US with the legal and accounting experience necessary to set up a trust fund to ensure the hospital's survival were ready to proceed, which didn't extract even faint praise from the IMB. Other attempts to raise money, even for a transitional period, failed. The four big Australian banks had all announced record profits, and I naively supposed that it might be possible to touch them for substantial donations. I decided to see if the AM and the OBE after my name were anything more than decorations, and carefully composed a letter to the chairman or CEO of each of these banks describing the excellence of the work done at Jibla and our acute financial need. I said that Australia's reputation in the Arab world had been damaged severely in recent times, and this needed to be countered in a convincing and tangible way. I asked them for $250,000 each, as a one-off while other arrangements were being made. I said that if they would so much as look at a rigorously costed request I would arrange for one to be prepared urgently.

One letter drew no reply, and two were answered with form letters signed by minor functionaries, one of them writing 'Dear J. Clezy'. Only Westpac's chairman put his signature to a sympathetic letter, but like the others he had to regret that his bank's charity budget was spent. He sent the latest brochure detailing Westpac's charitable work, which amounted to a great deal of money, not all spent in Australia. I accepted Westpac's refusal without anger, but was somewhat disheartened that in each case record profits apparently didn't allow for a proportionate increase in generosity.

We may never learn how vigorously the IMB consulted other Christian organisations that might have been in a position to take Jibla on. As far as is publicly known, the only expression of interest was from the People's Charitable Society of Yemen, chaired by Dr Abubakr al Qirbi, a pathologist and Yemen's foreign minister. After August talks between the mission, the PCSY and the Ministry of Health, the Society was to commence a takeover on 1 October and complete it on 1 January 2003. They would retain foreign staff and re-open the delivery room.

This rescue thrilled the IMB hierarchy, who declared it an answer to prayer, but their rejoicing was premature because nothing happened. The PCS chairman wouldn't return phone calls. Admittedly, he was overseas a good deal, but even when in the country he couldn't be contacted. A Sana'a lawyer was engaged to function as go-between, without effect. In early December Yemeni hospital staff fearing for their jobs, and Jibla townspeople fearing for their hospital, marched on the government offices in Ibb. They were promised a positive announcement within 48 hours, but again nothing happened.

A week before Christmas Bill had the word 'Baptist' painted out of the Arabic and English sign over the hospital entrance, a canny action that convinced Yemen authorities and Jibla residents alike that the IMB was serious about pulling out. An executive from another mission visited in November and was horrified that the IMB was walking away. He ran with the ball and by mid-December had come up with the skeleton of a possible rescue package, in association with kindred organisations. Our lawyer told the PCS that if they weren't proceeding there were others preparing to do so. This brought an immediate response: the PCS was still interested. It seemed strange that there had been no practical demonstration of this alleged interest, and I began to think that my suspicions about another agenda were correct. I saw the hospital closing and its assets stripped, enriching sharp local businessmen.

Meanwhile several SB and contract staff had decided that they wouldn't, or couldn't, continue working at Jibla under any new administration, and others who'd been prepared to stay became increasingly unsettled. I tried to assure waiverers, but without effect, that the sun would go on rising in the morning if and when the PCS took over. All this took place at the time of George W. Bush's increasingly bellicose posturing over Iraq. The CIA's recent bombing of a carload of al-Qa'ida members on a lonely Yemen road must have angered the government, although little was said publicly.

I wondered if the timing of the intended transfer meant something.

This gut feeling was reinforced by what Wolfgang, our travel agent, did when he booked us back to Yemen in May 2002 after our annual leave. We bought return tickets, but regulations meant that we couldn't book our return more than 300 days ahead, so I asked Wolfgang to make an open booking, but he had to specify a date, which we could alter if need be. He pulled 6 January 2003 out of his head.

On 20 December a Sana'a surgeon unknown to me phoned, offering me private work there, but I told him that when I left Jibla I'd be finished. He persisted and, with our accommodation in mind, asked how many children we had, so I said I was an old man whose children had long since left home. Puzzling over this call, it seemed that the only possible explanation was that he had inside knowledge that the hospital was closing. I was correct, because we now know that the government intended shutting it when the Baptists departed.

I put up a trial balloon on 21 December by phoning a Yemeni friend likely to know what was going on. Some of us wanted to know if the new administration would need us, I said, and personally I'd like to see something in writing by 28 December. Otherwise I'd take it that I wasn't required. If he recognised this for the little ultimatum it was, he ignored it. He assured me that all the confusion and delay was due to communication failure on the hospital's part, and implied that Bill was stalling, aiming to close JBH rather than hand it over to the PCSY. I took this to mean that if the hospital died, Yemeni authorities would duck for cover and allow the Baptists to be blamed for it. I saw this causing serious public displeasure, possibly with dangerous consequences, especially if the elements that we knew had long wanted to be rid of a Christian presence stirred up trouble.

Prevarication on Bill's part was a preposterous suggestion – the mission had been trying to extract action from the PCSY for months. What my friend couldn't know was that the IMB's London staffer driving the whole process was most embarrassed by what was (or wasn't) happening. If JBH closed and the details of the bungle got out, many of its longstanding friends in the Southern Baptist membership woud be sure to make their displeasure known to the hierarchy.

At Christmas we learnt that the PCSY had lost interest. Briefly we had some hope that the government would consider the Christian rescue package mentioned earlier, but this wasn't to be. One department was upset that we'd been talking directly with the PCSY! Soon we learnt that officials in the ministries for health and planning responsible for dealing with NGOs were agreed on one thing – it was the mission's business to transfer the property to the Ministry for Health, which alone would decide the hospital's future. This seemed to mean closure.

On Friday 27 December, Bill gave a sombre farewell luncheon for Yemeni staff, many of whom had been at JBH all their working lives. The men sat outside on blue plastic tarpaulins for an excellent meal prepared by the hospital kitchen, with the women elsewhere (as always) in our largest meeting room. The occasion brought visitors from Sana'a, including our office manager there, and I asked him to apply for our exit visas for 6 January. Yemen is as difficult to leave as to enter, and exit visas are essential.

As late as 28 December there was faint hope, in some quarters at least, that the hospital could be saved. Al Lindholm, in charge of Baptist work in Yemen, was on holiday in the US, but flew back to Sana'a in an attempt to persuade Yemeni authorities to keep us open. He thought he detected a whiff of success when government agreed to send a team of seventeen people, representing every department with an interest, to Jibla on Monday 30 December to meet with local SB leadership at 10 am. The agreement was that, after full discussion, government would make known its decision about the hospital's future two weeks later. Some of us (including Bill) felt we knew what that meant – a 'Don't call us, we'll call you' scenario.

In the expectation that we'd shut the doors at close of business on 31 December, admissions ceased on 16 December and our last outpatient surgery was performed a week later. My final clinic on 28 December was for reviews only, and a solemn morning it was. I knew some of these people well, having dealt with their problems for years. One greybeard came from Sana'a to say goodbye, not because he wanted treatment. I have no idea how he knew I was leaving, but it was a good illustration of the bush telegraph in action.

Then came the murders of 30 December, and hasty farewells before most of us went to our home countries, convinced that the hospital was finished. But the Yemen government reversed its decision, and reopened it on 1 February with a new name (Musteshfa Salaam – Peace Hospital), new manager (Abdul Kareem Hassan, an Ibb Health Department official with a long and warm association with JBH, where he'd had his early nursing training) and largely new medical staff (four Yemeni doctors, and a Romanian). They included Noaman al Mashraki, a promising surgical trainee who had worked for me for eighteen months in his spare time, without pay, and Abdullah al Matary, a Jibla man home after five years of postgraduate surgical training in Saddam Medical City, Baghdad.

Remaining doctors were Judy Williams, overdue for leave, Sara Perales, a Mexican lady skilled in paediatrics and dermatology, and Kumar Kamiraj, an Indian GP. Sara's sponsoring organisation didn't allow her to return after home leave, and Kumar sought employment elsewhere in mid-2003. Ten Indian nurses and ancillary staff also elected to stay, at least until their contracts with the Baptists expired.

One of the government's first initiatives was to install a metal detector at the hospital entrance. Early in February it pinged, identifying a man with a hidden gun. Despite his protestations of innocence it is difficult to believe he was merely a properly dressed Yemeni, an explanation accepted by the security service. Tension on the compound rose, and foreign staff again required a military escort to go outside the gate. They were moved to houses in the centre of the compound, with Yemeni staff occupying those on the periphery.

Patient numbers increased, and the cash flow in February/March allowed the reduced number of employees to be paid. In mid-April the government's promised funding still hadn't materialised, but this proved to be no more than standard administrative inertia, despite the presidential decree that the hospital be properly supported. The impoverished government of Yemen was deeply ashamed that the three Americans had been killed, and their sole means of demonstrating it was to spend the money that the Southern Baptists were unwilling to afford.

The case against al Hamidi was heard in May. An al-Qa'ida connection seemed proven. The defendant pleaded guilty but protested that the trial should be in an Islamic rather than a civil court. The judge's task was straightforward, and he sentenced al Hamidi to the official version of termination with extreme prejudice: public execution, with the body to be strung up for days afterwards. The defence lawyer appealed on the grounds that (assuming Jibla had been Christianising Yemenis) it was unjust to execute him for killing infidels. Marty wrote to the president asking that he commute the death sentence, but the killer faced a firing squad in Ibb Central Prison in February 2006.

Gwen and I had no difficulty filling in a few months at home, especially when so many people wanted to hear all about it. News out of Jibla seemed increasingly promising, so when Yemeni management and the Yemen Baptist Mission made repeated requests that we return, we agreed to do so. The Iraq War delayed our final decision, but as time went by we realised that Middle East instability would simmer on indefinitely, and if we didn't move soon we never would. Security officials in Ibb said they were unable to guarantee the safety of an American family living there, but foreigners on the Jibla compound seemed reasonably content. There were new recruits, Malcolm and Audrey Dunjey, who had seen us off from Madang when we transferred to Port Moresby in 1970. We hadn't seen them since.

We had several good reasons for returning. We'd been drafted out of Jibla in indecent haste, in effect abandoning friends and colleagues, with many goodbyes left unsaid. It almost looked as if we'd run away. Secondly, we knew that the journalists we saw every night on TV, reporting from trouble spots all around the world, lived far more dangerously than we did. Should Christian workers display more concern for their physical safety than frontline newshounds do? Thirdly, when so many in the Middle East seemed to believe that Christians were ogres of Caucasian origin who bombed them because they were Muslims, it was important to do what little we could to demonstrate that this wasn't so.

And I agreed with those who felt that the deaths of our friends demanded an ongoing Christian presence at Jibla, especially when Yemeni officialdom and most of the population were favourably disposed. So we left Australia on 30 June to find more Yemenis than foreigners living on the compound, morale good, and working relationships excellent. Professional camaraderie translated into social ease and warmth, and with our remaining Christian colleagues we were a brotherhood who had been through the fire together.

The reopened delivery room was busy immediately but the volume of major surgery recovered slowly. Even so, three surgeons found plenty to do, and in both July and August we put well over 500 cases through the operating suite. Burns, kidney stones, prostates, gallbladders, caesarean sections and hydatid cysts prevented boredom. Dr Abdullah was anxious to raise the standard of care and broaden the skills of our

Yemeni GPs, so organised grand rounds on Wednesdays at 8 pm. Most of our doctors lived on the compound, so this time was more suitable than it might seem. We always found enough worthwhile clinical material for discussion and teaching purposes.

Government believed that security remained a problem, especially for foreign staff, and decided that simply increasing the number of night watchmen was inadequate. The whole compound was floodlit as great expense, but whether this increased our safety is debatable. Other measures included altered parking arrangements so that vehicles could no longer stand near the entrance, and positive vetting of even the most innocent-looking local or foreign visitor wishing to enter the residential section of the compound. Whenever we went out, even for a stroll down the hill to the town, the duty officer recorded our details.

As 2003 rolled on none of this seemed excessive, given widespread public anger in Yemen, and right across the Muslim world, at what was happening in Iraq. The Bush administration seemed impervious to reason, and gave no indication that they'd ever paused to wonder why fifteen of the 9/11 bombers were Saudi nationals. Labelling them terrorists might be accurate as far as it went, but, as in so many situations, giving something a name didn't necessarily explain it. All but the hawks understood that nothing hurts like humiliation, and knew there were hordes of unemployed or otherwise unfulfilled, and often well-educated, young men in the Arab world who knew all about humiliation, and chafed restlessly under near-feudal autocracies. State security in many of these lands was such that thinking of rebellion was scarcely possible. (Try organising a protest rally in Saudi Arabia, for example.) Vicarious transfer of revolutionary sympathies to the Palestinian cause was easy – it was the only licensed grievance, to use Bernard Lewis's apt phrase – because Palestinians were perceived as being oppressed by a puppet state of the USA, the very same power that discontents held responsible for the survival of their own detested rulers.

Arab sympathy for the Iraq government is perhaps less easy to understand, because many aspects of Saddam Hussein's regime were widely despised in Muslim lands. He ran a highly secular fiefdom and played the religious card only when it suited him. His belated sympathy for the Palestinians is a case in point. And if the average US citizen didn't, many Arabs remembered pictures of a younger and less arrogant Donald Rumsfeld shaking Saddam's hand with great warmth and sincerity during the Iran–Iraq war. Then there was the First Gulf War, with Bush Sr's tragic abandonment of northern Kurds and southern Shiites in its aftermath, many years of sanctions, and finally the replacement of the old English proverb that blood is thicker than water with a new American version – oil is thicker than blood.

To top it all, but only just, there were those who saw the Second Gulf War as a poorly disguised crusade against Islam. While only a vocal few in the West took this view, the Arab world was full of them, understandable enough, given the Koranic concept of the theocratic state. It is this conviction that drives the suicide bomber, not the prospect of the delights to be provided by the seventy-odd big-breasted virgins awaiting each Muslim martyr.

As the Iraq conflict dragged on it was easy to see it as at least a preliminary draft of the first chapter of the clash of civilizations so eloquently predicted, described and explained by Samuel Huntington. No wonder foreigners living in the region took a keener than average interest in world news. We were in the Baghdad time zone and only two international borders distant. Every evening during the heightened religious awareness that goes with Ramadan we heard impassioned orations about the Iraq situation from the mosque on the edge of the hospital compound. It was painfully obvious that most Muslims would forgive Saddam long before they would forgive us, simply because he was one of them.

But the work went on, with Ramadan busier than ever, surgically speaking. In November 2003 Judy Williams went on long overdue leave, anxious about my capacity to keep going, as my longstanding backache had worsened. Fortunately our manager met a young local man in Ibb just home from Syria with his Master of Surgery degree, together with his Iraqi wife who was part-trained in obstetrics and gynaecology. He employed them on the spot, and they proved to be good doctors and delightful colleagues.

Gwen and I celebrated our golden wedding in Sana'a on 11 December 2003, the special feature being a lavish luncheon given by friends there. This event was unusual in a couple of respects, firstly in that no family member was present, which must be a record of a kind for a couple with four children and fifteen grandchildren, and secondly because we had a police escort for the two-hour drive from the hospital gate to the northern border of the Ibb governorate. As we approached checkpoints our flashers went on and we sailed through like royalty. When we returned two days later a police vehicle picked us up again.

Despite the tension in the country we decided to visit one of Yemen's most famous features, the Wadi Hadhramaut, before we left for good. This great *wadi*, bounded by 300 metre vertical walls, is a green ribbon two or three kilometres broad and 150 kilometres long in the otherwise barren south-east of the country. Thousands of years ago it was on one of the trade routes from Asia to Europe, and its rulers became filthy rich by taxing merchant caravans. This region produced most of the frankincense that brought a high price in Europe and elsewhere, and many Hadhramis amassed great wealth. Some of the oldest known artifacts come from excavations in the Hadhramaut, but for the ordinary tourist its particular claim to fame is its architecture, in which mud-brick construction is taken to its limit at Shibam, the so-called 'Manhattan of the desert'.

We made this trip in the company of Dutch friends with good Arabic, flying from Sana'a to Seiyun, in British times the capital of a pretentious treaty sheikhdom issuing its own postage stamps. The Kathiris ruled here for centuries and erected many imposing mud-brick buildings, the most striking being the Sultan of Seiyun's palace. An enormous square blockhouse several storeys high, it dominates the town. It is plastered a dazzling white and has round turrets on each corner. No sultan is in residence now because he and his entourage fled to Saudi Arabia during the revolution in South Yemen, and few furnishings remain to illustrate the pomp he enjoyed. The high bare rooms are a museum containing a remarkable collection of prehistoric local pottery, stone carvings and other relics of civilizations long gone, together with a unique collection of Freya Stark's photographs from the 1930s.

Tareem, a few kilometres eastwards, is notable for having the tallest mud-brick structure in the world, with the al Muhdar mosque's 50-metre minaret visible from all over town. Its sharp lines and intricate decoration are such that mud brick seems an impossible construction material. Tareem was home to families that made fortunes in the Dutch East Indies and returned to flaunt it by building splendid mansions. Again, these are of mud brick, with carved windows and doors in styles brought back from the east. These families too have fled, and years of dust and neglect have converted magnificent dwellings with up to 500 rooms to little more than ruins. Apart from its Islamic schools that recruit students from all over the world, Tareem is a dreary backwater. There must be few towns anywhere displaying such concentrated evidence of departed glory.

We imagined Shibam to be isolated and surrounded by sand, but the asphalt road snaking down the *wadi* from Seiyun passed through densely settled farmland dotted with villages, all with beautifully constructed houses of three or more storeys. Many householders settled for unadorned mud, but other homes were finished with almost every imaginable shade of plaster or paint. Some villages would be noteworthy guidebook material were they not completely upstaged by Shibam.

Much of the *wadi* is irrigated from bores, for intensive production of cereals and stock feed. Date palms are everywhere. This is picturesque enough, but the road takes a gentle bend and suddenly there it is, the unique UNESCO marvel that is Shibam, a compact little walled city occupying no more than half a square kilometre. At first sight it consists of houses ten storeys high, but this is an illusion because the ground is uneven, and the tallest is only eight storeys. These buildings are centuries old and require perpetual maintenance, but most are in amazingly good repair. Given that there is a wet season of a kind, it is almost incredible that Shibam is of mud brick.

Such tall houses mean that the narrow alleys of the city's interior are gloomy, except when the sun is directly overhead. Grubby children and smelly sheep were everywhere, with neither group paying attention to us or to the few other tourists, mostly Japanese, wandering around. We photographed a few intricately carved wooden doors, a Hadhramaut specialty, and then bought tickets that allowed us to inspect all eight floors of one showplace. We climbed the steep stairs with great care to avoid putting weight on the edges of treads where repeated repairs had been made. Secure maybe, but not worth testing. No handrails. With every wall half a metre or more thick and the stairway space three metres across, the house had much less functional living space than its external appearance suggested.

Out on the flat roof we heard a putt-putting far above us, amplified by perfectly synchronised echoes from the *wadi*'s sidewalls. We looked up to see a giant predator, like a cross between a hang-glider and a two-stroke motorbike, lazily circling Shibam to allow its occupant to take photos from otherwise impossible angles. For what we hoped would be our best photographs we settled for the traditional sunset view from high on the southern wall of the *wadi,* but the track was steep and awkward so we missed, by a few tantalising seconds, the best shots in the last rays of the setting sun, when Shibam's western walls glow gold.

Having seen this much of the Hadhramaut we came away with the feeling that it wasn't really Yemen at all. The photographs of President Ali Abdullah Saleh in his business suit displayed in every shop and on every second lamppost in our part of the country were absent. Such pictures as there were showed a much younger man, in military uniform or else in traditional dress, complete with a checkered *masheda* (foreigners call it a tea towel), the male headgear seen all over the Arab world. Women working in the fields wore steep conical straw hats unlike anything to be seen elsewhere, and men wore their shirts outside their trousers, Indian fashion.

From Seiyun we drove to Mukalla, a major fish-processing centre on the south coast. Our Hilux struggled up the steep road out of the *wadi* onto an undulating scree-spattered moonscape that looked like millions of acres of broken grey brick, brick dust and little else, apart from occasional spindly ground cover. For the first 100 kilometres or so the only sign of life was a lone woman walking towards a drab little clump of trees in a hollow. Farther on we saw another woman, miles from anywhere or anything, and then a thin donkey all alone, doing nothing. I've never seen such forbidding terrain – a desert, with its endless windblown screensaver patterns, is much more attractive – but occasional wheel tracks left the road, suggesting that some of the few little hollows in the distance were inhabited.

Like the approaches to many Yemeni towns, the road became a four-lane highway well outside Mukalla, a city with a strong Indian flavour, the older commercial area with its heavy cloistered verandahs resembling the back streets of central Mumbai. We slept in the rather isolated beachfront Holiday Inn but ate at cheap fish restaurants in town. The only 'sight' was the museum, closed long ago after looting during the revolution. It was a former sultan's palace like a huge derelict boarding house that had grown like Topsy, surrounded by what had once been lawn. The high wall of beautifully cut stone was much more impressive than the building it protected.

After the Hadhramaut, Jibla was worlds away. By this time the Iraq war was going badly, with so-called liberation becoming occupation. More important locally, the anniversary of the Jibla shootings was approaching. With al-Qa'ida's predilection for anniversaries known our security situation tightened further, and again we were advised not to walk in the town. In early January 2004 it was decided that things were as safe as they would ever be, and when Gwen first went down the hill Yemenis went out of their way welcome her.

Then came the Israeli assassination of the spiritual leader of Hamas in Gaza. This ratcheted up tension all over the Middle East, and when two women pipped our metal detector the very next morning foreign staff were sent to their houses while the incident was investigated. Each lady protested that she was simply and sensibly carrying her husband's gun, because soldiers sometimes asked for money before returning them, or else gave back the wrong weapons. One handed her gun to security staff easily enough, but the other's was strapped to her arm. This seemed suspicious, and in any case was in flagrant disregard of prominent notices prohibiting weapons in the hospital. Admittedly, the literacy rate is low, and Yemenis are not the only people on earth who sometimes choose to ignore public notices. After questioning both couples the police judged that neither had nefarious intent, but Security said we should again stop walking in Jibla town.

That day our only American nurse was chatting with a demure seventeen-year-old Yemeni nurse aide, as sweet a girl as one could find anywhere, and asked what her aim in life was. Calmly and earnestly she said she wanted to go to Palestine as a suicide bomber. They certainly don't have to be wild-eyed.

The defining moment of the coalition's occupation of Iraq came when the first notorious Abu Ghraib photographs were published. George Bush knew he had to say something, but his appearance on Arabic television was his Chappaquiddick, and he blew it. His failure to have his ever-so-clever speechwriters craft a convincingly abject apology was more than a monumental error of judgement, and his grudging partial apology via King Abdullah of Jordan a couple of weeks later only made matters worse. Such blunders confirmed the belief held by so many, that Bush and his advisers lacked the most elementary insights into Middle Eastern cultures.

In countries where sisters sleeping in the same room all their lives may go to extraordinary lengths to avoid undressing in front of each other, where male hospital staff much prefer to wait until the change room is empty before stripping to their underwear, and where the notion of husbands and wives being naked and unashamed together is sometimes all but incomprehensible, to millions of Arabs the Abu Ghraib images were proof positive of the fathomless cesspool of Western depravity. Gassing women and children was one thing; for the whole world to see a female American soldier teasing a naked Iraqi prisoner on a leash was quite another.

It is unlikely that anything Bush did or said could have been of significant benefit to anybody, apart from being evidence that at least he tried. As I watched the US administration's crass ineptitude in handling the fallout my conclusion was that the coalition had shot its bolt, and the sooner they all went home the better. How anyone ever supposed that a one-step transition from Saddam-style dictatorship to parliamentary democracy was remotely possible remains a great mystery. This would be difficult enough in a homogeneous state, but is preposterous in an artificial construct like Iraq, a doomed melange of three incompatible provinces lumped together in the post-WWI carve-up of the Ottoman Empire.

There are many old scores to be settled, and history teaches that they surely will be settled. One would think that America, having had its own civil war, would understand the near inevitability of Iraq having one too, but they blundered on, leading very unwilling horses to water, each gauche error serving to so alienate Arabs all over the world that it will take generations for anything like cordial relations between two bleeding, chafing cultures to develop.

As my time drew to its close I became ever more acutely conscious of the need to make sure that my Yemeni colleagues were able to handle the variety of work coming our way in increasing volume. Abdullah was managing kidney stones well without help, and both Fuad and Noaman were almost there.

We began collecting patients whose gallbladder operations performed elsewhere by inadequately trained people had gone seriously wrong. Abdullah's work in Iraq had included considerable experience of liver surgery so when we explored a young woman with three months' increasing jaundice due to something like shark line around her bile duct and hepatic artery, he was able to identify the structures to be dissected out before construction of a new biliary drainage system was possible. I see him being the local expert in these cases.

Until the others were ready to operate on them Judy was to take over the tracheo-oesophageal fistulas (TOFs). (In 2006 Dr Judy Williams returned to the US and other Americans at Jibla were deployed elsewhere after they and Yemenis close to them experienced months of what was perceived as increasing harassment by Political Security.) The TOF is a catastrophic congenital abnormality that comes in several varieties, most commonly with the upper end of the gullet ending blindly high in the chest, while the lower end forms an abnormal connection between the windpipe and the stomach. I treated one for what must be the last time about six weeks before we came home, under circumstances that illustrate some of the difficulties that most of us working in the Third World accept as normal.

One Monday morning a seventeen-year-old was delivered of her first child by caesarean section after prolonged labour at home. The baby was unusually bubbly and required energetic suction before she was fit to go to the ward, where she had attacks in which she went blue, especially when put to the breast. Sometime on Wednesday the young doctor rostered to look after sick neonates that day asked the nurse to pass a nasogastric tube for feeding purposes. She couldn't insert it more than a few centimetres and reported this unusual finding to the doctor, who wasn't greatly impressed. Attacks of blueness were treated with our homemade respiratory support apparatus, known as CPAP. This gave some relief but unfortunately the abnormal connection between windpipe and stomach meant that much of the air puffed into the lungs went on into the belly, and according to one observer, out the bottom end.

Alarm bells rang when I heard the bones of this story late on Thursday night. I found the baby as tight as a tick, and saw that one of the effects of the CPAP was to blow gastric contents, in this case including bile, back into the respiratory system, as evidenced by all the yellow froth around the baby's mouth.

The father was at home, hours away, and the mother couldn't produce a telephone number. I'm not even sure there was a phone in the village. The baby was far from fit for immediate surgery, and in any case there are good reasons for not operating on infants in the middle of the night if it can be avoided. I settled for tilting the mattress head down to help drain secretions from the mouth, and made sure that the nurses suctioned the baby properly overnight. By this time she was starving, and cried until morning, which was the best possible treatment for her bile-filled lungs.

Father appeared at midday Friday expecting to take his little family home, but shot through when he heard talk of an operation. The maternal grandfather was slower off the mark, but when the problem was explained and he was asked to sign permission for operation he refused point blank, said we should let the infant die, and slipped out of the hospital before I could speak to him. Meanwhile the baby's lungs seemed to be improving, so we settled down to try again on Saturday.

There was a Jibla convention that in a genuine emergency two doctors could give permission for operation when no male of the family was available, but in practice this was rarely necessary. And it's one thing to do it when a good outcome is virtually certain, but quite another when the patient has a TOF and double pneumonia.

Our manager Abdul Kareem Hassan heard about it and was waiting for the men of the family on Saturday. Grandfather came alone and again refused permission for operation, even when AKH told him we'd do it for free. His excuse was that the baby's father might have him sent to gaol. 'Sign here or I'll have you in gaol right now,' thundered AKH, which produced the desired result.

So Noaman and I settled down to correct the abnormality at 4 pm Saturday. It was his eyesight rather than mine that enabled us to dissect the abnormal area with appropriate precision and insert the necessarily very fine sutures into tiny structures exactly as required. The infant didn't turn a hair and went home on the following Saturday, sucking well, while I passed the message around that next time a baby was born in our hospital with a TOF we really should aim to operate on it before it was five days old.

The last few weeks flashed by. We had informal and formal farewells, on the compound and in the restaurant at the Taj Ibb, a new hotel plastered on the mountainside so high above the city that Ibb looked like a reflection of the Milky Way. Everything about our departure was so warm and friendly that we left Yemen with great sadness and reluctance, because in a few years Jibla had come to feel like home in a way that New Guinea hadn't in half a lifetime. And such was the numerically reduced state of the Christian community on the compound that the departure of even one couple, this or anyone other, would leave quite a hole. The only softener was the feeling that even if we didn't return to work, it ought be possible for us to make a social visit. So we applied for exit/re-entry visas, which would at least keep us on the Immigration Department's computers, and would simplify returning for any purpose. (We made one more trip, which we reduced to less than five months so that we could attend the wedding of friends in Melbourne.)

I couldn't dodge that fact that I was another surgeon who, come crunch time, was reluctant to lay down the scalpel. I'd known of too many others struggling on long after they should have called it a day, and I said repeatedly that I wouldn't fall into the same trap. But like them, I finished with complete conviction that I still had something in the tank. It would be a matter of leaving our future in God's hands, knowing He would open doors or close them, as a lifetime of experience has reminded us, over and over again.

Man of the Moment

Ken Clezy

Magnus Anderson, a world-weary Sydney obstetrician separated from his wife, is smitten by Sally, a beautiful but straitlaced Australian midwife. On her way to a woefully under-staffed mission hospital in Africa she convinces Magnus to join her as a short-term volunteer, despite his doubts.

Life in the confines of a hospital compound is a stark contrast to sophisticated Sydney. He faces the challenges of mission work in a Muslim land, opinionated colleagues, and an outspoken Islamist trainee specialist. And he continues to be drawn to Sally, fascinating but less responsive than he would like.

Just as Magnus settles into mission life, a tragedy in Sydney brings him home. Will this give him the clarity he needs to resolve the issues that plague him?

For more information visit www.wakefieldpress.com.au

Wakefield Press is an independent publishing and
distribution company based in Adelaide, South Australia.
We love good stories and publish beautiful books.
To see our full range of books, please visit our website at
www.wakefieldpress.com.au
where all titles are available for purchase.

Find us!

Twitter: www.twitter.com/wakefieldpress
Facebook: www.facebook.com/wakefield.press
Instagram: instagram.com/wakefieldpress

www.ingramcontent.com/pod-product-compliance
Lightning Source LLC
Chambersburg PA
CBHW051111230426
43667CB00014B/2537